TELL IT TO THE KING

Also by Larry King

Larry King

TELL IT TO

THE KING

LARRY KING

with Peter Occhiogrosso

G. P. PUTNAM'S SONS · NEW YORK

G. P. Putnam's Sons
Publishers Since 1838
200 Madison Avenue
New York, NY 10016

Library of Congress Cataloging-in-Publication Data

King, Larry, date.
    Tell it to the King.

    1. King, Larry, date. 2. Radio broadcasters—
United States—Biography. 3. Entertainers—United
States—Anecdotes, facetiae, satire, etc. I. Occhiogrosso, Peter. II. Title.
PN1991.4.K45A3   1988   791.44′092′4   [B]   87-29298
ISBN 0-399-13244-9

Typeset by Fisher Composition, Inc.
Printed in the United States of America
1   2   3   4   5   6   7   8   9   10

ACKNOWLEDGMENTS

This book never would have happened without the combined efforts of three very talented people. My writer, Peter Occhiogrosso, my book representative, Sterling Lord, and of course my editor, Neil Nyren. Peter asks good questions and leaves no stone unturned, and eats weird health foods. Sterling looks and acts just like his name. Nyren is now pretty much accepted as one of the five best editors in the country. I don't know who the other four are, but they have to go some to be in his league.

I'd also like to thank the three principal people I'm contracted to. Entrepreneurs all—all risk takers, all who have let me be me. They are Ted Turner at CNN, Norm Pattiz of Mutual Radio, and Al Neuharth of *USA Today*. Giants! My representative, friend, agent, confidant, is Bob Woolf of Boston. I used to be his lowest-paid client. (I'd wait on the hold button while he spoke to Larry Bird.) That is no longer true, thanks mostly to him—and everybody who works with him at Bob Woolf Associates. They are only the best.

On the personal side, a few deserve note. Miss Angie Dickinson of Beverly Hills, California, is a lot of things to me, the best of which is a good pal. Angie is always there. My oldest and dearest friend is Herb Cohen. We grew up together. He is an interwoven part of my life. He wrote the hit book *You Can Negotiate Anything*. They broke the mold after they made him. My brother, Martin Zeiger, of New York City, is a gem. We have gotten closer and closer over the years. All we have is each other. Both Herb and Marty are married to "Ellens," and both Ellens are lovely and smart and "with it." My son, Andy, and my daughter, Chaia, are always with me in thought if not in body. I adopted Andy when he was a young man in his teens, and Chaia's birth and subsequent growth to age twenty are the absolute joy of my life.

Andy's daughter, Dorian, will someday, I hope, be proud of her grandfather. My radio producer is one Pat Piper, assisted by Judy Thomas. They are a unique pair, as is Lorrie Lynch, my editor at *USA Today,* and Jeannie Williams, who now has her own column but was my editor for the first five years at MacPaper.

The staff under Randy Douthit at CNN are among the best in television. Dear friends I think of daily include the *Washington Post*'s wonderful columnist Chuck Conconi and the voice of the Baltimore Orioles, Jon Miller. Two exceptional people, who care about human beings rather than material things. If I left anyone out, I'm sorry. You know who you are and how much you mean to me.

This book is dedicated to
Tammy Haddad
My television producer, my friend . . .
for whom I wish all she wishes for herself

And to
Duke Zeibert
My friend, surrogate father,
and a guy who goes at life with both fists

CONTENTS

FOREWORD

I guess you could say I was riding for a fall.

For seven years I'd had angina and had taken nitroglycerin. Then I began noticing a shortness of breath and occasional pain. But did I go to see a doctor about it? No, the pain always went away, and so for several months I kept on the way I always had: running around, smoking three packs a day, getting by on a minimum of sleep.

And then on the morning of February 24, 1987, it all caught up with me. I was sitting in the car after my radio show, and the symptoms came back again, but this time they wouldn't go away. The pain just kept getting worse and worse—like a toothache running from my right shoulder all the way down my arm. I took myself to the emergency room at George Washington University Hospital, where they hooked me up to the EKG—and the pain stopped. I started feeling pretty foolish. The EKG was normal, I wasn't hurting, I'd made this big fuss. I was ready to get up and go home.

But the doctors wouldn't let me go. One of them, Dr. Warren Levy, didn't like the sound of my medical history and my bad habits, and he had a hunch. I guess that is what separates good doctors from mediocre ones. He said to wait and the pain would probably come back. So we were all sitting around, the cardiologist and the nurses and me, waiting for the pain to return. I sat there for five minutes, ten minutes, and sure enough the pain came back, this time worse than before. They took another EKG and a blood sample, and all the while the pain was mounting.

This is the part I'll never forget as long as I live. I was sitting up watching them across the room, four nurses and two doctors. They had the blood result on a piece of paper and they were reading the EKG as if it were a ticker tape. Then suddenly all six of them turned and came right for me—they were all walking *fast*. I remember thinking, This ain't gonna be muscle strain. They're not running over here to tell me I'm suffering from severe arthritis. One doctor said, "Mr. King, you're having a heart attack."

I didn't panic, but I did ask the doctor, "Am I gonna die?" The pain was that great.

"Asked like a good interviewer," he said. If I hadn't been in so much pain I might have laughed. He didn't say I wasn't going to die, and that bothered the hell out of me. On the other hand, my whole life didn't pass in front of me the way they always say it does, and I took that for a good sign. In fact, I remembered that Woody Allen line about the time he was on an airplane and it went into a dive and his whole life started flashing through his mind—and it was the wrong life!

I immediately thought of three things. I thought about what would happen to my daughter, Chaia, if I didn't make it. I fantasized her being there. I thought of my mother, who had died ten years earlier. And I knew right then that I'd never smoke again. I wasn't going to be like one of those guys I knew who had heart attacks and were smoking in the hall the next day.

"Am I gonna die?"

Instead of saying outright that I wasn't going to die, the doctor began to explain the situation. He told me that my chances of living were excellent, for three reasons: I was having my heart attack right in the hospital, my pain was on the right side, which is usually not terminal, and that hospital was one of twenty-five American hospitals using a new experimental drug called t-PA.

The drug t-PA is administered intravenously, and its basic purpose is to reduce the blood clot at the time of the attack. But because it hadn't been approved by the FDA, the doctor had to read me some information about it and I had to sign a consent form.

Meanwhile, I was still in pain. I had a vision. All my life I'd watched war movies in which some G.I. is always yelling, "Doc! Give me some morphine, please!" And when they give it to him, the guy smiles. So I asked for morphine, although I know now that morphine, the best painkiller in the world, won't help the blood get through the clot in the artery, which is what you really need. But when I heard the doctor say, "Okay, give him two cc's"—or whatever it was—"of morphine," I was already happy. For the first time in my life I was getting morphine.

The orderly came over and gave me the injection. Nothing. I looked at him and said, "Nothing."

He said, "It usually takes twenty seconds."

A minute went by and I could still feel the pain. They kept asking me, on a scale of one to ten, how bad the pain was. I'd say, "Seven, maybe eight." At times it felt like a nine. The doctor said, "Nine? That's pretty severe pain." I couldn't imagine what a ten would be.

He finished reading the consent form and as soon as I wrote "Larry King," the t-PA started going in. And it was then, as the medication was entering my system and the pain was beginning to slide back down from a nine to maybe a seven or a six, that I began the process of reevaluating the way I'd been living my life. I knew I'd be making some changes.

I was fifty-three years old. For thirty-three years I'd smoked three packs a day, had eaten whatever I wanted—the richer the better—and had never exercised. Besides that, I have always been a classic type-A personality. Another way of putting that is to say that I'm the worst person to be stuck with in a traffic jam. I start pounding the wheel, honking the horn, looking for a way out. If I can't find a moving lane, I start climbing the walls, which isn't easy in an automobile. If I have to wait on line in a store, at the doctor's office, the su-

permarket checkout, I get manic, turn my head up to the
heavens, and ask, "Why me, Lord?" When the saleslady at
Neiman-Marcus tells me that the store policy requires me to
wait a minimum of thirty minutes to have my purchase gift-
wrapped, I am overcome with a crazy urge to start breaking
glass objects—Steuben glass objects—until she decides to
make an exception in my case. In short, I'm no day at the
races.

As I lay there, I knew I'd have to change all that: diet,
exercise, smoking. Calm down. All right, I thought, I can do
that. But then I thought: Uh-oh, what about my job?

Many people would say that my job must be the most
stressful component of my life. I have a radio show, a television show, and a weekly column in *USA Today*. On a
Wednesday, when I'm working on my column, I write all afternoon, have an early dinner, and get to the CNN TV studio
in Washington by eight-fifteen. I go on the air with *Larry
King Live* from nine to ten. As soon as I'm off the air, I get in
my car and drive to the Mutual Broadcasting System's radio
studio across the Potomac in Crystal City, Virginia. I get there
around ten-fifteen and go on the air at eleven. The first two
hours of my radio show are taken up with interviews and call-
ins, the third hour, after the guests have left, is Open Phone
America, when I talk to callers from all over the country.

I go off the air at two A.M., drive myself home, and go to
bed. I live nearby in Arlington, Virginia, so I'm usually asleep
at two-thirty or three. I sleep only about five hours and then
I'm up by eight-thirty. If I'm lucky, I get a short nap in the
afternoon. The show is then repeated on tape at two A.M.

The pressure of that kind of schedule sounds killing, and I
wondered for a moment if I should cut back. But only for a
moment. The fact is, my job is not a pressure for me. Having
to operate on a patient whose life is in your hands, that's pressure; having to face Roger Clemens with the game on the
line, that's pressure. But I don't experience what I do as pres-

sure, mainly because it's too much fun. In fact, the time in my daily life when I feel the least pressure is when I'm on the air. Every night at nine o'clock on television and eleven o'clock on radio are the easiest times in my day.

Every day of my life, from Monday to Friday, I meet the most interesting people in the world—writers, politicians, film directors, historians, surgeons, lawyers, athletes, comedians, singers, psychiatrists—and ask them anything I want. And I get paid for it. On top of that, I talk to callers from all over the country and tell them what I think about any issue from the Middle East to the major leagues.

I can't control what the woman in my life does; I can't control my daughter; I can't control external events. But from nine o'clock tonight until three in the morning, I control my environment. I ask what I want to ask, and then I say good night to my TV guest and move on to radio and do the same thing. If I don't like what a caller is saying, I can redirect the conversation; in an extreme case I can cut off a call. It's my world—and I knew at that moment in the hospital that I wouldn't trade it for anything.

I want to welcome you to that world now, to tell you some stories about the great and not so great, the talented, the brash, the funny, and the frankly bizarre people who have passed through my professional, and sometimes my personal, life. They've given me plenty of laughs, some sadness, and a lot of surprises, and I hope they'll do the same for you. And maybe by the end of the book you'll see why even a heart attack wouldn't make me want to miss a single, solitary minute of it all.

CHAPTER 1

THE COMICS: LENNY AND THE GREAT ONE

The *Guinness Book of World Records* has determined that I've logged more hours on national radio than any other talk show host in the history of the medium; between radio and television I've probably interviewed more than thirty thousand people. Of all the guests I've interviewed over my thirty years in the business, however, if I had to choose my favorites by group, I would pick the comedians.

That's not as whimsical as it seems. As Tony Randall once said, "Comedy is a very serious business." If you're acting on the stage, you may sense how you're doing, but you don't really know for sure until the curtain comes down and you hear the applause. On some nights the audience's response may be less enthusiastic than on others, but you won't often get booed off the stage. In comedy, you *know* how well you're doing—or how poorly—at each moment. If you tell one joke and the audience doesn't laugh, you know you're not funny. Three such jokes in a row and you may start edging toward the wings. This could explain why so many comics appear so neurotic.

As much as I love comedians, I find certain comics too safe, afraid to offend anyone. Rich Little came on my CNN show one night after we had just finished a segment on the PTL, and I asked if he did an impression of Jerry Falwell. He started to do a little Falwell and then he stopped. I said, "Do you do Tammy Faye Bakker?"

"She'd be very easy to do," he said, "but I don't do her."

"Why not?" I asked.

"Well, you know, people are very funny about religion."

"And you don't want to offend?"

"Right. In my business, you can't offend."

Well, of *course* you can. That's what puts the best comics on the cutting edge. Rich is a wonderful interview, but he's careful. His material is careful. A caller asked him if Reagan or Carter or Ford ever got mad at anything he said. I laughed to myself. How could they?

Bob Hope is the same way. He may sound daring with his jokes about presidents and the military, but the last thing he'd want to do is risk actually offending anybody. The last time Don Rickles was on my radio show he said, "Larry, you can't hide anymore, you're more Jewish than ever. Kurt Waldheim could pick you right out of the line." Can you imagine Bob Hope saying that?

When I think about comics who run risks, Lenny Bruce leads the pack, and his friendship had a big influence on me. Because of him, I still get angry at show business performers who cop out. Because of him, the world never looks absolutely straight to me—there's always a tilt to it, an angle.

When you're walking around with a man who later becomes legendary, you never think at the time that he's going to be a legend. He's a guy who's funny—he's Lenny. I met Lenny when I was doing a disc jockey show in Miami in 1958. He came to the studio one morning about seven o'clock and said,

"I really dig ya" and invited me to see his show that night. Then I got a show at Pumpernik's restaurant in Miami Beach and he came on my show all the time. The idea of the show at Pumpernik's was to improve the restaurant's morning business by broadcasting live from the dining room. I sat in a glass booth and interviewed whoever came by, with no producer and no plan. It sounds crazy but it worked, largely because of the talent that was floating around Miami back then.

I sometimes had Lenny and Don Rickles on together—two different brands of American humor going at once. Lenny would wear a prison uniform that a friend of his had sent him from Raiford state prison. But Lenny wouldn't just *wear* it. He'd ask cops for directions in it, right outside Pumpernik's big picture window. We could see him out in the street talking to the cops in his prison uniform. Lenny would try to psych the cops by asking them for directions. He had it all figured out: a cop knew he'd look like an idiot if he reported that a guy in a prison uniform had come up to him on the street, but if he let the guy go and the guy really *was* a con, he'd look even worse. Lenny would come on my show and do an interior monologue about what was going on in the cop's head. "I'm an idiot either way," the cop would be thinking. "What's the way out of this? Gotta do it the American way. 'Uh, fella? See that cop down there on the next corner? Go ask him.'"

Sometimes Rickles would try to talk sense to Lenny, usually a losing proposition. "Lenny," he'd say, "are you crazy? Is this gonna help your life, Lenny? Is this a major thing in your life with the Raiford uniform? Maybe it'll get you beat up, and then you can walk around the streets and beg. Is this gonna be a bit? Lenny, wear a suit. Dress up, stand onstage, Lenny. Make a little money, take care of your mother."

When Dustin Hoffman asked me what I thought of his performance in the film *Lenny*, I said, "You were very good, but you weren't Lenny." He had never seen Lenny work. He said, "I understand. I would not go to see someone play someone I know. But tell me, what did we miss?"

I said, "You were very good. But Lenny was a very *funny* guy. That picture wasn't funny. You had his mannerisms cold, but I didn't fall down laughing. With Lenny you fell down. When Lenny was cooking, down on the floor you went. When he was not cooking, forget it—nobody was worse. But when he was good he was raucous. He was sexual. He had a way of moving his hands, his body."

Lenny was not known as a conventional joke teller. Once on my show, I decided to confront him about it. "Lenny," I said, "one of the complaints about you is that you never tell a joke. Everything with you is a weaving of stories and insights, but do you ever just tell jokes? Most kids who grew up funny grew up telling jokes to their friends."

Lenny said, "Okay. Joke. One of the great arguments of all time is between the environmentalists and the geneticists. The geneticist says, The way you're born is the way you'll be. The environmentalist says, The way you're raised is the way you'll be. Here's a story that maybe doesn't give you the answer but shows you the complexity of the question.

"A family goes to Yellowstone National Park on vacation— mother, father, and three children. On the way back to Los Angeles the parents look in the back of the car and, Holy Jesus! They forgot the one-month-old kid. Hey, it happens. You gotta clean up, gotta worry about Smokey the Bear, so they leave the kid.

"They're halfway home, and now here's the dilemma. If they turn back to get the kid, the father blows his sales meeting in the morning, the monthly sales meeting for the May sweep at the car dealership. He'll never get that day back, but he can always have another kid. They go on to L.A. and they leave the kid in the park, and the kid is raised by wild dogs for eighteen years. One day the dogs, in a fit of logic, realize they've done wrong and that the kid doesn't belong with them, so they leave him out on a highway and split. Now this kid, who's spent one month as a human child and seventeen years and eleven months as a dog, is picked up by a passing motorist. The kid enrolls in the University of Chicago, graduates Phi Beta Kappa. Valedictorian. He's called the most promising student in Chicago in ten years and is hailed by the president of the university as a young man with an unquestioned future. And *bam!* One day he's killed chasing a car."

Pure Lenny.

I became friendly with Lenny over time, and we used to hang out together. The only problem was that Lenny had some unusual traits. For instance, he loved to fish. He took me out deep-sea fishing, and I was scared to death. It was very strange for a Jewish boy from a big city to go fishing because I had had no introduction to it. And Lenny never stayed at swank hotels, even when he was making plenty of money. His favorite hotel in Miami was the Shoreham Norman, an old, well-kept Jewish hotel down on Fifth Street where most of the clientele were older Jewish people. Lenny *never* stayed at the Fontainebleau.

Another thing I liked about Lenny was that he was the first guy I knew who would just say anything. We were at dinner at Joe's Stone Crab in Miami Beach once. I was with my first wife, Alene, three other couples, and Lenny and his wife, Honey. We were talking about the merits of marriage and the subject came around to: What do you like best about your mate? The rest of us were saying things like "He has a great sense of humor" or "I like the way she thinks." Lenny sat there and said, "Honey is the best blow job in America." This was 1960. "That'll keep you home," he said. "Anytime I think of straying, I think: She'll go down on me anywhere. Would you pass the coleslaw, please?"

In other ways Lenny was very much like other comedians. He hung around with them—if he were alive tonight he'd probably be at the Carnegie Deli. Guys like Alan King and

Henny Youngman would say to him very sincerely, "Lenny, you're so funny. What do you need with the four-letter words?" Lenny once wrote a hilarious letter to Jack Carter, responding to an attack Carter had made on him in the press. Carter criticized Lenny's onstage profanity, and yet Carter was known for having one of the foulest mouths in the business *offstage*—he would curse out waiters, for instance, in the rudest, most obscene way. So Lenny wrote Carter a letter and sent copies to his friends, in which he used every obscenity he could come up with, explaining that none of this would mean anything to Carter since he didn't understand such language. It was all very self-effacing in a sarcastic way: "Dear Jack, I really appreciate the remarks you made, and I said to myself, That fucking cocksucker's really got my number."

Lenny was arrested only once in Miami and it had nothing to do with foul language. Dick Gerstein, the state attorney, loved Lenny and never gave him a hard time. Lenny found out about a leper colony, however—I don't know where it was—and formed an organization to help support it. That was fine, except that he raised the money dressed as a Catholic priest. He sent the money to the leper colony, he kept accurate records, he withheld the seventeen percent or whatever it was that he was allowed by law. The government never charged him with fraud, only with impersonating a priest. But he told me he never got laid so much as when he was dressed like a priest. He had a Cadillac convertible and he would visit these rich Catholic women to raise money for the leper colony. They would give him a nice donation and then they'd sleep with him.

But probably the most bizarre moment I ever witnessed in Lenny's act had nothing to do with obscenity, politics, or anything else that people usually associate with Lenny Bruce. He became dissatisfied with nightclubs, so he rented the show room in a Miami Beach hotel and put on the Lenny Bruce Show. The hotel was populated by old Jewish people in their sixties and seventies, but no matter. The show room was glass-enclosed, and all his fans came to see him there. The old Jewish people staying at the hotel would never go in—they wouldn't pay fifteen bucks to see a young comic they'd never heard of. But they'd watch the show through the window. One night Lenny said to his audience, "Hey, there must be forty of them out there looking in. I'll keep talking, but at the count of three I want you all to turn around and start picking your nose, pick your neighbor's nose—and we'll see what it does to them."

It got the effect he wanted. I saw one little old man running over to the desk clerk waving his arms. "You should see, there's craziness in there, picking each other's noses!" The manager asked Lenny about this later and Lenny said, "What's the matter with these people, are you crazy? I'm doing a comedy act. You think I could get grown men and women to pick their noses? There's something wrong with the people in this hotel, they're starting to imagine things."

"I know, Mr. Bruce, but that's what they said."

"Okay, maybe your own nose. But I could get you to pick your neighbor's nose? Come on!"

I met Jackie Gleason in the summer of 1964, when I went along on his famous train trip. When Jackie moved his television show from New York to Miami, he got CBS to hire a whole train to help him make the move. Instead of making chugging sounds, the train had a recording of Jackie's voice saying, "And away we go!" He'd stop at every little town and with a band and the Glea Girls and all that stuff would put on a show.

When we got to Miami, the first show he went on was my Sunday night television program. He'd seen the show before, and the night he was scheduled to appear, he got there early and rearranged the entire set. We went through the executive offices and found two new chairs. I had been using a swivel chair, but he told me not to use it because it focused attention on the swiveling instead of on the guest. Later everyone agreed that he was absolutely correct—when was the last time you saw a talk show with a swivel chair? Then he changed the backdrop and the lighting. He was that visually oriented.

I got to know Gleason's writers very well, especially Walter Stone and his head writer, Marvin Marx, who told me that Jackie was very difficult to write for because he was such a perfectionist. For instance, The Honeymooners never had a phone because the Kramdens were too poor to have a phone. Jackie had never had a phone in his apartment in Brooklyn as a kid. That one small thing created enormous problems for the writers. Any character they wanted to introduce had to come to the door or be shown on-screen in some way. And a phone is a great source of comedy—you can do takes off a phone. Walter Stone later complained to me, "Watch all the sitcoms and see how the phone is used. We had no phone, and we were limited by that."

In Brooklyn, there used to be something called a "rent party." When someone couldn't pay the rent, he would throw a rent party at which he supplied the potato chips and pretzels and the neighbors brought their own booze. When the guests came in the door they put some money in a tin box— they never handed it to him directly. One week, Gleason's writers put together a hilarious script based on Ralph's throwing a rent party. Now, the first thing you should know is that Gleason had a unique way of working on *The Honeymooners* in rehearsal. This was how it went: The show was broadcast live before an audience on Saturday night. The writers would prepare the script on Monday and Tuesday, Gleason would come in on Wednesday, and they'd read the script through for him. Jackie would make suggestions for changes and the writers would polish it on Thursday. Friday was a full rehearsal with the entire cast except Gleason. Gleason had a stand-in who looked somewhat like him and knew all his gestures and voice patterns and whom he had trained to react to the material the way he would. The stand-in worked for Gleason personally and Jackie paid him out of his own pocket. Jackie would watch the stand-in go through the rehearsal with Art Carney, Audrey Meadows, and the whole cast. The result was that when they did the live performance on Saturday, it would be the first time the rest of the cast were seeing Gleason react off them. He felt that this approach made things fresher and more spontaneous. I don't know of any other performer who worked that way.

When the writers read through the rent party script that Wednesday, Jackie was in stitches the whole way. They got to the end and he said, "Kill it. Tear it up and throw it away."

The writers were stunned. "Why?"

"Kansas City won't believe it," Jackie said. "Think of Kansas City. No rent, no rent parties. They won't know what that is. And Kramden wouldn't have one. Too proud. He'd steal first. He'd never let the neighbors know he didn't have the rent."

The writers were frustrated because they knew they had a great script. They tried everything with Jackie, even suggesting that Alice put on the party without Ralph's knowledge. But Jackie was adamant, and he always turned out to be right.

In truth, Jackie was the polar opposite of Ralph Kramden. He was extraordinarily bright and read everything he could— except fiction; he was interested only in nonfiction: history, religion, the occult. Jackie was Catholic, but he called himself a Roaming Catholic. I remember his saying that the Church did something to him. "They don't own you," he would say, "but they've got a part of you."

I asked him once if he liked challenges. "No, I don't want challenges," he said. "I want to do something I can do and have fun with. What do you think, I want to go skiing because it's a challenge?"

Jackie had a pretty good idea, though, of what led him to rise to the challenge of being an entertainer. When he was six years old his mother took him to a vaudeville show. He was sitting in one of the front rows and at the end of one of the acts when everyone started applauding, he turned around and watched the audience. He told me, "I remember at that moment saying to myself, I want to do that, and I want them to applaud me. That's the only difference between performers and nonperformers. There are nonperformers who are very funny, but they don't have the chutzpah to stand on the stage and say, 'I'm funny—put that camera on me, I'll make you laugh.' I've met hundreds of guys at cocktail parties who are funnier than I am. But they don't have that ego."

"Do you think you're conceited?" I asked.

"No," he said, "I'm not conceited. I *know* I'm good. Conceit is when you're *not* good and think you are."

Jackie was an insomniac and he used to stay up and listen to my radio show. He had my private studio number and would often call in with questions for my guests. Jackie was particularly interested in religion, ethics, and parapsychology. That doesn't mean he believed in parapsychology. He used to say, "I'll pay ten thousand dollars to anyone in the world who can come to my house"—and here he'd take a saltshaker, an ashtray, whatever was in front of him and move it a few inches— "and move that. I'll put it down on my table, you move it." He was absorbed by those ideas and by things like reincarnation. He had his problems with the Catholic Church, especially when he wanted a divorce and he had to find a way to have the marriage annulled. But Catholicism kept him interested because there were parts of it that made a great deal of sense to him. Christ made sense. "The Man gave His life," he would say. "He was some guy."

I spent a lot of time with Gleason, although not as much as I would have if I played golf, because Jackie golfed every day. We used to go to restaurants and clubs together. Of course, back in the sixties I wasn't in his financial league, so if we went to a fancy restaurant he'd pay for me. But I would take him to nightclubs in return, to hear new comics. He drank a lot when we went out but he was very sedate, and although he was a great laugher I had the feeling he laughed more out of courtesy than because a comic had surprised him with a joke. He had a quick mind and understood the mechanics of comedy, so it was hard to catch him off guard.

I took him to see Woody Allen once. Woody was always working at the Diplomat in Hollywood, Florida, back in the early sixties. I knew him because one day somebody had taken Woody to the dog track and then had brought him to my show later that night. Woody talked about how nervous he was onstage doing stand-up comedy. He kept saying to me, "This is not going to be what I want to do. I'm making a lot of money, but I'm scared every second I'm out there." Woody wore sneakers and a T-shirt, and people loved him, but he was uncomfortable. He said, "I want to make movies. I think that's my form of expression." Still, I think Woody's monologues, some of which were preserved on records, hold up better today than the work of any other comedian of that time.

Jackie had never seen or heard Woody, but he'd heard a lot about him. We went to the Diplomat and the owner said to Jackie, "Oh, I'll tell Woody you're here." Jackie said, "Please don't tell him. Some performers don't like to know that. I'll go see him after the show."

Jackie sat next to me as Woody did some of his now famous routines. One of Woody's funniest bits then was about a moose: Woody goes hunting in upstate New York, shoots a moose, straps it to his fender, and proceeds to drive back to the city. As it turns out, though, he's only creased the moose's scalp, and it comes to in the Holland Tunnel. Of course, there's a law in New York about driving around with a conscious moose strapped to your car, so Woody decides to take the moose to a Halloween costume party some friends are giving and ditch it. The moose mingles at the party, does very well, scores. Somebody tries to sell the moose insurance. When they give out prizes for the best costume, however, the moose comes in second—to the Berkowitzes, a married couple dressed as a moose. A fight ensues and the moose and the Berkowitzes knock each other out. Woody takes this opportunity to drive the unconscious moose back to the woods and dump it off. As fate would have it, he mistakenly takes the Berkowitzes instead.

"The following morning," the routine ended, "the Berkowitzes wake up in the woods in a moose suit. Mr. Berkowitz is shot, stuffed, and mounted in the New York Athletic Club—and the joke is on them, because it's restricted."

Gleason had never heard the routine before, but the minute it began he leaned over to me and whispered, "The moose has gotta be alive." When Woody mentioned that it was Halloween, Gleason leaned over and said, "Costume party." It was uncanny. The details about the party, the moose mingling, the guy trying to sell the moose insurance—all that put Gleason on the floor. But as soon as Woody said, "Twelve o'clock comes and they give out prizes for the best costume of the night," Gleason whispered to me, "Someone's dressed as a moose. Gotta be—the moose can't win." But Jackie didn't guess the end. The end of the bit fooled him completely, and he roared.

Still, I was impressed. Afterward he explained to me how he had known what was coming. It wasn't that he didn't respect Woody. He appreciated Woody's craft, but Jackie always thought in terms of comedy. "He's got a moose strapped to his fender," Jackie said. "Well, the story's not going to go anywhere with a dead moose." Jackie is the only comic I ever met who could analyze comedy like that.

Mel Brooks once told me the difference between comedy and tragedy: "If you fall down, it's comedy. If I cut my finger, it's tragedy." Gleason told me a story he'd heard from Charlie

Chaplin that further defined the thin line between the two. Chaplin said, "Suppose a guy in a tux at a swank party, looking very swank himself, is standing at the top of the stairs. He's a little inebriated, and as he begins to walk downstairs he misses the top step and sort of laughs. And you laugh. He's not really falling hard, he trips on the second step and he's got a little smile on his face, and he twirls his hat and you laugh again. He hits the third step and rolls over a little and now you think he's doing a bit. You're really laughing. When he hits the fourth step and turns around, there's blood trickling from the corner of his mouth. That's the moment when it changes from comedy to tragedy."

After repeating that story, Gleason went on to apply the principle to what happened to Jerry Lewis. Jerry Lewis was easily the greatest eighteen-year-old comic in the history of this country. Those early movies like *Jumping Jacks* and *At War with the Army* with Dean Martin were brilliant. The problem was, Gleason said, "He found taste." When Lewis found taste—that is, when he went on all the TV shows sounding very erudite—we no longer believed him as a nudnick. "The secret," as Gleason put it, "is that you must believe the character." You believed Jerry Lewis when he made those silly faces and spoke in that crazy whine, so he could take you where he wanted to take you. When Gleason was the Poor Soul, you believed him. Lewis just got too smart, so you stopped believing in the character.

One character that was definitely influenced by Jackie was Archie Bunker. I found this out when I asked Jackie if he thought *The Honeymooners* was a predecessor to shows like *All in the Family*. He said, "Carroll O'Connor called before the show went on the air and told me he was patterning his Archie Bunker on Ralph Kramden—a kind of Kramden of the sixties." Jackie didn't think Ralph was a bigot, though, and he called Archie Bunker "cheap laughs." He said he even told Carroll O'Connor so. Still, he was very proud that O'Connor would offer that kind of tribute to him.

As you can see, Jackie had very firm opinions about the business he was in and the people who were in it with him. Back in the sixties in Miami, there was a wild rock performer named Wayne Cochran who had a hit song, "Going Back to Miami." Cochran had a huge mane of bleached-blond hair and he looked like a wrestler. He had a swimming pool in his backyard, but there was no water in it—that was where he threw his garbage. Finally the police had to force him to do something about it because the neighbors were going nuts. He was in all the local papers, and one day Jackie said to me, "I've been reading about this guy Wayne Cochran. Let's go see him." So I went with Jackie, Art Carney, my first wife, Alene, and a couple of other people to the club where he was playing. Gleason and Carney were heavy drinkers, and they had a few that night. Wayne's act was absolutely outrageous— he gyrated and jumped around and punched out the ceiling. It was funny just to watch Gleason react. Jackie kept looking at me with his eyeballs rolling. Carney moaned, "The world is coming to an end." They couldn't believe they did essentially the same thing for a living. For his finale Wayne gyrated through the audience, and as he went by our table he tapped Gleason on the shoulder. Gleason looked up at him, pie-eyed pissed, and said incredulously, "There's no business like show business."

After Jackie died last year, Hank Meyer, his representative during all the years Jackie was in Florida, called and told me that Jackie had asked him to call and say goodbye. Gleason had said to him, "Call Larry and tell him I thought about him."

I told Hank that I had spoken to Jackie several times in the hospital. He said, "Yeah, I know, but he wanted to be especially remembered to you. He watched you every night. He watched your show Tuesday and he died the next day."

I didn't handle that too well. Jackie used to say he was

proud that he spotted me early on—he liked to tell people
that he knew I was going to be a national success someday—
and when I was sitting there working Tuesday night, a dying
Jackie Gleason was watching me.

It's like when Tony Auth, the cartoonist, told me about his
mother. Auth is one of my favorite cartoonists; he's won a
Pulitzer Prize and has had his work in the *Philadelphia In-
quirer* and the *New Yorker*. He came over to me at a party for
cartoonists and said, "I was going to call you, but I knew
you'd be here." Then he said, "My mother died last year. She
had cancer and it was very painful, the last two years especially. The only time she didn't have pain was when you were
on. The doctors had no explanation for it—they thought
maybe it was your voice. Anyway, she'd call me the next day
and tell me what happened on your show, because your show
became her life. She would say, 'It's seven o'clock, I'm eating
now. Larry's on at twelve, don't call me late.'"

Sometimes I'd mention Auth's name on my show because I
like his work so much. Then, during the news break, his
mother would call and wake him up. "She would never call
while you were talking," he said, "but she would call during
the news break to say that you'd mentioned my name. She
died very peacefully, mainly because they had her on a lot of
painkillers. My brother and sister and I were all around the
bed when she died, and we said goodbye. She said to me,
'Call Larry King and tell him thanks for giving me some
peace.'"

I absolutely did not know how to handle that. It's hard to go
on the air the next night and picture people lying on their
deathbeds listening. But it's a very real situation, and I can
see where a show like mine might help. What I'm bringing
them each night is something new, familiar but new: new
guests, new callers. I become a part of their lives, an institution—as anybody would who is on regularly. I had that feeling
for Arthur Godfrey when I was a kid, and for *Broadway Open
House* with Jerry Lester.

Jackie Gleason died a few days after Fred Astaire, and although Astaire was more famous for a much longer time, Gleason's death got bigger play in the media and evoked a more emotional response from people. The reason is simple. We didn't know Astaire; we had never heard him interviewed. But Jackie was family.

CHAPTER 2

THE COMICS: THE YIDDISH CONNECTION

Maybe I'm a traditionalist. Even though I have a lot of the new young comics on my show, I still really love the old Jewish comedians who aren't much in fashion anymore—the Borscht Belt types and the ones who came out of Yiddish theater. Maybe one of the reasons they're not so popular now is that not too many are left—although the few who have managed to survive, like Henny Youngman and Jackie Mason, still do very well.

I met most of the great comics in Miami. In the sixties and seventies Miami was a mecca for comedians and entertainers and opening acts of all sorts. Miami was a kind of Borscht Belt South, with all these jam-packed hotels needing an endless stream of performers.

That's where I first encountered Myron Cohen. Cohen was a salesman with an elegant voice—he was a talented linguist and did great regional accents—and he didn't start in show business until he was in his forties. People used to tell him he was funny, so he tried out a few clubs and then Ed Sullivan put him on. Sullivan made him. Cohen had a very classy, wholesome style on TV, but at private luncheons a whole other side of him came out. I heard him tell this joke at one such occasion, and I'll always remember it. It's not one you ever would have heard from him on TV, but it's classic Myron Cohen, and you'll just have to imagine the Yiddish accents as only Myron could do them.

"A synagogue is holding a raffle," he began, "with three surprise prizes. The word spreads that the synagogue has received some amazing gifts far in excess of the usual prizes and that they are now raffling them off. One member of the congregation decides to corner the market and assure himself of winning at least one of these fabulous prizes. It's a buck a ticket, and he buys half the tickets sold. Comes the night of the raffle, the cantor is handling the drawing, the synagogue is mobbed, every raffle ticket was sold, and this guy is sitting with half of them. The cantor announces that they'll draw for the third prize first. He calls the number and the guy with all the tickets doesn't have it. But he says to himself, I've got two more shots and now I'll find out what the third prize is. The third prize turns out to be a brand new Cadillac Eldorado, fully equipped. Now the guy is going crazy; he's got half the tickets and the *third* prize is a Cadillac.

"The cantor calls the second-prize number—and this time the guy's got it. He jumps up. 'Was I smart? Half the tickets? I got it.' The cantor announces, 'The second prize is . . . a cake baked by the rabbi's wife.' There's a hush in the synagogue. The guys says, 'A wha—?' A cake baked by the rabbi's wife. The guy says, 'Wait a minute. Third prize is a Cadillac Eldorado, and second prize is a cake baked by the rabbi's wife? That's crazy!'

"The cantor says, 'Just a minute, sir. A Cadillac, that's just a thing. This cake was baked lovingly by the rabbi's wife. She gave her time to it, she created it out of love and devotion—'

"The guys says, '*Fuck* the rabbi's wife!'

"The cantor says, '*That's* the first prize.'"

I had a chance to interview the great Menasha Skulnik, one of the classic Jewish comedians of all time. He was the one who played the manager of a hotel who whenever anyone asked him, "Are you the manager?" would throw up his hands and say, "I'm *not* . . . the manager. I'm the *manager*." That's hard to convey in print, even more so because everything Menasha did was inflection and body language. Jerry Lewis took some of his shtick from Menasha—that whining baby face and those contorted gestures.

Skulnik did a lot of Yiddish theater, and he once came to Broadway in a play called *Uncle Willie*. About that play Brooks Atkinson said, "This is probably the worst play ever to come to Broadway. It's a one-joke comedy with no depth of character, and its concept is not particularly unusual. However, if you do *not* see *Uncle Willie*, you will miss one of the great evenings in the history of American theater because you will have missed seeing Menasha Skulnik work."

Menasha told me about a friend of his who, he noticed, always wore either a light brown jacket and dark brown pants or a dark brown jacket and light brown pants. For the whole time he knew him, fifty years, he always noticed this. So one day on the train he mentioned his observation to his friend and said, "Explain this to me. In fifty years I've never asked you why."

"When I first came here, Menasha, I bought a brown suit," his friend said. "The pants wore out first. So I bought a new pair of pants. Then the jacket wore out. I never caught up."

Many of today's top comedians are descended in some way from those old Borscht Belt troupers, although ironically it

was another great Jewish comic, Lenny Bruce, who introduced the new kind of humor that eventually displaced them.
Lenny made possible the comedy of George Carlin (who not
only is a great fan of Bruce but does one of the best impres-
sions of Lenny I've ever heard), Richard Pryor, and Lily
Tomlin. But comedians like Henny Youngman, Mel Brooks,
Don Rickles, and even David Steinberg all descend in one
way or another from the great hotel humorists.

Henny Youngman is a nice guy who also happens to be a
schnorrer. He'll work for five hundred dollars or for six thousand dollars; he's over eighty years old and *must* work. He's a
great one-line joke teller, but not necessarily a funny guy sitting around a table. Henny's not quick-witted but he has a
great memory and a great store of jokes, and his timing is
impeccable. Woody Allen told me that Henny is his favorite
comedian. He said Henny does everything a comedian is supposed to do: surprise you, move you, make you laugh a *lot*.
But he's not someone of whom you would say, "Let's go have
dinner with Henny Youngman because we'll fall down laughing."

Don Rickles is a riot when he's on, but when he's not on
he's a generous, gentle, "What can I do for you?" kind of
man, which may surprise people who have seen his live act.
Two things about Don: First, if you haven't seen Rickles work
in a club, you haven't really seen Rickles. Nothing he's ever
done on television comes close to how outrageous he can be.
The other thing is that Don can be absolutely bizarre, even
when he's not onstage. Frank Sinatra told me about something Don did to him that I don't think anyone else on this
planet could have gotten away with.

There's one thing you have to keep in mind: if Sinatra likes
you, you can kid him to the end of the world. Any kind of joke
you want—if he likes you. Rickles had just gotten married; he
was in his late thirties. Frank was sitting in Chasen's with a
bunch of friends, eight or ten people. Rickles was in the res-

taurant and he came over to Frank, bent down, practically
kneeling next to him on the floor so nobody would see him,
and he said, "Frank. I just got married."

"I know," Frank said. "Congratulations."

Don said, keeping his voice down, "My wife's father and
my wife's brother—my new father-in-law and brother-in-
law—are tremendous fans of yours. They go ape for you. If
they knew that we're friends . . ."

"What do you want me to do?"

"Would you say hello?"

Frank said, "Sure, bring 'em over and I'll lay it on for you."

"Yeah," Don said, "I could bring 'em over. But you want to
give me a thrill? You come over to me. Do you know what
that would do for me, Frank? If you came over to me, this
would be on the list of big moments in my life, right up there
on top. I mean, we're only married two weeks."

"Okay," said Frank. "Where are you sitting?"

Rickles nodded his head toward his table. "Ten minutes,
okay? We just ordered. Come over in ten minutes."

Sinatra was telling me this story, and he said to me, "In ten
minutes, I remember, I get up and start walking over. I know
I'm walking through Chasen's and people are buzzing. I get to
the table. His brother-in-law's just eating his soup and they're
all talking. I decide I like Don so much I'm really gonna put it
on for him. He's a nice guy, he deserves this favor. So I don't
just say hello, I *throw* my arms around him and say, 'Don,
how the hell are ya?!'

"Don looks at me and says, 'Frank, this is fucking personal.
Get outta here!' Never acknowledged me, never introduced
me. The brother-in-law spits out the soup, the father-in-law's
jaw drops, and Rickles goes back to the conversation as if
nothing happened. I walked away and thought to myself, That
fuckin' guy. Only Don could do this and play it out. Never
introduce me. And six tables hear it. I gotta like him for that.
All I can do is shrug my shoulders and walk back. Meanwhile,

people are saying, 'Did you see Rickles: "Frank, get the fuck outta here, this is personal"?'"

To which I should add that only Rickles could do that—and go up a peg in Frank's mind.

I was in the club the night Sinatra first caught Rickles's act in a lounge in Miami Beach. Sinatra came in with his hangers-on—Joey Bishop and the whole crew. Rickles got onstage and started his act, and then he saw Sinatra. He said, "Frank, you're an old man. Come on, Frank—the chambermaid? The lady's cleaning the room, you gotta grab her? What, you can't go ten minutes? Frank, my mother, she's seventy-one years old, come on. A Jewish lady, Frank, whaddaya want, to set records? Why don't you go upstairs, have some graham crackers, a little warm milk, you're an old man."

Sinatra was laughing. Rickles looked down and said to Joey Bishop, "Joey, you can laugh. Frank says it's okay."

Then there are the Brooks brothers, as I call them, though of course Mel and Albert aren't related. As a comedian, Mel Brooks is in a class by himself; he has that special kind of genius that allows him to get into a character and improvise. On any given night Mel might come on my show, for instance, and be the two-thousand-year-old man. He would find a way to fit the character to the circumstances. Mel was my guest the night the United States put a man on the moon. I said to him, "We're on the moon. What a historic night. You're two thousand years old. How do you feel about this?"

"Ah, I love the moon," he said. "The moon is my favorite thing in the whole universe."

"Why?"

"For three hundred and eleven years, I thought I had a cataract. One day a guy named Irving said, 'Isn't the moon beautiful tonight?' I said, 'The wha'?' He said, 'The moon.' I said, 'The moon? It's not a cataract?'"

Then I asked him if he knew Moses.

"I helped him," he said. "Helped him get out of Egypt."

"How?"

"Moses had a speech impediment. He stuttered. When he was standing in front of the Pharaoh it was embarrassing. There was 'Luh, l-luh, l-luh, l-luh.' So I hit him in the back. 'Let my p-puh-people go.' He died a hunchback."

"He died a hunchback? From what?"

"From carrying the tablets. 'Thou shalt not' *alone* was eighty-three pounds."

What I love about Mel is that you can ask him a question that's impossible to answer, and he stays right in character. I asked him if he was there the night Christ died.

"Yeah, I was there," he said. "I was on the hill at the Crucifixion."

"How'd you feel?"

"Terrible. I went home—couldn't eat my rice pudding. I couldn't eat it, couldn't touch it, couldn't go near it."

Out of character, however, Mel can be even funnier. I once showed him a picture of my daughter, Chaia, and he said to me, "This is a curse."

I said, "What do you mean, a curse?"

"The worst curse in the world is a pretty daughter," he said. "This girl is gonna break your heart. With an ugly daughter, she's always there: 'Pa, whaddaya need?' Saturday night she's home. 'Whaddaya need? I'll make you dinner, Pa.'

"I'll tell you another thing," Mel said. "You got an ugly daughter, you don't need a clicker to change the television channels—she gets up and does it for you. She'll sit there and turn it all day long. This one," he said, looking at the picture, "this one, you'll be in a nursing home when you're fifty-five years old. She's gonna visit you. She's gonna come visit you in the nursing home, in a Porsche, with a guy named Lance. Lance is gonna look out the window the whole time he's there, with sunglasses on, impatient. She's gonna bring you gifts you can really use, like a Gucci belt. And she's gonna lean over and say, 'Don't dribble your food down your mouth, Pa—Lance doesn't like that.'"

All that out of one photograph.

Albert Brooks came as a complete surprise to me. He called to ask me if he could use an excerpt from my radio show in his movie *Lost in America*, and then he came on my show to talk about the film. There was no way that I could be prepared for the wildness that followed.

I don't know why Albert isn't more popular than he is, because he's one of the funniest people I know, right up there with Mel Brooks and Sid Caesar. I've heard that he can be manic, that he's a perfectionist, but he's been nothing but hysterical with me. He does the kind of imaginative things that I don't think anyone but a top-flight comic mind would dream up. On my show he did Walter Cronkite going up in space as the first journalist-astronaut. His premise was that Cronkite would be selected to go on a shuttle flight but that he'd have a nervous breakdown because he was too old—and that we would have to hear it. Albert does a great Cronkite impression, so you have to imagine Walter's booming voice and dramatic inflections:

"Oh my God Almighty, get me down! I have made a *horrendous* mistake! No, but I'm not *kidding*, God Almighty, Houston, land *please*, I'll *pay* you! I cannot see! I have made a horrible, horrible mistake. I want to throw *up* and I don't even know *how*! Please, my God, I beg you. I'm wealthy beyond your *wildest* dreams! I have property in Sweden—land this!! I'll pay for the fuel! I'm having a *bad time*. Something's wrong, seriously. I'm questioning my whole *career*. Oh my God, I'm *freaking out*! I never wanted to see the earth like *that*. I just wanted to see it behind me, *flat*."

Albert told me that he played for the Beverly Hills High School football team. His real name is Einstein, Albert Einstein. He said, "We never won. An all-Jewish football team, no blacks. What chance did we have? But we had a Porsche bus."

There are two more people I want to mention here, though one of them, strictly speaking, isn't a stand-up comedian.

Paul Lynde came out of the *New Faces* show. Every year, Broadway producer Leonard Sillman put on a show called *New Faces: New Faces of 1949, New Faces of 1950,* and so on. Each year, he would launch a talent search and usually come up with a pretty good cast, but there was never a show like his *New Faces of 1952.* Paul Lynde was in that show and did a bit that brought down the house and established him as a major new comedy talent.

It almost never happened, though. The problem, Paul later told me, was that he was not a stand-up comedian. He was an actor, and he couldn't get into *New Faces* as an actor because it was all music or comedy scenes. So he wrote a monologue.

He came onstage with a cast on his leg, bandages around his head, his arm in a sling. He limped to the podium and said, "Members of the Wilkes-Barre Rotary Club, I want to thank you for your wonderful two-week, all-expenses-paid trip to the Congo—no, let me amend that. My late wife and I want to thank you . . ." Then he stopped for a moment. "All we found was her shoe," and he started to cry. "I don't want to say, gentlemen, that it was dirty, and I don't want to say that the helicopter ride was a little hairy, but it's just that we didn't know they were gonna throw us out the door . . ."

He became an overnight sensation and went on the road. The only problem was, he didn't know what to do in a nightclub. His monologue took only twelve minutes and then he had to do Shakespeare because that was all he knew! He survived, though, and had a great career. He never did stand-up again, but in his movies and on television shows like *Hollywood Squares,* his delivery was never less than brilliant.

And then there's David Steinberg. David does a lot more producing and directing today, but he used to do classic stand-up, and if there was a hall of fame for comedy sketches, his crazy psychiatrist bit would be there.

Miami was where I first met him, too, performing before those Borscht Belt South audiences, and the first thing I said to him was "David, how would you describe a Jewish man?"

"A Jewish man," he said, "is someone who, if you wake him up with a phone call in the middle of the night and say, 'Sorry I woke you,' will say, 'It's okay, I was reading.' And a Jewish woman is someone who would never open her eyes during intercourse because she could not stand to see someone else having a good time."

Henny Youngman is eighty-two, Milton Berle is eighty, Bob Hope is eighty-five, George Burns is ninety-two, and whenever I've asked any one of them about age they have given me nothing but flippant answers. I've said to each of them, in effect, "Your motivation can't be money, and at this point it can't be acceptance. I can understand that you might want to perform once in a while because it's fun. But George, why do you want to fly to Kansas City for twenty-two thousand dollars and stand on a stage and do two a night?"

And they do lines on me. George will say, "What else are you going to do in Kansas City?"

I asked Berle, "Why don't you think of retiring?"

"To what?" he said contemptuously. "Retire to what? What am I going to do?"

I don't think they want to deal with retirement, and I also think they see stopping as death. I'm fifty-five years old, and I've had a heart attack. I know I'm never going to reach ninety-two. And I know that if someone said to me right now, "Let's shake hands, you'll make seventy-five, but on your seventy-fifth birthday you've got to die," I would take it in a minute. That would sound like a good deal to me: twenty more good years. But I know George Burns doesn't think he's going to live to be a hundred and fourteen. What keeps him going?

But none of those comics will say anything believable, such as that they're afraid of dying if they stop. They don't want to dwell on it. They remind me of what Casey Stengel once said: "Most of the guys I played with are dead at the present time." They'll kid each other about it all the time, as long as they can keep it flippant. Milton Berle once said on my show, "George Burns is here. He'd love to be on but he's too far away—he's in the lobby."

Believe me, if Burns had been in the lobby, he'd have been at that microphone in nothing flat. And if asked why he bothered at his age, he'd have said something like "Because I need a long-term contract. If I'm a hit here, maybe they'll sign me for five years."

CHAPTER 3

MADNESS TO THEIR METHOD

If there's one person I'd give anything to interview, it's Laurence Olivier. I've done so many interviews *about* him, I've had so many actors discuss him, that I don't think I'd ever run out of questions. Tony Randall said he'd swim the Atlantic to work with Olivier for free. Charlton Heston said his biggest thrill in show business was not receiving the Academy Award. It was completing a scene with Olivier in the movie *Khartoum* and hearing Olivier say, "Great work, Chuck."

Dustin Hoffman tried to explain Olivier's greatness to me. I interviewed Dustin on my television show, and while we were off-camera he told me this story.

"Did you see *Marathon Man?*" he asked.

That's the movie where Olivier plays an Eichmann-type Nazi living in Argentina and Dustin is a sort of innocent bystander whose brother is a CIA agent. The Nazis have a cache of diamonds that they want to dump on the world to get money for their organization, and there's a scene where

Olivier has to go to Forty-seventh Street in Manhattan to have some diamonds appraised. He is a concentration camp killer, and Forty-seventh Street is where the Hasidic Jews have their jewelry stores. Dustin came to watch the shooting of the scene on Forty-seventh Street even though he wasn't in the scene—which is probably the greatest respect any actor can pay another.

Dustin heard the director explain the scene to Olivier: he's outnumbered forty thousand to one by the Hasidic Jews, and there's a good chance some of them may recognize him from the camps, as someone later does. The director told Olivier he had to project fear and loathing at the same. Dustin said to me, "Watch that scene, watch what Olivier does with his eyes as he walks down the block. He got both emotions at once: scared to death and feeling superior to everyone on the block."

Olivier is not a Method actor. He works off a higher intelligence, according to Anthony Quinn, who told me a funny story about Olivier. They were doing *Becket* on Broadway, and Quinn was thrilled because he was working with Olivier and because his name and Olivier's were both above the title on the marquee—which any actor would kill for.

"When you're an actor," Quinn told me, "you naturally assume that other actors work the way you do. Rehearsals were going very well, and I assumed that Olivier was going back to his dressing room and *becoming* Becket. I was certainly becoming the King, which was my role. So I'm tough to live with the last two weeks, because I've become the King. I start to think about what the King was like when he was a child, what the King would have done the morning of this scene, and so forth. I assumed that Olivier was doing the same thing because we were really cooking in rehearsals.

"And now it's opening night. And I am as much the King as I can be—I'm ninety-eight percent the King. It's the first act, I'm sitting on the throne and there's electricity in the house. Olivier is standing next to me, and the Archbishop is stage center making a speech and I'm listening to him. Olivier is also listening to him, and then he will respond in about a minute.

"Suddenly Olivier starts tugging at my robe. This isn't in the scene. I don't know what to do. Has he forgotten something? He keeps tugging. So I lean forward and he leans over to me and he says, 'Tony, where the fuck do you get good English beer in New York?' The next minute he's talking to the Archbishop, perfectly in character. I couldn't believe it.

"Then the death scene. We're almost finished, it's nearly the last scene in the play, and the rest of us are standing backstage. I'm still recovering from this incident about the beer, which has told me he's not only not a Method actor but he can be anywhere he wants and still be brilliant. Olivier does a death scene that brings down the house and the crew and all of us. We're listening backstage and tears are coming down as he makes this death speech—he knows that his friend the King has killed him—and then he dies. There is a blackout before the final scene, and as Olivier passes the stage manager in the wings, he says, 'Tomorrow we move the blue light.'"

Gleason worked with Quinn and Olivier, so he had a great perspective on them. Method actors drove Gleason crazy; he found them so difficult to work with because they always have to know what's motivating their characters. That was why he loved working with Olivier. The two of them made an HBO movie a few years back, and I asked Gleason if he had ever discussed motivation with Olivier. The only time it came up, he said, was when they joked about it. "The only people who talk a lot about acting techniques are the new school of actors—and interviewers," Gleason told me. "Mostly, we just did it, and we talked about broads, Hollywood, booze, and England."

Anthony Quinn was a different story. As Gleason put it, "Quinn don't act; he marinates. You know: you gotta become the part."

When they were making *Requiem for a Heavyweight*,

Quinn played the heavyweight and Gleason was the manager. They were shooting a scene in the Bronx in which Quinn was supposed to have just finished a fight and walk into the dressing room.

"I can't just walk into the dressing room," Quinn said to Gleason. "I've just fought twelve rounds."

"Well, what do you want to do?" Gleason asked.

"I'm gonna run around the block five or six times," Quinn said. "You start shooting the scene, let the director wave to me as I pass, and I'll come right in."

Jackie was incredulous. "You're gonna do this, huh?"

So Quinn went running around the block, they signaled, he came in, and Gleason purposely blew his lines.

"We had that guy spinning around the block all day long," Gleason told me. "By the time we finished the take, we had him huffing and puffing like it was a forty-eight-round fight."

Surprisingly, Gleason's attitude toward Method actors was not unlike John Houseman's. The old school of actors, stage or screen, never dealt with motivation, Houseman told me. They dealt with things like projection. As great as Orson Welles and the Mercury Theatre actors who made *Citizen Kane* and *The Magnificent Ambersons* were, Houseman pointed out, none of them ever asked for motivation: "Why is Kane doing this?" No one would ever say, "Kane comes through the door and he's very angry. Why is he angry?" They would ask instead, "How do I play the anger? Is it vicious anger, is it anger for the moment?" But never "Why?"

I'll tell you an Olivier story that most people probably don't know. Olivier was originally supposed to play the Godfather. He was all set to go, and then he got sick and nearly died, and they gave the part to Marlon Brando. Coppola had originally called Olivier and said, "Larry, I think you'd be perfect for this. But I want you to be comfortable and I don't want anyone to be embarrassed. Would you mind doing a test?"

Olivier agreed and Coppola had him do what was essentially the opening scene, at the wedding. Robert Duvall told me Olivier was *incredible*. He didn't put anything in his cheeks, but he had a perfect Italian accent. Duvall said, "He had a sneer on his mouth with happiness in his eye."

Duvall also told me what it was like working with Brando. I asked him, "When you're working in a scene with Marlon Brando, is he the character or is he Brando?"

"That's a good question," Duvall said. "We're actors and we react off each other, but we're sane human beings, too. We know there are lights and a crew, and I know that that's Marlon and he knows I'm Robert. So when he was acting in those scenes, we all knew it was Marlon Brando. Except sometimes."

I asked him what he meant.

"Sometimes he was so great," Duvall said, "that he was Don Corleone, and he scared us. There was this scene where he turned around and said 'No!' We had suggested something and he was *supposed* to say 'No.' But we all stopped cold— Caan, Pacino, and I. We were frightened to death: Corleone was mad at us. It was because of moments like that that we all came to watch Brando when we weren't in the scene with him."

Duvall discussed Brando's death scene near the end of the movie, where Corleone is playing with his grandson. Just before that scene he has a conversation with Al Pacino on a bench. In the script, while Don Corleone is talking to Michael, a servant comes by and asks if they'd like some wine. And they're supposed to say, "Go away, we're talking." Duvall told me that when they went to shoot that scene, the servant came by with the wine, Pacino was talking, and Brando *took* the wine. The actor serving the wine didn't react, he just asked Pacino if he wanted some wine. Pacino said no. Brando ad-libbed, "I don't know. Lately, I drink a lot of wine."

Duvall told me, "We all fuckin' fell down, it was just so perfect."

This may seem odd, but Marlon Brando's best friend was

Wally Cox, the skinny, meek actor who is probably best remembered for creating the title character of *Mr. Peepers* on
television in the 1950s. They were roommates when they
were both struggling to make it in New York. Karl Malden
said the saddest man he ever saw in his life was Brando at
Wally Cox's funeral. He was inconsolable.

Malden and Brando are also great friends, of course. Malden loves Brando and has worked with him a lot on the stage.
But Brando is by nature a practical joker. He has a riveting
stage presence but he loves to play tricks on other actors. In
the biggest scenes he'll do things like dig his fingernails into
their knees under the table.

Malden told me that one night when he and Marlon were
doing *A Streetcar Named Desire* on Broadway he decided to
get even with Brando. They were backstage, and he knew
that Brando wasn't paying attention because they were talking
about something else. All Malden said to him was "Marlon,
it's your cue."

Marlon runs onstage and immediately knows he's not supposed to be there. The two actresses playing Blanche and
Stella are in the wrong place. They're shocked at his coming,
and he knows that Malden screwed him up backstage. All he
does is say, "Stella, you got a cigarette?"

"No," Stella says. And he says, "God *damn*."

He walks off and says to Malden, "Don't play games with
me."

Brando is a little out of it now, though. Tommy Thompson
told me a revealing story about him. Thompson was a gifted
author who wrote *Blood and Money* and later died of cancer,
and Brando was his best friend. *Apocalypse Now* had just
come out, and it was playing to wildly mixed reviews: they
loved it, they hated it. Francis Ford Coppola was conducting
film lectures around America in which the whole discussion
was about *Apocalypse Now*. Pauline Kael did thirty-two pages
on the film in the *New Yorker*. Meanwhile Brando was in Ta-

hiti. Tommy Thompson flew to Tahiti and Brando met him at the airport and drove him back to his place in a pickup truck.

"I wanted to say something nice to him," Tommy told me. "So I said, 'Marlon, I saw you in *Apocalypse Now*. You were terrific.'

"And Brando said, 'Is that the one where I was bald?'"

Rod Steiger has his own Marlon Brando story. The role Steiger is best remembered for—next to *The Pawnbroker*—is Marlon Brando's older brother in *On the Waterfront*. Steiger told me about a problem he had shooting the famous "I coulda been a contender" scene with Brando in the back of the car. "Marlon was there for his scenes," Steiger said, "but he wasn't there for my talk-back. The way they shot that scene was that first the camera was on Brando while he delivered his speech, then the camera was on me during Brando's speech for my reaction shots, then they did a two-shot of us during the same speech. Finally the camera was on me for my lines to Brando while he responded to me. But when it came time to shoot my lines, Brando left, so I had to sit there talking to an empty seat with nobody to react to."

David Dukes told me a similar story about having to film over-the-shoulder scenes with Frank Sinatra in *The First Deadly Sin*. Dukes is a fine actor who was in the play *Bent* with Richard Gere some years ago on Broadway. In *The First Deadly Sin*, he played a mad killer and Sinatra was a detective, and there was a scene where they confronted each other. Dukes sat through the scene when they were shooting Sinatra, giving back his lines for Sinatra to react off. Then it was Sinatra's turn to give back his lines. When they shoot scenes like that, the second actor does not have a mike, but he usually speaks his lines as a courtesy for the first actor. Unlike Brando, Sinatra stayed for the reaction shots, but instead of saying his lines for Dukes, he said things like "Gee, David, you're a terrific actor." Dukes's line would be "I've killed, and I'll kill again," to which Sinatra would say, "We'll go to Vesuvio's, we'll have some nice spaghetti carbonara . . ."

Franchot Tone was the opposite of anything that had to do with Method acting. He was a classic example of the old school. I asked him once, "What if you're in a scene and a fly lands on your shoulder? Do you brush it away?"

"Never. Was the fly in the script?" he asked.

"No."

"If it's not in the script, I don't brush it away."

I asked, "Wouldn't the character brush it away?"

"I don't guess for the character. The character moves stage left and says —. He comes through the door and says —. That's what I do, I move stage left and say —. The script didn't say, 'scratch your shoulder,' so I don't scratch my shoulder."

Henry Fonda explained the art of acting to me better than anyone else. "Acting is reacting," he said. "Children are wonderful actors until they're about eight or ten years old, because they don't know what's going to happen. When they play cops and robbers they're fantastic—until they know that they can get hurt when they fall, and then it's not fun anymore. It's fun when you don't know about your knee; kids do better falls than actors till they're ten."

Fonda gave me a hypothetical example of a scene in a restaurant that will end when the actor walks out the door of the restaurant and is shot by a killer waiting outside. "Ninety-nine percent of people will act during the dinner as if the shooting is coming," he said. "A professional actor knows the shooting is coming, but if he's good he doesn't act it. He plays the minute, and he plays his minute off your minute."

I did two hours with Fonda in Miami, and what I remember most is his telling me that he loved playing Mr. Roberts on Broadway because he was nothing like the character in real life—even though his public image was. Henry said he was an alcoholic and a roustabout and that he never really knew how to love a woman, but his image was such that people raised their kids to be like Henry Fonda. He never could live up to that image, except as Mr. Roberts, and it galled him. "There were times," he said, "when it would be three in the afternoon and I would think, Gee, I wish it was eight o'clock so I could be Mr. Roberts again."

Fonda took his craft very seriously until the end, and he could talk acting all day. The same is true of Robert De Niro and of someone that De Niro reminds me of—Paul Muni. I always think of De Niro and Muni together because they submerge themselves in their characters, they become the people they play. Whether it was in *I Am a Fugitive from a Chain Gang* or *Scarface,* Muni worked on his own makeup and did everything he could to merge with the character, which made for great individual performances but denied him a "star" identity. In the same way, we have no real image of De Niro. When I think of him, I think of Jake La Motta in *Raging Bull* or Travis Bickle in *Taxi Driver* or Al Capone in *The Untouchables*. Bogart and Mitchum became stars by always playing themselves in a way. Gary Cooper is always Gary Cooper; De Niro is never De Niro, Muni is never Muni.

Paul Muni was greatly loved by other actors. He came up in the Yiddish theater, where he was known by his real name, Muni Weisenfreund. He didn't acquire the name Paul Muni until he appeared on Broadway in *This One Man* and then *Counsellor-at-Law*. After he became famous through his movies, he continued to act on Broadway. But he instructed the theater managers that anyone who came backstage and said, "I'm a friend of Paul's, I want to see him," was not to be admitted. His friends all called him Muni, and he never used the name Paul except professionally.

Tony Randall told me about doing *Inherit the Wind* on

Broadway with Muni as Henry Drummond and Ed Begley as
Matthew Harrison Brady. In the stage version, Randall played
the newspaperman E. K. Hornbeck, who talked to the audience. The opening scene had Hornbeck sitting alone
onstage, and behind him was the shadow of the train as it
pulled into town carrying Henry Drummond. Muni would get
off the train and enter carrying his bags: Drummond has come
to town to try the case. Randall said to me, "I'd always get a
little thrill during that opening, to think that I was on the
same stage with Muni, the greatest actor of my time."

About eight months into the run of the play, Randall went
onstage as usual. He settled into his chair, the train whistle
sounded, the audience hushed, the shadow came against the
backdrop—and Ed Begley walked out carrying his bags. Muni
and Begley were getting bored, so they had switched roles,
and they didn't bother to tell Tony.

"I just said to myself, My God!" Randall told me. "They
were perfect playing the opposite roles. And then they began
to switch off from time to time so that the program eventually
said something to the effect that 'We do not know who will
play the part of Matthew Harrison Brady and Henry Drummond tonight.'"

If Paul Muni was an actor's actor, Eugene O'Neill was an actor's delight. His work seems to bring out the best in stage
performers, from Jason Robards to Jack Lemmon to Colleen
Dewhurst. I recently asked Dewhurst about acting in O'Neill
plays, which she has done many times. She has even played
his wife, Carlotta, in a one-woman show. I said, "What quality
did Eugene O'Neill have as a writer that makes actors want to
perform his plays?"

"He forced you to get into the character," she said. "You
couldn't use actors' tricks. The little raising of the eyebrow
wouldn't do. And he was able to touch women to an extraordi-

nary degree. He never wrote a woman's character that wasn't very real and very penetrating, and therefore very painful."

"All humility aside then, would you say you have to be a great actress to play those parts?" I asked.

"Not necessarily," she said. "But you have to be someone who can really get in touch with your feelings."

Obviously, great actors are usually able to do that. But some very good actresses, she felt, might have a tough time with O'Neill. And what she couldn't get over was that a man had written those astonishing women's roles. Many of them were mad or drunks; he was a drunk himself and a little mad, yet he was also a macho guy and not at all feminine. "But he understood," she said.

"To act O'Neill is both a joy and an immense effort," she said. "If you do eight performances a week, in four of them you'll think you hit it, and in four of them you'll think you missed."

Ernest Borgnine is one of the great character actors of our time, and with one exception he never really broke through to become a leading man. On my show he talked about the days when he was beginning to make it and how he longed to be more than a character actor. Working with Spencer Tracy in *Bad Day at Black Rock,* one of the great unsung movies, was the biggest thrill of his life, he said. But when they finished that movie, Borgnine was concerned about being typecast and was looking for a movie in which he could play something other than the heavy. Tracy gave him this advice: "Stay here in Hollywood. You'll have a great career as a character actor. You'll have a wonderful life, you'll always work, and you'll make a lot of money. And we'll fool around and have a lot of laughs together."

But Borgnine had been offered the lead in a small movie to be shot in New York in black and white, written by an un-

known author named Paddy Chayefsky. The film was *Marty*.
Ernie told the story like this:

"I said, 'Spence, I'm gonna go do this movie.' He said,
'You're making a big mistake. You're gonna make a little black-
and-white film, no one's ever gonna hear of it, you're gonna
think you're a star and you're not gonna be a star. I'm telling
you, Ernie, I love you, but it's a mistake.'

"And I said, 'Spence, if I don't try it now, I'll never know.'"

So Borgnine made *Marty* in two and a half months and was
nominated for the Academy Award for best actor. Tracy was
nominated in the same category for *Bad Day at Black Rock*.
Of course, Borgnine won, and as he was walking up to accept
the Oscar, he passed Tracy, who said to him, "You never listen, do you?"

Richard Dreyfuss told me that I could act if I wanted to. He
said, "You'd be very good. You could do all the Neil Simon
plays because he writes parts for fifty-year-old Jewish guys
with hang-ups, like you. You'd be a master. And you have one
edge that an actor has to be born with—a great voice."

Dreyfuss said he always wanted to do radio drama because
it makes an actor rely totally on his voice. "None of the tricks
work on radio," he said. "The raised eyebrow doesn't work.
The nice gliding movement doesn't work. I come into a room
well; *that* doesn't work. All I've got is my voice. What I've got
to learn to do with my voice—which you're doing all your
life—is to express terror, happiness, pathos, anxiety, surprise.
And no face to help me. I give a lot of credit to those radio
actors."

That was all very nice of him to say, but I think my mind
would get in the way if I ever tried acting. I think I would be
guilty of what Fonda talked about. I would know I was going
to get shot when I went out the door. So the whole time I was
supposed to be eating dinner, oblivious to my fate, I would be

sneaking a look at the door between bites. And my nature would be to change my lines, which would throw off the other actors. Like a jazz musician, I don't say anything the same way twice.

On the other hand, Pete Fountain told me that when he worked with Lawrence Welk—which he considered the most important two years of his life—he learned that he could sit every night "and just play the note." It was a useful discipline for him. He told me I should try acting, if only as an exercise. "Do a play for three months," he said. "Do the same lines every night and it'll be a great discipline." Needless to say, I haven't taken him up on his suggestion.

Bette Midler gave me another perspective on the question of improvisation when she was on my show. Bette said that Zero Mostel drove her crazy when they did *Fiddler on the Roof* together. Bette played the oldest daughter in the Broadway version, a fact that a lot of people forget. "He was a great Fiddler," she said, "but there was no play—it was all Zero." It was a bravura performance, and he amazed the other actors on the stage, but they liked it better with Herschel Bernardi. Often the cast got better reactions from the crowd when somebody other than Mostel played the lead, even though the audience didn't tear the house down the way they did for Mostel.

"When Zero did 'If I Were a Rich Man,'" Bette said, "we'd time it. Some nights eleven minutes, some nights thirteen minutes—the shtick he did, the little extra business with the audience. Herschel was an actor. With him, 'If I Were a Rich Man' took eight or nine minutes every night. The applause was never as big, but they were applauding Tevye; when Zero did it, they were applauding Zero." That unnerved the actors, and Zero was apparently not popular during the run of *Fiddler*.

I liked Herschel Bernardi very much. He had a marvelous

voice; of all the roles he played, including the one in *Peter Gunn*, the most money he ever made was as the voice of the Jolly Green Giant. Once you get an established voice, where *they* need *you*, then you've got it made in the commercial world. Herschel was able to do plays he liked because he always had the Jolly Green Giant to fall back on. He told me that he would walk into a room and say hello to someone and kids would turn around and yell, "The Jolly Green Giant!"

Hanna-Barbera once asked me to do a voice: God. They were creating a series on the Bible and wanted me to do the voice of the Old Testament God. I asked them why they saw me in that role. Hanna and Barbera are crazy guys; when you're doing cartoons, you've got to be a little crazy. They said, "We think that the God of the Old Testament smoked and that he had a raspy voice. He wasn't a crystal-clear announcer. Your voice isn't the best voice, but we always know it's your voice. It doesn't sound like any other voice, and God would have had a voice like that."

Jon Voight is a classic Method actor whom I've gotten to know very well. When he did *Midnight Cowboy* he lived in a flophouse in Tulsa for two weeks to learn the correct Oklahoma accent. Gleason would have said, "Call up a guy from Oklahoma, listen to him for two minutes, and do him. It ain't a big deal, pal."

William Hurt is another Method actor I admire a great deal, and he's also the epitome of the New York actor who tolerates Hollywood only as long as he absolutely has to in order to make a living. I was backstage with him after a performance of *Hurlyburly* on Broadway one night, and he told me that whenever he does a film in Hollywood he keeps the return ticket to New York in his pocket during every scene. Even when he was in a prison cell in *Kiss of the Spider Woman*. And if they tell him that they're not shooting the next day, to come back the day after, he goes right to the airport. He can't *stand* southern California. That's his rule. If he's wearing only a bathing suit, they've got to put the ticket somewhere. He wasn't kidding—Jerry Stiller later confirmed this. Hurt has to know that there is *on his body* a plane ticket to New York.

He never carries bags when he goes to California. He keeps an extra set of clothes in California, which he moves to wherever the film studio is putting him up—toiletries, shoes, the whole bit. He never socializes in L.A. and when they break for the weekend, he's gone. He even knows the airline schedules by heart. When I was standing backstage with him that night, he said to me, "Hey, United flight 79? It goes at 7:40 now." There's a guy who loves New York.

Kirk Douglas is the son of Russian immigrants and is definitely an actor from the old school. Kirk starred in *One Flew Over the Cuckoo's Nest* on Broadway and owned the rights to it. It bombed on the stage, and his son Michael Douglas said to him, "Dad, I don't know how to tell you this. It's a terrific play, but you're a lit-tle too old for it." That was about fifteen years ago. Kirk was around fifty-five then and Michael pointed out to him that the lead character is thirty-three. As Kirk told me the story, he then said to Michael, "You know better?"

"I'll buy it from you," Michael said, "and I'll produce it Off-Broadway." He eventually bought it, packaged it, put Jack Nicholson in it, and the movie went through the roof and won five of the top Oscars.

One of the things I enjoy about meeting people like Kirk Douglas is that they are larger than life to me. And while I'm not in awe, I have great respect for their craft. I asked Peter Ustinov what it was like to work with Kirk Douglas in *Spartacus*, the Stanley Kubrick movie based on the book by

Howard Fast. Ustinov said the best part of it was watching
Douglas hopping around. Apparently, Kirk is as hyperkinetic
off-screen as on. "Even when we had lunch, he'd be jumping
around," Ustinov said.

Parenthetically, from that same film Ustinov added another
story to my Olivier file, this one about Olivier's uncanny ability to steal scenes. "I had a great scene in *Spartacus*," Ustinov
said. "Olivier plays the head of the Roman guard and he
comes to visit me. I'm a wealthy landowner, and I have all the
funny lines in the scene. I'm putting him down. The scene is
mine. The thing is, I don't like watching rushes, so I hadn't
seen the final outcome until I went to the premiere. Then I
saw that Olivier had spent the entire scene chewing grapes
and picking his teeth. I was so busy being witty that I never
noticed what he was doing. But during the scene the audience
is watching Olivier, who is having trouble getting part of a
grape out from between his teeth."

Kirk Douglas is also a real old-fashioned family man. His
Jewish heritage is very important to him. He doesn't talk
about it much, but he goes to synagogue on the High Holy
Days, and his family is the most important thing in his life.
Yet he talked about the problems of getting older, having
trouble landing good parts, and having a son who is suddenly
a heartthrob and a bigger hit than he ever was. In fact, when
Michael Douglas and Karl Malden were starting *The Streets
of San Francisco*, Kirk told me he called up Malden and said
to him, "Don't let my son get a big head. If he's got big
scenes, tone him down a little. Let him go along slowly."

Burt Reynolds has his own theory of why actors make it or
don't make it in the movies. To Burt, it's all a question of
whether the camera likes you or not. He said, "The camera
likes me. I don't know what it is, but it likes me."

So every day of his life when he's working on a movie set,

absolutely the first thing he does in the morning is go to the camera and say, "I love you. Like me today. Please, like me today." He told me that Universal dropped him and Clint Eastwood on the same day, along with about a dozen other new actors, saying they had no chance of success. "But if the camera likes you," he said, "you can get away with an awful lot. And if it doesn't like you, you could be the greatest actor on Broadway, but you'll never get anywhere in the movies."

Tip O'Neill isn't an actor, but he does have great stage presence and a commanding voice. Tip once told me about the time he met Robert Redford in an airport bar in Denver. Redford came over and said, "I'm a great admirer of yours." Tip had no idea who he was. Clearly, Tip doesn't go to the movies. He noticed that a lot of people were looking into the bar and he thought they were watching him. But when Redford left, they all followed Redford. Tip said to the bartender, "Who is that?"

"That's Robert Redford," the bartender said.

"Who's *that*?"

"He's an actor."

Tip filed the information away and left. He had told Redford, though, that if he was ever in Massachusetts or Washington to come by and see him. Some time later in his office in Washington, Tip's secretary came running in to him. "Mr. O'Neill!" she announced. "Robert Redford is here to see you!"

By now Tip had forgotten the name and had no idea who she was talking about.

"He said he met you in the airport in Denver," she added, "and you told him to come by."

"Oh, yeah," said Tip. "What does he do?"

"Mr. Speaker, he's a movie actor."

Tip greeted Redford very heartily, but, he said, he could tell that Redford knew he didn't remember Denver at all.

Two days later, Tip was in the Madison hotel in D.C., heading out through the lobby, when he spotted Redford walking across the street. He remembered the face this time and the attention Redford got everywhere he went. Tip may have been planning to retire, but he was still a politician. "Twice I didn't know who this guy was," Tip told me, "but I wasn't going to let it happen again. I go running right out into the street, go past my limo that's waiting for me, and throw my arms around Redford. 'Bob, good to see you again!'

"And Redford said, 'Tip, good to see you—and you just killed twelve hundred feet of film.' I had run right into the middle of a scene and never noticed the cameras, but Bob was very gracious about it. After all, this time I remembered his name."

CHAPTER 4

THE NAME
OF THE GAME

According to Jackie Gleason, what killed Elvis Presley was
Presley's inability to cope with his overwhelming celebrity.
Gleason knew, because he had to cope with it himself. While
Jackie was obviously not heartthrob material, his visibility on
the new medium of television made him one of the most popular figures of the fifties. He told me about an experience he
had after taking over the *Cavalcade of Stars* television show
in New York in 1950. He was out one day in Coney Island,
walking along the boardwalk to get a couple of hot dogs at
Nathan's. He was with a few of his pals and when they turned
around, they noticed that a huge crowd of people had begun
following them. "What the hell is this?" Gleason said.

And the people were all yelling, "It's Jackie Gleason!"

Jackie said that right then he made a decision: "I'm still
going to go to Nathan's. I'm still going to eat where I want to
eat." Presley didn't make that decision, he said. Presley decided, "I can't hack that."

I once asked Frank Sinatra what he missed most as a result of being a celebrity. "Shooting pool," he said. Sinatra liked shooting pool in pool halls and he can't really do that anymore. But if he wants to have dinner at the Palm tonight, he'll go have dinner. Yes, there will be four guys with him, but if people come over to the table he'll usually be gracious and say hello.

Johnny Carson once told me that being a television celebrity is very different from being a movie celebrity. "If I'm in a restaurant," he said, "there's nobody who doesn't feel free to come over to me. And no one ever calls me 'Mr. Carson.' It's 'Hi, Johnny.' But if you see Paul Newman sitting at another table, you don't go over. You point. Because Paul Newman is eight feet by ten feet. I'm twenty-one inches. You're comfortable with me; he's larger than life. He's a movie star and therefore unreal."

Television talk shows have worn down the mystique of movie stars. Mystique is what the old moguls like Goldwyn and Mayer understood. They would never have let Clark Gable go on television. It's what Colonel Tom Parker understood. If Presley had done *Larry King Live* and all the other shows, he might have lived twenty years longer, but they couldn't have charged fifty bucks a ticket for every show.

The question is, where do you draw the line in terms of the press? When Sinatra was married to Mia Farrow, a particular photographer used to follow them around trying to get pictures of them, not just in public places like restaurants, but in supposedly private places like their boat. It bugged Frank, and he got the photographer's name. Then he hired three photographers of his own to follow the guy all over for a couple of weeks, around the clock. They'd take pictures of him wherever he went, take pictures of his house all night. It was all perfectly legal, and it drove the guy crazy.

People are always saying that if you make a decision to be in show business, you're making the decision to have those pictures taken. But is it true that, as Willy Loman says in *Death of a Salesman*, it comes with the territory? Buddy Rich put it to me this way: "What if I just wanted to play the drums? All I owe you is the best drum playing I can give. I don't want my picture in the paper; I just want to play drums. Why are you determining for me that I entered show business to have my picture taken?"

The best example I can cite of that fine line between what you owe your fans and what sense of privacy the public owes you is an incident that happened to me not long ago. If nothing else, it made me understand how some of those celebrities must feel at times. I had just started seeing my ex-wife Sharon for the first time after my heart attack and after going out with Angie Dickinson for some time. Even though we are no longer together, at that time I wanted Sharon back, although I knew she was seeing another guy, and it had been a rough couple of weeks. We were out having brunch and were discussing whether we should spend the night together again. We both were hesitant, but we had decided that we were going to go ahead and do it anyway. We were in the process of choosing a hotel when someone approached our table. "Larry King! Larry King!" he shouted. "I'm from Cleveland and I'm your biggest fan."

The guy was really thrilled, but he was also one of those effusive types any celebrity dreads. "Listen," he said, "my wife, Mildred, is just crazy about you. We watch you on television, we listen to you on the radio, and we read your column. She's in the ladies' room but she'll be coming out in a minute. We *gotta* take a picture."

I thanked the guy and turned back to talk to Sharon. He wouldn't go away. "Who's this?" he asked, looking at Sharon.

How exactly do you introduce your ex-wife, whom you've divorced and are starting to see again? "This is Sharon," I said.

He half-whispered in my ear, "Hey, how's Angie?"

By this time, I was just hoping he would leave. Sharon was trying to ignore him and drink her coffee but I could practically hear her teeth grinding on the cup. The guy started yelling for his wife, as if she could somehow hear him in the recesses of the ladies' room. "Mildred!"

Then, to me, he said, "Hey, no bother, is it?"

What we don't realize when we think about celebrities is that there's also a boring, everyday side to their lives. When people see me on TV or hear me on the radio, I don't think they visualize me having to run down to the convenience store in my building to buy toilet paper and cereal. I remember Walter Cronkite telling me about the time he went down to the 7-Eleven because his wife needed milk. He got the milk and the milk carton broke as he was handing it to the clerk. It caused a major commotion in the store. Everyone was gawking, as if to say, "Walter Cronkite has broken a milk carton in the 7-Eleven—that's not supposed to be!" What he was saying to me was "Why *can't* it be?"

And it was at a 7-Eleven that Peter Ueberroth discovered he was *Time*'s Man of the Year. *Time* doesn't tell its Man or Woman of the Year that he or she has been selected. In fact, *Time*'s staff works four or five stories at once so even the writers don't know. Ueberroth had been on a fishing trip with his son, and on the way back he stopped at a 7-Eleven and asked the clerk if the new *Time* was in yet. The clerk said that he still had last week's issue. Peter was about to leave when the manager called out, "Hey, they came in. They're right here, lemme just clip 'em open."

He clipped open the pile, tore the paper away, and Ueberroth saw his picture on the cover: Man of the Year. He said to the manager, "Can I buy ten of these?"

And the manager said, "Hey, I got customers! I can't sell no ten to one guy, you crazy? Two, three, maybe."

*   *   *

Life magazine did a survey of the most identifiable images in
the world, and the most identifiable of all was Muhammad
Ali. Ali came out two points ahead of the Coca-Cola symbol. I
think something like ninety percent of the world identified
him. What is it like to be *that* famous? There are probably
quite a few places that Sinatra could go in the world and not
be recognized, but Ali was identified by African tribesmen,
Australian backwoodsmen, Chinese schoolchildren. Yet of all
the celebrities I've met, Ali is the only one I ever heard say
flatly, "I earned it, I wanted it, I liked it, I want to give it
back, I want to use it for good things, there's nothing wrong
with it."

When I was growing up, the ultimate celebrity for me was
David Kaminski from Brooklyn—Danny Kaye. And sometimes he acted like it. When I interviewed Danny, he told me
he was a success because of his own craziness. He said the
public school system didn't know what to do with him—he
made jokes, he made tummel, he kidded in the gym, he got
up in class and imitated the teacher. So they threw him out.
Schools don't know what to do with that kind of kid. He decided that he would go *to* his craziness, let it be his strength.

How crazy could Danny Kaye get? On a whim, he would go
down to the airport, get in his own plane, fly to San Francisco, walk into the back of Johnny Kan's restaurant, give the
chef the night off, and cook the meals that night for the customers. There are people walking around who have eaten
Danny Kaye's moo goo gai pan and don't even know it. He
was the only Chinese escoffier cook in the world who was not
a professional chef.

Danny was a licensed pilot and he knew the president of
United Airlines. Every so often he would go down to the airport and fly an empty DC10 from Chicago to Denver. He

couldn't fly passengers, and a couple of pilots would go along with him, but he'd fly left seat the whole way. Danny's approach to anything he was afraid of was to learn as much as he could about it. He was afraid of flying so he learned how to pilot a plane. He was afraid of medicine so he studied it. Michael De Bakey, the heart surgeon, used to let Danny stand in the operating room and observe. Danny knew everything that happened to him when he had his heart surgery, including what went wrong.

Because of all that, Danny could sometimes be a real pain in the ass. He had a know-it-all attitude that would irritate the hell out of professionals. Mike Marshall of the Dodgers would step out of the batting cage and Danny would say to him, "Keep your elbow up, you're dropping it too low." And Marshall would say, "Thank you, Mr. Kaye."

"Hey. Hey. *Hey*," Danny would say. "I'm not some old schmuck. I know what I'm talking about." He'd have his cane and his little hat. "You're dropping your right arm." I don't know if he was right or not, but you could see the players getting a little frustrated. Or he'd say to Mariano Duncan, "You don't have to throw right away. Hold the ball a second. I saw Billy Cox play. Tell him, Larry. Tell him about Billy Cox." Cox was the great Dodger infielder who was so quick he could virtually read the signature on the baseball before gunning the hitter out at first. Danny would say this in a way that wasn't rude exactly but that implied, I know and you don't. Celebrity can do that to you—it makes you feel that the rules don't apply, that you can do anything you want.

I've always had some affection for the performer, even when he was a son of a bitch. If someone gives you joy, I figure maybe that's all he owes you. Sinatra doesn't owe an interview to Liz Smith, but he owes you a performance. If he produces, if he makes you happy, what's the difference if he's not nice? I think the worst son of a bitch I've ever heard of was Al Jolson—I've never heard a good word about him. As

George Jessel told me, "Jolson's funeral was widely attended by those who wanted to make sure." Ty Cobb was probably right up there with Jolson. There were four baseball people at Cobb's funeral, and only one of them was a former player. What was the line that Jack Mann wrote when Cobb died? "Now all we can add is that he's dead." Cobb was supposedly a racist, a skinflint, a cutthroat ballplayer who always went into a base spikes high. He was a nasty guy, but what did it matter if he won games for your team?

To quote Buddy Rich again, "All I owe anybody is my drums. I don't owe you a hello, and I don't owe you a good-bye." Mel Tormé, on the other hand, said, "I learned the hard way. I was a rat-fink sort of guy, but I think a performer owes the audience. I owe the public honesty and compassion, because they do pay my livelihood. I owe them more than my voice."

It's an ongoing debate. I've interviewed both Rich and Tormé many times on the subject; they were very close friends and they totally disagreed. I think I come down more on Rich's side, if only because, based on my own experience, I understand how insecure performers can feel.

I'll never forget the time when, after a series of financial blunders, I was forced to declare bankruptcy in Miami. Desperate for some new source of income, I flew out to Los Angeles to look for work. I spent several weeks there, but after visiting every radio and TV station in town, I still couldn't find a job and I was feeling pretty beat. On my last day, all I had left was my ticket back, my rental car which I had no money to pay for—and three dollars.

I had four hours to kill, so I drove to the Beverly Hills Hotel, walked one flight down to the coffee shop, and had a milk shake to fill myself up. The check for the milk shake was three bucks, so I couldn't even tip the countergirl. When I got my car from the valet, I said, "I just ran out of the hotel without my wallet, so I can't tip you, I'd have to go back." I

had half a tank of gas. I figured if I stopped anywhere and
something happened, I'd panic, so I drove straight to the airport and dropped the car off. It was on a cash deal, back in
the days when you could rent a car for cash, but I told them
they'd have to bill me—which is probably why they don't rent
cars for cash anymore. I went into the terminal and I still
had a few hours before my flight, so I approached a friendly-
looking guy and asked if I could borrow some money. I said I
needed a couple of bucks to buy newspapers to read on the
plane, and he gave me five. "Here, get yourself a bite to eat,"
he said. I got on the plane and flew back to Miami, still out of
work and completely broke.

Now we dissolve to 1987, the eighth annual Ace Awards,
cable television's highest honor. The awards were given out at
two ceremonies, one at night in a theater in L.A., the other at
a luncheon at the Beverly Hills Hotel. Alexander Cohen was
the producer and I was the emcee, for which I was paid five
thousand dollars. My escort was Angie Dickinson, and we
drove up in her car, a Mercedes. We arrived, the cameras
started snapping, and we went inside—where I not only
would emcee but would win an award as the best talk show
host on cable TV. As we were walking down the stairs, that
whole scene from 1973 suddenly flashed in front of me. I
asked someone, "Is the coffee shop still here?"

It was, although it's not really a coffee shop so much as a
gleaming brass counter. Milk shakes were four dollars now;
they'd gone up a buck. The minute I hit those stairs, everything came back to me, and I must have gone into a daze
because Angie said, "Is something the matter?"

"I'll tell you later."

That was one of the proudest moments of my life, but also
one of the weirdest. And six weeks later I had a heart attack.

My other proud moment came when I won the Peabody.
For one thing, mine was the only talk show that had ever won
it, but what made it for me was what Alistair Cooke said be-

fore he presented the awards. "There are all kinds of people in the broadcast industry," he said, "and ninety-eight percent of them can be put in a category: they follow. You do something, they repeat it. They're careful, this ninety-eight percent. They take no risks, they're never late, they're never early. Ninety-eight percent. The other two percent are in this room today."

That made me feel pretty good. The Peabody is probably the most valuable award I've ever won, but what happened to me at the Ace Awards, on the stairs of the Beverly Hills Hotel, was the most personally significant. It made me realize how far I'd come—and how far I could drop.

If you may not owe them hello and goodbye, as Buddy Rich said, you do owe them the drums. I think Lenny Bruce made a major mistake near the end of his career. Lenny owed us a performance, and he didn't give it at the end. His audiences weren't paying to hear a diatribe. He just stopped being funny. The irony is that I don't think Lenny ever had a conviction upheld; he may have had a misdemeanor, but never a felony. But all he talked about on the stage in his last few years was how he was being persecuted, and I think he was wrong.

The opposite of that would have to be what I witnessed when I went to see Steve Lawrence and Eydie Gorme perform on Cape Cod in the summer of 1986. Their son had died under unusual circumstances not long before. He was twenty-three, and he died of crib death, almost unheard of in adults. He had slept at his girlfriend's house in Los Angeles and was getting up to go to work. He turned over in bed, pulled a pillow around himself, and said, "I'm going to sleep an extra five minutes." And he died.

Steve and Eydie were performing in Atlanta when they got the news. Somehow Frank Sinatra heard about it and called to tell them he was sending his private jet to bring them back to L.A. "You don't want to take a commercial flight at a time like this," he told them. The doctors couldn't come up with an explanation other than that the young man had somehow asphyxiated himself.

I called on the day of the show to let them know I'd be there that night and to ask if they wanted to talk. Their publicist said they hadn't been doing any socializing lately, but they'd see me after the show.

They were absolutely the same as ever onstage, and they even called me up with them and introduced me to the crowd. As I was going back to my seat, Steve said, "We'll see you backstage."

It was a kind of tent theater and they had a mobile dressing room. When I went backstage, I felt like I was walking into a wake. Eydie was sitting on the couch and she hugged me as I came in, held my hand, and said, "Larry—my companion every night when I can't sleep. I'm up all night, I even listen to the replay of your show." And Steve kept saying, "I don't know, Larry, I don't know. Twenty-five years old, never took a drug, in perfect shape. Maybe God meant it to happen."

Then Eydie, who is Catholic, said things like "Fuck God!" or "Don't give me that God crap!" And Steve would say, "Don't say that." Steve still goes to synagogue, looking for answers. He said Kaddish and he still says Yizkor.

Backstage on Cape Cod, Steve was saying, "Tell me anything. Tell me it was a car; tell me he was drunk; tell me someone shot him. Give me a reason." Then their other son, who travels with them and plays piano in their show, came in. He said to them, "You know, sometimes I feel like I wish it were me." Somehow they were all able to hold together and draw strength from one another, even in their separate suffering. And I believed their frustration: How do you deal logically with the illogical? A defective car, a brick falling off a building—terrible bad fortune, but those things happen. People don't lie in bed and die at the age of twenty-five.

Steve and Eydie gave a hell of a show that night. That's all they owed us, but they did owe us that. What if they had

gone onstage and said, "We're only going to sing fifteen songs
for you tonight, and they're sad songs. And then we're going
to tell you about our late son"?

Jimmy Hoffa was a celebrity of a different sort. He was not
the kind of guy you'd love, but I didn't dislike him. He was,
however, the kind of guy you'd want to have on your side. I
liked his anger. "Every time they say I used strong-arm
guys," he told me, "I'd ask them, 'How do you think the
whole union movement began? Management guys tried to
beat up strikers!' Why didn't they ever put management on
trial and ask them why *they* dealt with the mob? The mob had
to be in management for management to survive. When the
mob was called in by management to hit union people over
the head with bricks, the government never said that the
president of the company was doing business with the Mafia.
But if Hoffa hires an ex-con, Hoffa's tied up with the mob."
Jimmy liked to refer to himself like that, in the third person.
    Lenny used to say, "If God lines people up, Jimmy Hoffa's
ahead of J. Edgar Hoover. The first virtue according to Christ
is to forgive. Well, Hoover punished, Hoffa forgave." What
Lenny meant was that Hoffa would always hire guys who had
been in jail and put them to work. Of course, that was because his boys were always getting into trouble with the law.
    I interviewed Jimmy just after he got out of prison and he
was really caught up in prison reform. I said, "How could a
Jimmy Hoffa, so used to running things, take incarceration?"
    "I can take anything life deals me," he said. "Nothing keeps
Hoffa down. They can send me anywhere and I'll make my
place. They ain't gonna break me." He talked about the conditions in jail. "Blacks are tough in prison?" he asked rhetori-
cally. "Wouldn't you be? By the way, we didn't have no
segregated unions when Jimmy Hoffa ran the Teamsters. We
had black truck drivers in Mississippi."
    It was ironic that Bobby Kennedy went after Hoffa, be-

cause the Kennedys had no knowledge of what the workingman was up against and what value a Hoffa had to someone
trying to earn a decent living. In fact, I'm convinced that the
Kennedys sent the Teamsters to the Republican party. As a
result of Bobby's persecution of the Teamsters, they supported Nixon in 1960. They supported Johnson against Goldwater only because no union could support Goldwater. They
supported Nixon against McGovern, they stayed out of Ford-
Carter, and then they came in for Reagan twice.

The night I had Marcello Mastroianni on my radio show, he
was the second guest of the evening. He arrived early, so I
went out to greet him and introduced him to my friend Herb
Cohen. Marcello speaks English with a heavy accent, but he
and Herb started chatting away, so I left them alone and went
back to do the show. I later learned from Herbie just how the
conversation had gone. Herbie had started off innocently
enough by telling Marcello that he'd recently been to Italy.
Marcello asked Herbie where he'd been and Herbie said he'd
been to Venice and he'd just come back from Milan.

"Milano?" Marcello said with a sneer. "Those people suck."

Herbie said, "What?"

"Milano suck, Venezia suck, even Roma suck. They oppress
southern Italians."

"They do?"

"Yes," said Marcello. "Where do you live?"

Herbie said, "Chicago."

"You know where the airplane fly from Chicago? She go
from Chicago to Milano and then Roma. Milano first! Roma
second."

Herbie was startled. "Yeah, I think you're right," he said.
"I think it does go there first."

"Three hundred and fifty years ago," Marcello said, "when
there was no opera in Milano, when there was no concert, in

Napoli we had a thriving theater. We were known throughout the world. Those people treat us like dirt, they oppress us. Southern Italians are warm, wonderful people."

Poor Herbie had only been in the north of Italy, and every time Marcello asked him what other cities he'd seen, Marcello would say they sucked. After a while, Herbie was afraid to name any more cities.

When Marcello came on the air, I asked him how he liked doing all those love scenes with some of the most beautiful women in the world. Did it turn him on? He said, "Turned on? First, the positions they put you in for the camera are impossible. How can you get turned on when they're sticking the camera in your ribs? You never get an erection! You're in bed in a room with sixty-three people and the director has the camera under the woman's armpits, you don't get turned on."

I have my own story that relates to that. A lot of unusual things happen to me on the air, but nothing compares with what happened one night in the fall of 1975. You may remember Marilyn Chambers, the star of *Behind the Green Door* and other adult movies. Well, Marilyn was on my radio show in Miami, talking about—what else?—sex. She said, "Sex is a commodity to me. You have your voice, you use it. I have my body, I use it. It doesn't mean any more than that to me."

She stayed till the end of the program, and we were getting ready to break for the news. Perhaps to illustrate her point, she asked me, on the air, "Do you want to make love during the news?"

While I was fumbling for an answer and trying to find my voice, she added matter-of-factly, "How long is the news anyway?"

"Six minutes," I said, grateful for a question I could answer with a straight face. "And another minute of local."

"Let's do as much as we can in seven minutes," she said—

and then she began taking off her clothes. Finally, all she had on was a slim gold chain around her waist.

I didn't know what to do. Chambers certainly was attractive, but—make love? Right there in the studio?

"Come on," she said. "The subject of this show is sex, isn't it? Don't you think it's appropriate?"

So I gulped and said okay. I broke for the news and I asked the engineer to leave the control booth. The idea was that we would make love and then I would talk about it on the air after the news. Except, well, you know what comes next. I couldn't do anything. It was just too public, too exposed. It was *weird*.

When the news ended, we went back on the air and talked about what happened. She said, "Why couldn't you get excited? I was willing to do anything. In fact, I like you. We could have fun. Do you want to go out after?" I said no, thank you.

When the morning disc jockey came on, she was still naked. She started dancing around for him and then went over and danced right into his face. The poor guy didn't know what to do. She said to me, "It's like you taking your elbow, Larry, and rubbing it up against somebody."

Well, maybe not exactly.

Speaking of public performances, Alan Jay Lerner told me a story about Richard Burton. Burton was the lead in Lerner's Broadway musical *Camelot*. Lerner's admiration for Richard Burton as an actor was extremely high. But his admiration for Burton as a drinker scaled all heights. Burton was perfect during rehearsals and on opening night. The show had gotten mixed reviews, but because of Burton it was sold out. Elizabeth Taylor was showing up in the audience, attracting even more attention. The third night of the performance, however, Lerner got a call in his apartment around seven o'clock. Burton hadn't arrived backstage yet and he was usually there by six. The curtain was at eight.

Lerner ran down to the theater, which was near his apartment. He knew that the capacity audience would be lining up to return their tickets if Burton didn't show. At seven-thirty Burton finally arrived, so bombed that he didn't know who Lerner was, wasn't sure what theater he was in, and had no idea what play he was supposed to be doing. They were pumping Burton full of coffee and Burton was ranting on about never having missed a performance in his life. Just as he finished saying that, he fell flat on his face, out cold.

By ten of eight, Lerner couldn't take any more, so he left the dressing room and stood in the back of the theater to wait for the inevitable announcement: "Ladies and gentlemen, due to illness tonight, the leading role . . ." followed by a chorus of groans and a stampede for the box office. Instead, the overture began. The curtain went up and there was Burton, in costume and in character, delivering a flawless performance.

Sometimes events are connected in eerie ways that I don't even try to unravel or explain rationally. When Liza Minnelli was on my show she talked about how strongly attached to her mother she was, the effect her mother's neuroses had on her, and the difficulties of growing up the child of such a famous woman. A few weeks later, I went to see Liza in concert, and after the show I was standing backstage with her, my wife, and Dr. Michael Halberstam and his wife.

Dr. Halberstam, the brother of author David Halberstam, was a cardiologist and he was talking to Liza about death— how you deal with the death of a parent or loved one who had as much an impact as Liza's mother had on her. The only good thing about the death of a loved one, he said, is the finality of it. Unlike a broken love affair, death doesn't leave any doubts.

A week after the concert Halberstam's house was robbed, and he was foolish enough to chase the robber down the street in his car. He cornered the guy, got out of his car, and the thief shot and killed him. It seemed eerie to me, not only because he had just been talking about death but because his wife had heard the conversation and then had to deal with *his* death. She watched him die in front of her. What a tragic irony.

Liza and I also discussed the relative advantages and disadvantages of fame—in her case not only her own fame but also her mother's. My experience with being recognized in public has, thankfully, been limited. I've been on national television only for a few years, and because Washington, D.C., isn't wired for cable, I can walk the streets there without too much recognition. On the other hand, my job does have its benefits, and I don't mean just getting a good table in a crowded restaurant. I get to meet a lot of interesting people in my line of work, and one of the most interesting was an actress from North Dakota named Angie Dickinson.

Angie Dickinson was a true fantasy of mine. When I saw Angie in *Dressed to Kill,* I was with my wife, Sharon, and I told her, "If she calls me, I'm gone." And Sharon said, "If she calls you, I'd understand your going." It was like a little joke between us. After Sharon and I were divorced, however, Angie came on my show, and I felt I had to take the opening—I asked her out.

The first time we dated was a scene I'd never experienced before, because I took her to a restaurant where the waiters all knew me—but everyone in the place knew Angie Dickinson. It's hard to say whether that was more exhilarating or humbling, but it sure was wild. Later, we went to a nightclub, and as we were getting ready to leave, Angie got on line to go to the ladies' room. I could see people whispering,

"That's Angie Dickinson, waiting on line!" The women were trying to decide whether they should let Angie ahead of them. You know, what's the polite thing to do when you're on line ahead of a movie star? But Angie waited her turn like everybody else, and nobody on that line spoke to her. I guess Johnny Carson knew what he was talking about.

That night, we were at her house and I looked over at her and I thought, I want to call Herbie, I want to call one of the guys, and I want to say, "*Holy shit*! Larry Zeiger, the kid from Brooklyn with the glasses, is sitting here with Angie Dickinson!" That's what I wanted to do.

Just then, she looked over at me and said, "You know, it's so strange."

"What is," I said.

"That your voice is over here," she said, "and not over there in my radio."

And I thought to myself, Christ, she had the same fantasy about me that I had about her. She listens to me every night, and she must like my voice. I can't tell you what that sort of thing does for your insecurities, but I recommend it highly.

One of the terrific things about Angie is that we have both a romance and a friendship. In fact, sometimes it's hard to tell which comes first—and here is one of the strange ironies of life. Fourteen years ago I was out of work, alone in California and looking for a job. My friend jockey Bill Hartack was riding that day at Santa Anita. I went out to the track with him and naturally, since he had business to do, I was alone all afternoon, wandering around the track. I had no money to bet, there weren't any laughs. As I was strolling through the clubhouse, I spotted Burt Bacharach and Angie standing at the bar, having a drink. I thought how lovely she looked. I actually fantasized that it was me standing at the bar with her and quickly left because it was a little too much to take. Who would have believed that fourteen years later, Angie and I would have spent the day together at Santa Anita, having lunch and betting horses, visiting friends? As we were leaving, heading toward the valet parking area, we passed by the bar—the bar from fourteen years ago. It is impossible to describe that feeling.

The weird side of going out with someone like Angie, though, is that you sometimes feel as though you're conducting your courtship to an audience. I remember once walking into a hotel lobby in Washington with Angie on my arm when a fellow came up behind me, tapped me on the shoulder, and whispered in my ear, "You know, Larry, there are forty million guys in America who'd die to be in your shoes right now."

That sense of being followed—maybe stalked is a better word—is something I've often witnessed firsthand. There is a group of five people who wait around outside CNN headquarters whenever I have a celebrity on the show. It's always the same five people and they always show up together. They seem to lurk in the shadows, armed with bound autograph books and a camera, and they won't go away until the guest signs five autographs and poses for a photo or two. They are never there for, say, a U.S. Senator; but if it's Gary Hart, they'll be out there. Since I usually leave the CNN building the same time as my guests and often walk them downstairs, I've encountered the group on numerous occasions. They dress like street people, and although they never bother me, they bombard my guests and there isn't much I can do about it.

The one time it got a little scary was the night Alan Alda was on. We had finished at CNN and I was to drive him to Mutual to go on my radio show. As we left the building and started walking to my car, sure enough, those same three women and two men were waiting for us with their camera and autograph books, only Alan wasn't having any. He flatly refused their requests, which must have come as a rude surprise to the autograph hounds who may have thought of Alda the way most Americans do—as a sweet, uncomplicated guy. They were in shock that he could refuse them, and started following us to the car. That's where it got a little weird. Alda got in and they were sticking their faces against the window. He rolled it down and said to them, "To give an autograph is demeaning to the person who gets it. I will not demean you."

They all looked at each other as if to say, "Who is this nut?"

In a way, I can see it from both sides. Those people probably thought Alda was being a wise-ass, because if getting an autograph is demeaning, they'll take it. But I believe he was sincere. After all, he took longer to explain his position to them than it would have taken to sign the autographs. And he kept talking about it in the car as we drove to Mutual: "What do they *do* with all those things?"

That's the trouble with celebrity, of course: it exposes you to everybody in the world, even when you just want to be in a corner by yourself. Usually, you can finesse the situation by being polite and noncommittal, but that doesn't always work.

Take this instance. Duke Zeibert's is one of Washington's power restaurants. Sometimes things happen at Duke's just because you have fifteen or twenty Washington heavyweights in the room at one time, and that creates a charged atmosphere. I've been present at a number of such scenes at Duke's and they can be a lot of fun, but one of the weirdest involved millionaire Jack Kent Cooke.

Cooke is one of the richest men in the world. He used to own the Los Angeles Lakers, the L.A. Kings hockey team, and the Forum in Los Angeles, and he still owns the Washington Redskins. But unfortunately, he's a horse's ass. He was holding court at Duke's after a Redskins game, with a whole crowd of media people and hangers-on, staging what I like to refer to as the Jack Kent Cooke Show. David Brinkley was

there, along with Lesley Stahl and William Safire, all around
Cooke's table. After a while, Sam Donaldson came into the
restaurant and sat down with his wife at a corner table. Right
away, Cooke yelled, "Sam! Sam, come on over here!"

Donaldson looked up, a little chagrined, but didn't say anything. "Sam Donaldson!" Cooke screamed again. "Step right
over to the Jack Kent Cooke table, Sam. Come on!"

Donaldson gave a little wave but didn't move. Then Cooke
really started acting crazy. "Sam, dammit, I said come *over*
here!"

By now people like Brinkley and Safire were getting embarrassed at Cooke's antics. I was sitting at a table about midway between Cooke and Donaldson, and I started saying,
"Stay, Sam, stay."

Another guy started chanting, "Go, Sam, go!"

Finally someone said, "Two to one he goes."

They began laying odds, but Donaldson never moved. It's
always inspirational to see a man like Donaldson refuse a boor
like Cooke. The typical reaction of most Washington people
would have been to get up and go over because the Lord had
summoned them to the Sermon on the Mount.

Cooke once invited me to sit in his box for a Redskins
game, and the same day he also invited Larry L. King, the
author of *The Best Little Whorehouse in Texas*. Jack thought it
would be cute to have the two Larry Kings in his box. Since
I'm also a friend of Edward Bennett Williams, however, who
doesn't like Cooke, it became an issue of choosing sides, like
children. I declined. Cooke was furious. Apparently, nobody
declines Jack Cooke. He called me in a rage, with the same
tone of voice he had used on Donaldson: "What do you mean,
you won't come?"

Cooke is a self-made millionaire who built his fortune all on
his own, and I have to respect him for that, but as Edward
Bennett Williams said, "He gives being rich such a bad
name."

*   *   *

For all the ups and downs of celebrity, though, it does have its perks. Dodger manager Tommy Lasorda has made a business out of his own celebrity. He has never picked up a check in his life that I know of. I once emceed a dinner in Baltimore honoring the Dodgers. After I spoke, Tommy said to me, "Don't eat here, we're going to find our own restaurant."

We drove around town and Tommy picked out a pricey-looking Italian joint. We were with Jeff Rimmer, the Baltimore sportscaster, and Johnny Podres, the great Dodger pitcher who beat the Yankees in the 1955 World Series. None of us had ever been in this place before, but as we were going in, Podres whispered to me, "No chance we pay."

We went in and Lasorda asked for the owner. "Hey, I heard about this place!" he said when the owner appeared.

The guy was beaming. "Tommy Lasorda!" he said. "Hey, this is great!"

"Right," Lasorda said. "So bring us the real stuff."

The owner started sending out platters of food, his best wine, the works. We never paid. Tommy had brought along a couple of glossy photos of himself, which he inscribed to the owner, all the payment necessary.

Tommy sometimes does that. He carries around photographs, eats in restaurants for free, and signs the pictures. The owner hangs the picture on the wall like an endorsement and thinks he's getting a great deal.

One time Tommy asked me to make reservations for dinner at the Palm in Washington, where he was taking a couple of reporters from the White House press corps while he was in town. They know me at the Palm, so I arranged for a nice table for Tommy and his crowd, and then I met them there after they'd eaten, just to chat for a while before my show. When it was time to leave, the waiters gave Tommy the check. Paralysis set in—it was something he'd never experienced before. He said to me, sort of under his breath, "Larry, what's this?"

I said, "I made the reservation in your name, like you asked me to."

"Yeah, I know, but—"

"We can't give it to the White House guys," I said.

"No, can't do that. What the fuck we gonna do?" As if the idea of actually paying the check never occurred to him. *I* wasn't going to pay it—the three of them had dinner and I had a cup of coffee. I said, "Jeez, I don't know. Maybe the radio network will pick it up."

"Yeah, yeah, that's a good idea! The radio network, they'll pay, won't they? What should I write down?"

"Write down Tommy Lasorda, Mutual network."

"Okay. I'll add the tip on, too."

And there are moments when celebrity can be fun. Some years ago, after I'd broken up with my second wife, I was seeing Gail Sheehy. Gail is married to Clay Felker now, but at that time they weren't seeing each other. I was working in Washington and she was in New York, and we decided to spend Labor Day weekend driving around Connecticut and Massachusetts together. So on that Saturday morning I took the early shuttle up from D.C., she met me at the airport in her car, and we started driving up to Massachusetts. It was raining and we were hoping to find someplace where it was dry and we could just enjoy a nice day in the country.

Not long after we left the city, we drove past Mamaroneck and Gail said, "I grew up in Mamaroneck. Do you know that I haven't been back here since I graduated from high school and went away to college and my parents sold the house? It's been more than twenty years."

So I decided to get off at the Mamaroneck exit and we drove past the high school, the playground, and finally we got to her old house and I parked the car out front. I said, "Do you want to go inside?"

It was pouring rain, Saturday morning at ten o'clock. She said, "Oh, I couldn't do that. I couldn't just go up and ring the bell."

"Hey, I don't know about you, Sheehy," I said, "but I'm a Jewish kid from Brooklyn, and I'm goin' up to the door."

I rapped on the door and this guy answered. You couldn't ask for a more perfect character: Aaron Rosenblatt, sixty-eight years old. His wife was sixty-five, he was retired, the kids were gone, and he'd lived in this house with his wife for fifteen years. I said, "Mr. Rosenblatt, you see the lady sitting in the car? She grew up in this house. Do you think it would be okay if she came in and had a look around?"

He nodded affably, I waved to Gail, and she came in. Mr. Rosenblatt called to his wife, "Honey! This young lady grew up in the house. Show her around, come on."

The woman took Gail upstairs and I could hear Gail saying, "Oh, yeah, this was my bedroom. And they moved this over there, it used to be here," and so on. Meanwhile, I went into the kitchen and the guy made me a cup of coffee. He said to me, "Did anybody ever tell you you got a voice that's a *double* for Larry King?"

"I *am* Larry King," I said.

He went, "Eeee, my God!" Then he pointed to the radio. "See the radio dial? Seven-ten, WOR. You were just on the air. Four o'clock this morning, I heard you. What are you doing in my house at ten A.M.?"

I started explaining to him, and while I was talking I saw a bookshelf behind him. Gail had had three books published at that point, and they were all on the shelf together. I decided I wasn't going to say anything. But then the guy brought the coffee over and started nudging me—this is so Jewish—saying, "So, uh, uh?"

"What?"

"You know, uh, who's the girl? I mean, I know you're divorced. You're entitled. But, uh, so is she a friend, what?"

I told him she was a writer.

"A writer, oh."

"Writes for *New York* magazine. And she writes books."

"Books? So who is, if I may ask?"

I pointed to her books. He screamed, "Gail Sheehy!"

The wife came running downstairs and he said to her, "You know who this is sitting in our house? This is Larry King, and that's Gail Sheehy!"

"Gail," she said. "Your books changed my life!"

They started hugging us now, and he ran out and came back with flour and bacon and everything, and they started making breakfast. We didn't leave until twelve-thirty.

CHAPTER 5

POLITICS:
AES, HHH, JFK

The first vote I ever cast for president was for Adlai Stevenson. One day during the 1952 presidential campaign, I sat in the last row of Madison Square Garden at a rally and watched him speak. Frank Sinatra introduced him. At that time, Sinatra was a real Democrat—he told me how he used to stuff ballot boxes for Al Smith when he was a kid.

In 1957, I got to meet Stevenson. I hadn't been in radio two weeks, and here I had a chance to interview a hero of mine. Stevenson always liked being called Governor. Later he became ambassador to the United Nations, which most people would consider a more prestigious post, but being governor of Illinois would remain very special to him. Mercedes McCambridge later asked me, "Don't you agree he has the most beautiful blue eyes you ever saw?" It was easy to see why women adored him—his eyes were crystal blue and they danced. I was definitely in awe of the man, so when we went on the air I said, "I must say, Governor, how much I respect you. My first vote ever cast for president was for you, and to be in your presence is a singular honor."

I would never say anything like that on the air today, because I don't like to gush, but I was full of admiration for him. And I was pretty young. Anyway, Stevenson replied, "Mr. King, we have never met. Yet when I walked into the room tonight, I said to my companion, 'I have a feeling this man is one of the great judges of character we will ever meet.' How unfortunate that there weren't ten million more of you."

After Stevenson, and before Mario Cuomo, my favorite politician was Hubert Humphrey. I met Humphrey at a fundraising party at Pompano Beach. I normally avoided those things because I was a broadcaster, but I went to this one and for a while there I tended bar. Humphrey came by and said, "Larry King tending bar for me? Now I know I've made it." I was just a local personality then, so he had no need to be nice to me. It was just Humphrey's way. As Barry Goldwater said to me, "Hubert was American."

Goldwater was right. Nobody better embodied an American than Humphrey: the son of a pharmacist who went on to become mayor of a city, then senator, then vice-president, a self-effacing man who maybe talked a little too much.

I once emceed a debate between Humphrey and the president of the American Medical Association, Dr. Ed Annis. The question was whether there should be Medicare, Humphrey arguing for it and Annis, a right-wing conservative, arguing against. The AMA was violently opposed to Medicare at the time. After the debate, the three of us went out to dinner together. We were talking about the debate and I complimented them on how well each had defended his position. Humphrey said, "That's because we've studied each other's position. Nothing the other guy says surprises us." And just to demonstrate, they reversed the debate during dinner, Humphrey arguing against Medicare and Annis for. They were each just as forceful, just as well informed, just as convincing.

I may have been one of the few people on earth to hear Hubert Humphrey say a bad word about Medicare.

Over the years I got to know Hubert very well and came to love him for his humanity as much as for his political convictions. The last time I interviewed him was a few weeks before he died. We were discussing loneliness and greatness and how the public's impression of fame or greatness can be so different from the private realization—as we learned that Lincoln was a manic-depressive or that Churchill, too, had moments of great depression. In that last interview, Humphrey told me he had checked in to Sloan-Kettering just before the holiday season—they had diagnosed cancer and were going to begin treatment—and he called his wife, Muriel, and said, "Go visit the kids. I'm going to start this treatment tomorrow morning, I want to be alone and get a good night's sleep. No sense your staying here."

"So I'm in this private room in Sloan-Kettering Institute," he told me, "and I pick up the phone and call the switchboard. I say, 'This is Senator Humphrey. I'd like not to be disturbed.' Then I read a little, and I've just turned off the light to go to sleep when the phone rings. I say to myself, Damn. I pick up the phone, and it's Richard Nixon. He's in San Clemente recovering from phlebitis and he's all alone. He's waiting to go spend time with the kids. And we talked for two hours. We talked about old times, we talked about cancer, we talked about Watergate. We were just two old warriors."

I was almost crying when Humphrey told me that story. Here were two men who'd run against each other for the presidency in one of the closest elections in American history and who couldn't be more different from each other. Now it's nine years later: one of them is dying of cancer, the other is out of office in disgrace. And they're both alone before the holidays, commiserating with each other.

When Humphrey died, I watched his funeral on television.

It was also Nixon's return to Washington, the first time he'd been back since he had resigned. He was in the third row of mourners, and when the camera panned to him and then came in close, that scene crystallized in my mind: two guys all alone, commiserating. I wondered how many people seeing Nixon at the funeral knew what was really going through his mind that day.

Incidentally, I'm convinced that Goldwater voted for Hubert Humphrey against Nixon in 1968. I was with Barry at the Republican convention that year, when Nixon's people threw a party the night before the nomination. It was virtually a victory party because everybody knew he was going to win. Barry and I left the party with Edward Brooke, the former senator from Massachusetts, and a couple of others and went to a restaurant for dinner. I remember, as we were driving over, Goldwater saying with much disdain, "Who wants to give Nixon a party?" Judging from his tone of voice alone, I would bet Barry couldn't pull the lever for Nixon.

That was a pretty wild night, as it turned out. We all had a lot to drink and started talking about women, as men do when they have too much to drink. Goldwater started telling stories about a German girl he'd slept with five or six years earlier.

Shortly after Kennedy had been in Germany giving his famous *"Ich bin ein Berliner"* speech, Goldwater went over on a fact-finding tour, which is the prerogative of the ranking Republican favored for the nomination. He said, "There was this German girl, a secretary from our embassy, who was unbelievably gorgeous." He described a cross between Ursula Andress and Romy Schneider. "I was over there alone for seven days and on the sixth day—Barry did it." That's the way he spoke about himself—in the third person, like Jimmy Hoffa.

"Now I'm back," he said, "and as the opposition party

leader, the perfunctory courtesy is to call on the president to discuss *my* visit to Germany. And then we're supposed to hold a mini–press conference in the Rose Garden to discuss Germany for ten minutes. I walk into the White House, and Dave Powers meets me in the Oval Office. Kennedy comes out of the shower—Jack showered four times a day; he had a thing about it, showered and changed clothes four times a day—Jack's brushing his hair and he looks right at me and says, 'You made her, huh? You son of a bitch, you made her.'

"'What are you talking about?' I say.

"'Ursula.'

"'Ursula?'

"'Yeah, Ursula. The embassy secretary. I tried for five goddamn days. I had Jackie go shopping, I sent her notes. Nothing. And you, older than me, with your white hair, you made her.'

"So I say, 'How do you know?'

"'I'm the president, how the hell do you think I know?'

"So then he says to me—and this was what I loved about Kennedy—he says, 'Barry, you don't want this job. You don't want to run against me. There are a lot of good things about it, but there are certain things you won't like.'"

After that, all Kennedy wanted to know about was Ursula. Dave Powers said, "They're expecting you in the Rose Garden."

Kennedy finished dressing, he put his arm around Goldwater, and they walked outside. "We have no statement to make," Kennedy said. "Just tell them the senator and I discussed, at length and in depth, German-American affairs."

George Smathers told me a story about Kennedy's sexual fixations that was even more bizarre than Barry's. Kennedy was speaking at the Fontainebleau at a dinner honoring Claude Pepper's return to Congress. Kennedy decided to stay over at the hotel rather than fly out late at night, or at least that was the story they gave the press. A prominent young movie actress and sex symbol with whom Kennedy had been carrying on a serious flirtation—one who's still alive, I should add—was in Palm Beach at the time. Kennedy had decided this was his chance to spend the night with her. Smathers had a home in Miami Beach. A conservative Democratic senator, he was a close friend of Kennedy's, and they had played around a lot together. So Smathers arranged to have the woman come down from Palm Beach to his house. He left her there and drove himself to the rear entrance of the Fontainebleau.

Kennedy was staying in a suite on the top floor of the hotel, guarded by the Secret Service. Not long after he arrived there after the dinner, Jack and two Secret Service agents left the suite, walked the seventeen flights down a back staircase, out a back entrance, and into Smathers's car. Smathers in turn got out of his car, walked up the seventeen stories with a third Secret Service guy, and was brought into Kennedy's suite, where he spent the night. Kennedy drove to Smathers's house, where *he* spent what was left of the night with the young actress.

At five-fifteen the next morning, Kennedy drove back to the Fontainebleau in Smathers's car, got out, and, bad back and all, walked up the seventeen flights to his suite. Smathers walked down, got into his car, and drove away. I've never asked the actress if the story is true, but it's too convoluted for Smathers just to have made it up. I do know the actress worshiped Jack and believed that Kennedy would have married her sometime during his second term. Robert McNamara, Kennedy's secretary of defense, confirmed that she was everything Kennedy wanted in a woman but insisted that Kennedy never would have left Jackie, and I have to believe that too. If the story proves anything, it's that you have a better chance of getting away with really outrageous behavior if you are already president.

Jack Kennedy's ambition was to buy one of the Boston papers and write a column in it three days a week. He's the only president I know who liked newspapers. He liked having them around; he liked the press room, the typewriters, the pads and pencils. I think that's why he was so good at press conferences. Pierre Salinger told me that he never once heard Kennedy demean the press in general or a particular newspaper or reporter. The White House did cancel delivery of *Newsweek* at one point because it had been highly critical of Senator Smathers, even though Smathers voted against Kennedy eighty percent of the time in Congress. But then, Jack had other reasons for liking George.

When Robert McNamara did my show, I said to him off the air, "You all knew about the women, didn't you?"

He said, "Yeah, but it was a different era."

"How wrapped up in women was he?" I asked.

McNamara then told me this story about Kennedy that took place at the height of the Cuban missile crisis. "Khrushchev had sent us two conflicting cables," McNamara said, "and we came up with the brilliant idea of sending a cable back as though we'd never received the second one. Khrushchev's second cable contained a proposal that we couldn't accept, and the implied threat at the end of the cable was 'Give me an answer or it's war.'

"It was Robert Kennedy who came up with the idea of sending a cable back as if we hadn't gotten the second one. Kennedy's cable put forward *our* proposal and closed, 'Let us know within twenty-four hours.'" That gave Khrushchev an out with his people."

So now, according to McNamara, they were waiting to hear from Khrushchev. And it was coming down to the twelfth hour, when there could be a real threat of starting World War III. People were running back and forth between the briefing room and the Oval Office, and there in the office were McNamara and Rusk and the Kennedys and the Chiefs of Staff. In the middle of all this, a good-looking lady walked in with a bunch of files and dropped them on McNamara's desk. John Kennedy looked up, looked down, looked up again. Then he said to McNamara, "Who's that?"

"She's filling in today," McNamara said. "You know, we're really swamped, so they sent her over from Commerce."

Kennedy leaned over to McNamara. "Bob, I want her name and her number," he said. "We may avoid war here tonight."

It's hard for us now to look back and see that, probably as early as 1966 when Paul Fay's book, *The Pleasure of His Company,* came out, America knew that Kennedy had screwed around while he was in the White House—but nobody cared. When I had Fay on my show to discuss his book, which said nothing directly about Kennedy's sex life, he told some stories about JFK's proclivities that he hadn't included in the book. We didn't get one outraged phone call. If anything, Fay made people love Kennedy even more. For instance, he told me he was in a motorcade in Manhattan with Kennedy when he was running for president, and a woman ran up to the car. Fay said to me, "It's ten years later, and she's still the prettiest woman I've ever seen. She grabbed Kennedy's hand and said, 'Senator, anything you want, anything I can do, please let me know.' The motorcade kept going and Jack turned to me and said, 'Go back and get her name—we could lose.'"

But it was not a big deal to anyone the way it is now, and I would have to guess that it's at least partly the influence of the women's movement on our thinking. Why did McNamara go home and tell everybody he knew that story about the missile crisis? It just didn't matter.

When Teddy Kennedy pulled out of the presidential race in 1984, he threw a party for his Secret Service men in his home in McLean, Virginia. He invited Ronald Reagan because the same agents were once in Reagan's detail. Reagan stayed till two in the morning and they got drunk and told John F. Kennedy stories. Teddy said, "As critical as I've been, the Reagans have always been nice to me and my family." Jackie has been to the White House during the Reagan administration, though that story is generally not well known. Oddly enough, I think the Kennedys are the couple that the Reagans most see themselves resembling. They were in the same age group—Kennedy would be seventy now. Nancy must have thought of herself in Jackie's image then and is still very much like her in some ways, from the designer gowns to the extreme thinness.

One of the Secret Service agents who worked for John Kennedy told me a story about Kennedy's first night at the movies after being inaugurated. When John Kennedy was in the Senate, he used to go to the Key Theatre in Georgetown fairly often because it was his neighborhood theater. (In fact, he was responsible for attracting attention to Georgetown back then. Georgetown and McLean properties both took off because of the Kennedys.) Three days after Jack moved into the White House, he told the Secret Service that he wanted to go to the movies. This agent said, "You can order any movie you like and have it shown here in the White House."

Kennedy said, "Yeah, but I want to see this picture tonight, and it's playing at the Key Theatre."

So they took a limo to the theater. That day he had held a meeting of the cabinet, and he had told all the members that his cabinet was going to be a different kind of cabinet from previous ones. His cabinet was going to be a twenty-four-hour-a-day cabinet. "You are always on duty," Kennedy told them. "If you can't give me Saturdays, Sundays, and nights, then please don't serve in this cabinet."

Kennedy got on line at the Key Theatre. The Secret Service guys couldn't believe this. They said, "We never get on line." People started looking up; he'd been there before, but not as president. And he didn't have money—Kennedy never had any money on him—and the Secret Service had to lay out for him. He went in and sat down, and sitting right in front of him was Douglas Dillon, the new secretary of the treasury, and his wife. Kennedy leaned forward and tapped him on the shoulder. "I said we work twenty-four hours a day," he said to a startled Dillon, who did the wildest double take the Secret Service men had ever seen.

Kennedy was in Miami the week before he was killed in Dallas, and I heard him speak at the Americana. The same week I did an interview on presidential security with the Miami Beach chief of police and with a former Secret Service agent. We covered all the relevant questions about protecting the president. For instance, they told me, one standard procedure was to change routes—have the newspapers publish one route and then go a different way. But they didn't do that in Dallas because they wanted a crowd. In Miami Beach, people knew he was coming, but it wasn't a motorcade, so they printed that his route would be from the airport up Collins Avenue; he never went up Collins, he went up 95. They sent a limo with flags and troopers up Collins Avenue, but it was a dummy. Obviously, a parade creates different problems, however. They had to print the route of the parade in Dallas because they didn't want thousands of people lining the wrong streets.

The police chief and the agent discussed the frustrations of trying to protect a president. For instance, if the Secret Service decides that the motorcade shouldn't stop at a particular corner because it's too dangerous, and the president says he wants to stop there, they stop there. If he wants his bubble top down, it comes down. If there had been bad weather in Dallas, Kennedy might have lived.

The day Kennedy was shot, I got Grant Stockdale on the phone. Stockdale was Kennedy's ambassador to Ireland, and they were old friends. His wife was a poet and his daughter was an actress, and they lived in Coconut Grove. When I asked Stockdale for his thoughts on Jack Kennedy that day, however, he started to weep inconsolably, and we weren't able to use any of the tape. Four days later, he jumped to his death from the tallest building in Miami. And then we discovered an astonishing story.

Grant Stockdale was born into a good family and never had to work too much in his life. He was part of the Boston gentry. As ambassador to Ireland, however, he had run out of money. He was on a government budget, which he had exceeded with lavish parties and so on, and he was broke and in debt. As a last resort, he had come back from Ireland for a private meeting with John Kennedy and had explained the situation to him. After all, they were old friends. Kennedy apparently agreed to advance him a substantial sum of money—the figure I heard was a quarter of a million dollars. "Here's what we'll do," Kennedy told Stockdale. "I have to go to Dallas this week. Meet me here next week and I'll have a check for you."

I don't know whether it was going to be a personal check or from government funds or what. But after Dallas, Stockdale was broke and embarrassed, Kennedy was dead, and no one else knew of the conversation. He didn't know Bobby well enough, didn't know Lyndon Johnson at all, and anyway he was distraught over the death of an old, dear friend. So he killed himself. When the police went to the hotel room from which he jumped, all they found was a copy of *Life* magazine with John Kennedy on the cover.

CHAPTER 6

POLITICS:
MARIO AND MO

I first met Mario Cuomo when he was lieutenant governor of New York. I was doing one of my many remote broadcasts from New York City, and he came on the show, told me what a fan he'd been, and said that, because he didn't sleep very well, he'd listened to my radio show for years. For my part, I was impressed with his gentility and his brains and I thought: This ain't no ordinary New York politician.

After that we began to talk by phone and to correspond, and at the 1980 convention, when Carter was nominated, Cuomo appeared on my show again. When he ran for governor in 1982, I found myself rooting for him. And when his *Diaries* were published, he came down to Washington and went on the air with me. We later did speaking engagements together, and our friendship grew. Herb Cohen, whom I've known since we grew up together in Brooklyn, became part of that friendship, and we discovered that Herb's wife and Mario's wife, Matilda, had gone to the same high school. Herb is a professional negotiator, and with his combination of

street savvy and political insight he was right at home with
Mario. We all spent nights at the governor's mansion—we'd
fly up on a Thursday and stay over the weekend.

Five days before Mario delivered his famous keynote
speech at the Democratic convention in 1984, he read it to
me over the phone.

"What do you think of this?" he asked me. "You like this
'city on the hill' idea?"

Cuomo reminded me that it is the job of most keynote
speakers to rack up the incumbent. "But I always call him
President Reagan in this speech, I never slam him personally," he said. "Do you think that's okay?"

"It sounds fine to me," I said. Who was I to advise him on
his speech? Besides, I thought the whole thing did sound
pretty good and we were confident it would go over.

"After the speech," Cuomo said, "I'm not going to stay for
the convention. I'm going to fly back that night and let the
lieutenant governor head the New York delegation. It's something he's wanted to do all his life."

I told Mario that I was going to be at the convention and
asked if he'd do my show afterward. He said sure. When he
gave his speech, I went out on the floor and stood next to the
Oklahoma delegation. I was hearing words that I had heard on
the phone five days ago, which was a real kick, but for the
first time I heard the *way* they were being delivered, and I
knew that magic was happening that night. Anybody standing
in that audience knew it. They knew that a new figure had
emerged on the American scene. The speech was delivered
like a summation to the jury by a great trial lawyer: his voice
was soft yet strong, his hand motions almost pontifical. Mario
made a case for independent Americans—and the only reason
his case wasn't strong enough to prevail with the electorate
was that his defendant was Walter Mondale.

When he finished, a guy in the Oklahoma delegation
turned to me and said, "You know him?"

"Yeah."

"I never heard of him," he said, "until tonight. Jeez, I'd love to know him. There's two things he made me feel tonight: He reminded me why I'm a Democrat. And he made me think of my mother—she passed away three years ago. She died in a nursing home and Medicare paid for that nursing home the last two years of her life. I couldn't have afforded it. Reagan didn't want Medicare."

I went back to the studio feeling exhilarated. Herb Cohen's son Stephen was working for Mario that summer as an aide, and the same day as Mario's speech he had taken his LSATs to get into law school. Meanwhile, on his way over to do my show after giving the speech, Mario had been stopped by every network. They too knew that a star had been born. As Mario walked into the control booth, Herb Cohen phoned on my private studio line to congratulate Cuomo on the speech. When he came in, I said, "Mario, Herbie's on the phone." It could not have been more than twenty minutes after the speech.

Cuomo picked up the phone and the first thing he said to Herb was "How did Stephen do?"

During the festivities celebrating the anniversary of the Statue of Liberty in 1986, Mario joined me on the air while I covered the events over WOR in New York. He had to bring Reagan a union card so that the president could throw the switch lighting up the statue. New York is a closed shop, and Reagan had to join the union, so Cuomo had his card with his photo and number on it. Reagan signed it and Cuomo kept it as a souvenir of the event.

At one point in the broadcast, I described what it meant to me—because, like Mario, I'm first-generation American—to know that my parents had sailed into that harbor. I gave what I thought was an eloquent little speech. And then Mario said, "It's easy for us to talk. We did okay. How about all the peo-

ple for whom the promises weren't kept, whose dreams
weren't fulfilled? How about all the parents whose children
are on welfare? Where are the streets of gold? Sure, you and I
can wax sentimental. We can say, 'Did our parents ever think
this would happen for us?'

"You know what we should do? Twice a year we should turn
that statue around—if we could move it—and point it in, and
let people read what it says to show them what we're promising. And we should put another statue in Los Angeles or San
Francisco for the Asian Americans and Mexican Americans
who have no association with the Statue of Liberty in New
York Harbor."

I love the way Cuomo's mind works, turning a concept
around like that. He's an eastern version of Humphrey. Humphrey had a knack for taking an established practice and turning it on its head. He once said to me, "The whole system is
out of whack as far as mortgages go."

"What do you mean?" I asked.

"When my wife and I started out," Hubert said, "we had a
little place where we raised kids and were cramped, but we
had those big mortgage payments. Then as we prospered, we
got a bigger house. The kids left because they were grown—
we didn't *need* the big house then. When we need the big
house is when we have the kids. We ought to work out a way
by which new parents can get bigger houses, and we ought to
do it with scaled mortgages. So on a thirty-year mortgage, the
first ten years is three hundred a month, the second ten years
is seven hundred a month, and your third ten years is a thousand a month. And *all* of it in the first ten years is interest—
so what? This way children could have room to play in."

Cuomo is capable of that kind of idea. Unlike Humphrey,
however, he has the oratorical power to make people believe
it's possible. How powerful a speaker is Cuomo? Every year
on Lincoln's Birthday, Lincolnphiles from all over the country
gather in Springfield, Illinois, to hear speakers who they feel

embody Lincoln's oratorical qualities. They've been doing that ever since Lincoln's death. Some presidents have been invited and some have not—Franklin D. Roosevelt and John Kennedy spoke, but Carter wasn't invited. You don't have to be president, of course; Oliver Wendell Holmes spoke there. But the only man in the history of that event to be invited two years in a row was Mario Cuomo.

One night at Grossinger's, Mario proved to me exactly how well he can control a situation and how he can move an audience in just about any direction he wants. We appeared together at the 1983 awards ceremony of the New York State Broadcasters Association. I was the introductory speaker and Mario was to follow me and present the awards. Station owners, general managers, program directors, announcers, everybody in broadcasting in the state was there. When I was a kid, I used to dream that I could stay at Grossinger's one day; it was a mythical wish, a mountain resort hotel. And there I was, the featured speaker, introducing the governor.

I was really *on* that night. I couldn't believe the things I was saying, all of it pegged around Mario. Mario has a cutting wit, but more often than not he can laugh at himself. I've heard a lot of reports about his testiness when kidded by the press, but I've never found him that way personally. And certainly not that night at Grossinger's.

That night, I told stories about the neighborhood. "When we were kids," I said, "there were only two kinds of kids who lived in my neighborhood in Brooklyn, Jews and Italians. Some blacks, an occasional Irish on the fringe. I didn't meet my first W.A.S.P. until I was nineteen.

"But Italians and Jews have an inborn rift. Christ was the cause of the rift, and every Thursday the Italians in our neighborhood let us know it by beating us up. So that it shouldn't be a surprise—why kick a guy who's going on a date Saturday night?—we decided to make it every Thursday at four. It was easy: Jews lined up, Italians formed a gauntlet; they smacked you in the face, said, 'You killed Our Lord,' and it was over. All things considered, Mario had to be doing the same thing over in Queens. Had to be, it was part of the culture. So here's a man who is governor of New York—and he's what? fifty years old?—so we're talking thirty-two years ago Mario Cuomo was punchin' Jews."

Cuomo was on the floor by that point. "One Thursday," I said, "one of us decided this had gone on long enough and he confronted the designated puncher, whose name I think was Guido Russo, and he said, 'Stop!' Guido was shocked. Everyone in the line was shocked. The kid said, 'I confess. We killed your Lord. But, to quote Lenny Bruce, the statute of limitations is up. In fact, my uncle did it, so I absolve all others Jews on this line.' Now, Guido had a rough time dealing with that. For one thing, he didn't know what 'statute of limitations' meant."

And then I leaned over and said to the governor, "Mario, your people ain't too bright."

The audience loved it, Mario loved it. I was amazed by what I was getting away with—in fact, I hoped I wasn't going too far. Finally, I finished and Cuomo stood up.

"Thanks a lot," he said, "for asking me to follow an act like that. One of the things that made this country great is that we're constantly faced with a set of impossible challenges to make a democracy work—to meet in Philadelphia to construct a Constitution, to be an Italian and have to follow Larry King, a Jew who has reminded us of our heritage. And how many times tonight I've been reminded that we are inferior to them."

He picked up on the humorous note, but then he took the whole thing, turned it semiserious, and moved that crowd with him. And all he did was say, "You know, seeing Larry King here tonight, the son of immigrants, standing up before this audience made up of the top broadcasters in the state and making them laugh, makes me think about the American dream. The one thing you have to say about this country is that the dream is possible."

Then Mario fantasized about going back with camera crews to Ellis Island in 1906 and recording the arrival of a poor immigrant from Italy—Immaculata Cuomo, his mother. He took us through the whole interrogation routine that she had had to go through, pointing out that her husband was without employment or education, or even a place to live, that neither of them spoke English very well. He ended by having an official ask her what she planned to do for America in exchange for letting her into the country. Of course, the punch line was "I'm-a gonna have a son-a be governor-a New York."

From that moment, Cuomo had the crowd in his pocket.

Those stories Mario tells about growing up the son of poor immigrants are no exaggeration, by the way. My favorite of all of them is the one about his father. He owned a grocery store, but he had never been to school and barely spoke English. Mario would come home from school every day and work in the back of the store. One day when Mario was about eleven, he was working in the store with his father when Mario's teacher—whom his father had seen only during open school week—walked into the store. The teacher took one step inside, the father looked up and saw him and immediately ran over to Mario and whacked him across the face. Mario was on the floor when the teacher got to his father to tell him that Mario was doing so well in school that he wanted him to appear in the school play. His father had assumed that if the teacher was there, his son must be in trouble. And he didn't know how to apologize. He just nodded at the teacher.

During his campaign for governor, Mario told me he got a call from his mother. "Mario," she said, "are you against capital punishment?"

"Yeah, Ma."

"Mario, the whole neighborhood's for it. Everywhere I go they're for it."

"Well, I'm against it. What do you want me to do, Ma?"

"Say you're for it," she advised, "and then don't pull the switch."

Mario called me once after he read in the papers that I was going out with Angie Dickinson. "You're dating Angie Dickinson?" he said. "Christ, that's heavy."

"Mario," I said, "she would love to meet you. She regards you as very sexy."

"You're kidding," he said.

"No, Mario, honest, she'd love to meet you."

I knew he was going to give a speech in San Francisco the following week, and Angie had been bugging me to introduce her to him, so I thought I'd set up something long-distance. "You're speaking next week in San Francisco," I said. "Tell me where, she'll come to hear you, and then she'd like to meet you after the speech."

"Larry, I'm a guy on a diet and you're offering me a charlotte russe? I know what'll happen," he said. "Matilda isn't coming with me to California. The speech will be over, I'll be nice and courteous and I'll say to Angie Dickinson, 'Do you need a ride home?' And ten years from today at the Cuomo hearings . . ."

That was two months before the Gary Hart–Donna Rice scandal. Cuomo would never give in to that kind of emotion. However, where he runs the risk of giving in to emotion is as a typical raised-in-the-streets New Yorker. That's why Mario yells at the press, and it gives him trouble. I said to him once, "You're walking down the street and a guy on the corner says, 'I made your sister pregnant.' Your sister's in a convent; you know she's not pregnant. But you go over and beat up the guy. You grab him, push him up against a lamppost. You would do that, Mario, right?"

"Yeah."

"This guy doesn't even know your sister, but you can't walk on. In other places you can walk on, but not in New York. So for you, the press conference never ends. You walk along the street with it. If a reporter says to you, 'The Mafia runs you,' you gotta scream, 'There is no Mafia.'"

That is a trait of his. He's also completely family-oriented. Harry Truman once wrote an angry letter to a Washington music critic who had knocked his daughter Margaret's perfor-mance as a singer. Truman called the critic a son of a bitch. It got enormous headlines at the time—a handwritten letter from the president using that kind of language. It caused quite an uproar. Cuomo defends his family the same way.

Well, you can't do that in a presidential campaign. But New Yorkers do. That's the street corner speaking. We were up at the governor's mansion one night, Mario, Herbie Cohen, and me, and the butler came in about one A.M. and said, "Would you gentlemen care for a liqueur before retiring?"

We ordered an after-dinner drink, the butler left the room, and Mario turned to us. "Did you ever in your whole life think that anyone would come over to you and say, 'Would you care for a liqueur before retiring?' Franchot Tone had that said to him—not an Italian from Queens and two Jewish guys from Brooklyn. That ain't the corner."

On another occasion I was having dinner with Cuomo, sports announcer Bob Costas, Ted Turner, and a couple of other people. It was before Cuomo had announced that he would not seek the Democratic nomination in 1988, and there was a lot of speculation that he not only would seek it but would get it. Turner was sitting at the other end of the table from Mario. He leaned across and said, "Mario, I'm a great admirer of yours, and I'm prepared to support you in any way possible. I can't use CNN to your advantage, but I can give you all the money you need and help you in any way I can with my friends. I just have one question. Answer the question and I'm all yours. The question is 'Are you in favor of total world disarmament?'"

Mario said, "Ted, any person listening to that question from someone like you—Reagan, Haig, Gorbachev—would answer yes. You've given me the promise before you've asked for the answer. You haven't just brought it up in conversation, you've dangled something." Mario paused for a moment, again like a trial lawyer setting up his summation. "Disarmament, yes. Major weaponry, yes. But total disarmament will never work. I would never be dishonest with you. And while, if I ran, I would appreciate contributions, I wouldn't want favors. I hate when people give favors, because it entwines you with them. Anybody would appreciate your support, and anybody would be crazy not to admire all you've done. But *you* did it. You didn't do it because people set conditions for you."

Turner sat there and said, "You're my man." It hadn't been what Turner wanted to hear, but he liked it even better. If that were George Bush, can't you picture the rest of the evening, all spent buttering up Ted Turner? But I don't think Mario said another word to Ted about politics. In fact, the only other time Ted and Mario talked was when the Atlanta Hawks, Turner's basketball team, came up. Mario knew a player Ted didn't know he had. Ted's a good sports fan, but not a great one. He owns a lot of things, so it's possible for him not to know the last man on his NBA team.

But Mario never played to him, never brought up disarmament again, never talked politics. And he had the best line of the evening. Bob Costas, who had never met Cuomo before, said jokingly, "You couldn't hit the curveball, eh, Mario?"

"Who can?" Cuomo said. "If we could hit the curveball, somebody would bat .500. It's a question of how well we hit the other pitches—and occasionally we hit the curveball. You can't hit a curveball for better than a .250 average. It's a round ball and a round bat, and the ball is moving."

Here is Herb Cohen's opinion on why Mario wouldn't run for president. Cuomo went out to Los Angeles to give a speech and held a press conference afterward. The first question a reporter asked him was "Governor Cuomo, one of the reasons people are saying you won't run is that you don't have fire in your belly. Is that so?"

Cuomo said, "I'll tell you one thing. If I did have fire in my belly, I'd get some seltzer and I'd put it out." He didn't get a laugh. The press conference went on for over half an hour, until an aide announced that Cuomo would take one last question and then have to leave to catch his plane. A reporter asked, "Why did you come to Los Angeles? You gave a speech, but you didn't announce for the presidency. So really, why'd you come?"

Cuomo answered, "I came here to test the political seltzer." And again nobody laughed, no one got the joke, which left him feeling nonplussed. It was at that moment, Herbie says, that Cuomo realized he was going to have a problem communicating in a lot of places outside of New York.

But in the long run, I don't think either his defensiveness with the press or any difficulty communicating to non–New Yorkers is going to be as much of a drawback as his penchant for surrounding himself with young aides. Mario loves young people, but when I think of the political minds who have told me they would volunteer to work for him, I have to believe he should widen his circle. I'm talking about Pierre Salinger, Arthur Schlesinger, Sol Linowitz, Zbigniew Brzezinski, Robert McNamara. Cuomo could have a circle that would dwarf Kennedy's Camelot. People I talk to are more interested in hearing about Cuomo than about any other politician or celebrity that I say I happen to know. I was on a plane with George Bush's son when I mentioned that I knew Cuomo and the son said, "*Gee,* I'd like to meet him."

Mario has never told me he wants to be president. We all guessed for him. One night at dinner there was a lull in the conversation, and out of the blue I said to him, "Mario, cut the bull. Are you gonna run for president?"

"Nobody ever asked it like that," he said. Then he added, "Larry, I don't know how to tell you this: governor of New York ain't bad. When we were kids, if somebody had said to you that you were going to host a national radio and television show and have a national column, would you have said, 'Not worldwide?' A couple of years ago I was working in the back of my father's grocery store. I'm governor of New York—it's all right, Larry. If I never did anything else, this is okay. Some interesting people have been governor of this state.

"Besides," he added, "do you realize that if I'm elected president, the summer White House is in Rockaway?"

Next to Mario Cuomo, my favorite contemporary politician is Mo Udall, Democrat of Arizona. When I think about great politicians passed over for second best, I have to list Mo. Udall has served thirteen terms in the House of Representatives and once played for the Denver Nuggets in the NBA. He probably finished second in more presidential primaries than anyone in history, and I think it's a shame, because he would have made a great president.

Like both Stevenson and Cuomo, Udall has an unerring sense of humor. Mo told me jokingly that he was the only man ever elected vice-president by acclamation in the primaries. Everybody wanted him number two. He could have finished second in the *Republican* primaries. He said, "Maybe I have the personality that fits a vice-president: I'm able to nod agreeably at whatever you say. I appear to show great interest while being totally bored and am very good at funerals and get-togethers. And I can talk basketball off the top of my head—one of the essentials of being a vice-president."

The odd thing is that, although Mo never won a primary, I don't think he ever finished third either. Jerry Brown beat Carter in five primaries, and Udall was second. Carter beat Brown seven times, Mo was number two. Kennedy beat Carter, Mo was number two; Carter beat Kennedy, Mo was number two. Mo told me that he is convinced that thirty-six percent of America adores him.

He never got the vice-presidential nod because he was from Arizona and wouldn't have dressed up anyone's ticket. He was also considered *too* funny, the same rap that Stevenson got, so even his humor worked against him. Bruce Catton, the Civil War historian, told me that Lincoln's sense of humor was not politically appreciated in his day either. For instance, when people complained to Lincoln about Grant's drinking, Lincoln reportedly said, "I've been looking at the record of the war thus far, and if anyone can tell me General Grant's brand, I'd like to send a case to our other generals." In responding to how the cabinet could approve certain measures that were unpopular, Lincoln would say, "The vote was nine to one, but *I* was the one." Statements like those caused an uproar. His humor was not appreciated, and the same may be true of Udall.

The difference between Udall and Cuomo is that Cuomo can be funny in public, but he has the ability to match the wit to the occasion. Udall would be humorous at a funeral. People don't know how to respond to that. The public is more comfortable with politicians like Gerald Ford who have no wit at all. I was broadcasting from Detroit during the 1980 Republican convention, when Ford came into town amid rumors that Reagan had picked him as a running mate. (I remember Mark Russell wondering what would happen if that ticket were elected. If they came to a dinner together, who sits where and how do you address them—is it "Mr. President and Mr. President"? If there's an assassination attempt, who does the Secret Service jump in front of first?) Reagan was going to make his decision the next day and it was the talk of Detroit. Ford came on my show and, after I introduced him, I asked, "What brings you to town?"

He looked at me sort of puzzled and said, "Well, the convention is here." That's what Johnson meant when he said Jerry must have played football without a helmet in college.

General John Singlaub said to me off the air one night, after Mo Udall's name had come up, "Oh, I don't agree with Mo on anything, but of course I'd vote for him."

I asked him why. "Because he's a national treasure. You never throw treasures out."

Mo acknowledged that he was friendly with fellow Arizonan Barry Goldwater despite their political differences. He told me that Goldwater once said to him, "I got beat by Lyndon Johnson by sixteen million votes and you couldn't win a primary from Jimmy Carter. Between us, we've made Arizona the only state in the union where mothers don't tell their kids they can grow up to be president."

Barry Goldwater loved Mo Udall. He liked Jacob Javits, too. This may sound surprising, but I've come to believe that senators and congressmen like colleagues who are bright, make them think, and are honest with them. In his heart, Goldwater doesn't want some jerk who might happen to agree with him politically to beat Mo in an election, even though Mo may disagree with Goldwater on just about everything. Javits went in and spoke for Goldwater in Arizona. They didn't agree on anything, but they were great pals and they appreciated each other for what they had. One of the things that most amazed me when I came to Washington was how much value is placed on friendship here, on whether someone calls up and talks to you about issues rather than about their ideological beliefs.

The first time Mo came to the Mutual network studios— which are in a building in Crystal City that has very tight security and a maddeningly complicated procedure for getting in—he said to me, "Rickover's offices are in this building, right? No wonder he's the way he is. Getting into this build- ing is a major effort, and if I had to do it every day, I guess I'd have a personality like his."

Mo told me about the time he was campaigning for the presidential nomination. "The first town I was in, the car got stuck in a parking lot in the snow. The woman driving the car said, 'You go into that barbershop, Mo, while we're pulling this car out of the snow, and say hello to that old man in there whose mouth is going all the time. He's very influential.' I stuck my head in and saw a couple of old guys in there whit- tling. I said, 'Excuse me, sir. I'm Mo Udall from Arizona and I'm running for president.' One of them said, 'Yeah, we know. We were laughing about it this morning.'" Albert Gore, Jr., uses that story now, but it was Mo who told it first.

Udall has been a collector of political humor over his thirty years as a trial lawyer and politician, and his collection ranges from anecdotes to quips and bloopers. "One of my favorites," he told me, "was when Jerry Ford said in a House debate some years ago, 'If Lincoln were alive today, he'd be turning over in his grave.' The other classic is that Lincoln was born in a log cabin which he built with his own two hands. Con- gressman Gephardt said of the Middle East that he didn't see why the Arabs and Jews couldn't sit down and settle this like good Christians."

Udall was on my show around the time the Marcos scandals were exposed in the Philippines, and I asked him what he made of it all.

"It's unbelievable," Mo said, "that a man who started out being honest and being for his people could get so corrupt. I noticed in the morning paper that apparently he was contributing money to U.S. election committees. The charge was that in 1980 Marcos had sent fifty thousand dollars to Carter and fifty thousand to Reagan. That reminds me of the story about the judge who came out to the bench and said, 'Gentlemen, before we start this trial I want to make an announcement. Yesterday the defense attorney came to my office and gave me five thousand dollars. This morning the plaintiff's attorney came to my chambers and gave me *ten* thousand dollars. I want the record to show that I'm giving five thousand dollars back to the plaintiff, and we're going to try this case strictly on the merits.'"

CHAPTER 7

POLITICS:
AND A CAST
OF THOUSANDS

In 1957, every southern senator signed something called the Southern Manifesto, a going-on-record statement against the 1954 *Brown v. Board of Education* decision, pledging their undying efforts to uphold "the principles of the Constitution"—which to them meant segregation. Lyndon Johnson would not sign it, but every southern senator did, including William Fulbright. When I had Fulbright on my show, I asked him, "How could someone as progressive as you—in favor of unilateral disarmament and food stamps and against the war in Vietnam when almost everyone else was for it—how could you have signed the Southern Manifesto?"

"I gave Arkansas what they wanted in one area," he said, "and they gave me what I wanted in all the other areas."

"Isn't that a cop-out?" I asked.

"It probably is," he said. "But I felt that my position on foreign policy, on Vietnam, was so important that it wasn't worth losing my Senate seat to someone who would have

been just another segregationist. An integrationist wasn't
going to win in Arkansas in those days. So I stand up boldly, I
don't sign the Southern Manifesto, and now a new guy comes
in who doesn't feel the way I do about foreign policy."

It's an interesting question from a moral-ethical point of
view, and I have asked it of college professors: If you are ad-
vising Fulbright, and you want a man who is chairman of the
Senate Foreign Relations Committee who can stop the war in
Vietnam, do you advise him to vote segregationist in order to
keep his seat? I interviewed members of the Americans for
Democratic Action, and they had an enormous dilemma with
Fulbright—who embodied everything they loved—because
he had signed the Manifesto. I also interviewed Sam Ervin,
who signed the Manifesto but who continued till his death to
believe in its principles. Ervin may have become a hero
through the Watergate hearings, but he was a bred-in-the-
bone segregationist. Fulbright didn't believe in that; he believed in the Civil Rights Act. But he acted pragmatically.
Was he right? It's a question readers might ask themselves.

Richard Russell was a giant in Georgia, called by many the
brightest man in the Senate: he had leadership, vision, a one-
world outlook. And yet he signed the Manifesto, too. The
irony of southerners, as I learned from interviewing them,
was that they were all in favor of the New Deal. Roosevelt's
biggest supporters were the southern Democratic bloc because that was the poorest part of the country then.

Take George Wallace, for example. I used to get mad at
him a lot, but he was a populist. He always kept the sales tax
down because it hurt the poor people of his state. Alabama
introduced junior colleges in America and, next to California,
today has more junior colleges than any other state; it is second only to California in free education. George was pro-
union, he was free-spending on public projects—he was so
populist that he was even occasionally accused of being a so-
cialist. And on the subject of race, George was a phony. He

told me once, years ago, "When the blacks in Alabama get fifty-one percent of the vote, you gon' see an integrationist." Indeed, once blacks became the majority in the state voting polls, he had black aides and a black public relations man.

The other side of that irony is that it was Eisenhower who appointed the most liberal judges and initiated the integration movement in the South. The only Republican votes in the South at that time came from black voters—what few were able to register—because the Republicans were the party of Lincoln. A lot of the southern judges who stood up and reaffirmed the Civil Rights Act and had crosses burnt on their lawns were Eisenhower appointees. They weren't part of the entrenched Democratic establishment, and they weren't heads of the Rotary Club. They tended to be young and somewhat idealistic. The blacks I had on my show in the fifties and early sixties, like Jackie Robinson and Wilt Chamberlain, were for Nixon and against Kennedy. They didn't trust Kennedy with his upper-class ways. How it changed, how the Republican party disowned the blacks, is an interesting story.

During the sixties, I got to know and interview most of the major black political leaders, including Martin Luther King, Jr., Stokely Carmichael, Malcolm X, H. Rap Brown, and Huey Newton. A common feeling ran through most of them, which I can best describe by telling a story. Stokely Carmichael was one of the brightest kids I ever met, but he had already started to sound vicious around the time I was interviewing him, so I asked him about it: "Why are you so angry?"

One simple question. And in response he told me about the time they were integrating a school down South and he took his six-year-old niece to kindergarten. The cops weren't about to let them integrate. One cop grabbed Stokely's niece, put the girl on the ground, put his boot on her neck, stuck his gun in her ear, and said, "This is the last time I'm gonna tell ya. You're never, nigger lady, gonna go to school with white boys."

Carmichael took her home in shock. She was a basket case, and Stokely told me he decided then and there that he would never let a boot hold down the neck of another black person again, that he would kill the person wearing the boot rather than let it happen.

The black leader who opened my eyes the most was probably Malcolm X. He gave me a great understanding of the black movement. There was a fire in Malcolm, and I thought of him as the poet of that movement. He was very light-skinned with red hair. "Do you think, Mr. King," he said to me, "that if you were my color, you'd have your job? In your wildest dreams?"

That put things in perspective for me. Malcolm was the first to say to me, "I never see my people in a commercial. Did you ever think about that, Larry?" Before he said that, I had never thought about it. Now we take these perceptions for granted, but just twenty-five years ago they were unheard of.

I flew back from Chicago recently and the pilot and copilot were both black. Twenty-five years ago, there would have been panic on the plane. Even as recently as ten years ago, something happened that I'll never forget. I was flying to Dallas first class, and sitting next to me was a white pilot who was "deadheading"—flying to Dallas to pick up his plane. He recognized me and he happened to be a fan. He said, "Larry, you know who the pilot is today?"

He was a black pilot flying left seat. There weren't many black left-seat pilots back then because they had been very late getting into the system. "Watch this guy," he said. "He puts on a good show."

I had no idea what he meant. After we got up into the jet stream and were cruising along, the black pilot came out, put his pilot's hat on the shelf, and stretched so we could all see his captain's insignia. Then he walked out into the aisle where everyone could see him plainly. "Ain't dis a lovely day to go flyin'," he said in his best Uncle Remus accent. "Holy Moses, what a day we's been havin' up front in de cockpit. Ain't it

wonderful, folks? I's flyin' dis plane to . . . uh . . . uh . . . uh
. . . Dallas. That's where we's goin', Dallas." This is a true
story. That was one nervous first-class section for the rest of
the flight.

I got to know Harry Belafonte very well when he was in
Miami, and he told me quite a few revealing stories about
race relations in the sixties. Among other exploits, Belafonte
broke the color line in Miami Beach, nearly embarrassing
Jackie Gleason in the process. A new hotel had opened, called
the Beach Parker Hilton, and Gleason owned a piece of it.
For the hotel's opening act in 1964, they booked Harry Belafonte. He showed up with a whole troupe, more than forty
musicians and crew. Blacks were just starting to integrate in
Miami, but prominent and affluent blacks still stayed at the
Sir John Hotel, a very prominent, swank, all-black hotel.

Harry didn't arrive until the morning of the opening, and
he brought his whole troupe into the Hilton. The desk clerk
said, "We've made arrangements at the Sir John."

Harry said, "If I don't stay here, I don't sing here."

The clerk began frantically making phone calls. He came
back to Harry and said, "Okay, you can stay, but the rest of
your troupe—"

"No, no, no. This is the Harry Belafonte Group. I stay, we
all stay."

Finally the manager called Gleason, who was the only one
of the owners he could reach, and Jackie immediately said to
him, "What the fuck are you doing?" Harry, with his entire
troupe, broke the color line that day.

After the Civil Rights Act was passed in 1964, Lyndon
Johnson hosted a party at the White House for black leaders.
Martin Luther King, Jr., headed a guest list that included just
about every prominent black civil rights advocate of the day.
There was a receiving line, and the black leaders were shak-

ing hands with LBJ and saying thank you. And why not? Johnson had certainly made a great speech at Howard University and had pushed through the Civil Rights Act that Kennedy couldn't get past Congress.

They were all moving down the line shaking Johnson's hand and saying, "Thank you, thank you, thank you."

Belafonte stuck out his hand, took Johnson's hand, and while he was holding it said, "Wait a minute, Mr. President. Forgive me, but do I have to thank you for my birthright?"

And Johnson said, "Of course you don't."

Then Johnson stopped, looked around the room, and said to everyone within earshot, "Isn't it something that you had to thank me for what should have been guaranteed you?"

The party took on a completely different tone from that moment. Johnson stopped being president and started being a guy mingling at a party. And they served black food, which was also Johnson food: southern fare like chitlins and fried chicken. The other guests in the room, from the eastern liberal establishment, didn't know what to do with the food, while LBJ was picking it up with his fingers and really digging in.

Richard Nixon took a much more pragmatic view of race relations. In all the times I've interviewed him, I've never picked up any sense that he was a racist. He certainly had more than his share of problems—Watergate, Vietnam, campus riots, plumbers, you name it—but racism: I didn't feel it. I'll leave it to others to disagree.

One of the most interesting aspects about Nixon to me— and I know it sounds trivial—is his love of sports. It's a passion. On one show I did an hour of Richard Nixon on sports— no political questions at all—and decided that if Nixon ever wanted to go into another line of work, he could make a good sports talk show host. Reagan is constantly invoking his days as a sportscaster, but he doesn't know sports at all. He couldn't even pronounce the names of the Boston Celtics when they were at the White House. Nixon knows the nuances—the difference, say, between hit and run and run and hit in baseball. He can discuss the relative range of short-stops.

I once asked David Eisenhower, "How's your father-in-law?" The first thing he said was "Oh, he's fine—we went to the Mets-Phillies series together last week." He meant it: all four games of a four-game series.

Nixon is on a Rotisserie baseball league with Eisenhower. He is the general manager, David owns the team. For readers who aren't familiar with it, Rotisserie baseball is very popular in America right now. A dozen or so people get together to form a league and they each put up a certain amount of money—say, two thousand dollars apiece—some of which goes to the computer firm that keeps the league's records and updates them biweekly. There are maybe eight teams in the league, and they draft "players" from the current pool of pro baseball players. Each team might have a budget of eight hundred dollars to spend on ballplayers, whose prices are based on their relative value as determined by the computer. At the end of the season, the winner gets most of the money that's still in the kitty, maybe as much as ten grand.

Drafting players is the crucial part of Rotisserie baseball. Some ballplayers go for three dollars, but you might have to pay a hundred and eighty dollars for a Don Mattingly or a Tim Raines. Remember, you've only got eight hundred dollars. After you pick your players, the computer takes over. All the players' stats are fed into the computer, and the performance of your team, your aggregation of players, is based on the continuing performance of those players in real baseball during that season. The computer figures out the league standings based on those performance ratings—batting averages, ERA, and so forth.

Believe me, playing Rotisserie baseball changes your whole appreciation of the real game. Eisenhower told me he went with Nixon to see the Yankees play the Angels, and they didn't care who won. All they were concerned about was the players on their Rotisserie team because those players' performances would directly affect their team's standing. The fun of it, he said, is that you feel part of the league. The bad part is that you're all over the board—you read all the box scores every day and you begin to go berserk.

Rotisserie baseball is a game for rabid fans, people who follow every team and practically every player in both leagues. Nixon is like that. If you asked Reagan about Rotisserie baseball, he'd probably think it was something you eat at a dinner party. Nixon would know the name of the third-string catcher for the Seattle Mariners.

When Stanley Sporkin was appointed to a federal judgeship, William Casey and Stanley and I went to lunch at the Palm to celebrate the appointment. Casey was a big backer of Sporkin—who had worked under him at the Securities and Exchange Commission and the CIA—and had convinced Reagan to appoint him. Sporkin later testified at the Iran-contra hearings that he had advised the CIA to stay out of that whole mess because he didn't like the sound of it—but naturally they had ignored his advice.

At any rate, we had lunch to celebrate the appointment in 1986. Casey, who came to the lunch with a couple of security men, was a big, gruff New York Irishman with a deep New York City accent. He was a surprising character in a lot of ways. For instance, he liked Mario Cuomo quite a bit, which shocked me. A lot of people don't know that Casey and Cuomo are both alumni of the same university, St. John's in Jamaica, Queens. "I met Mario at a St. John's alumni dinner, where I sat next to him," Casey said. "I had a great conversa-

tion with him. Mario's my kinda guy. Maybe I don't agree
with him on everything, but I could like him."

"What about Bush?" I asked him.

"Wellll," he said, "I'm not so sure Bush is my kinda guy."

I asked him how he thought Cuomo would do in an election
against George Bush and Bill said, "Cuomo would murder
Bush. He'd wipe him out."

"You're kidding," I said. "You'd pick Cuomo over Bush?"

"No contest."

The conversation got around to politicians' weaknesses and
I asked him what he thought Ronald Reagan's biggest weakness was. Casey said, "Ronald Reagan is totally incapable of
firing someone. And he's absolutely incapable of dressing
someone down. He can get mad at a situation and say, 'What
went wrong here?' But he could never call you into the office
one on one and dress you down."

When David Stockman blasted Reagan's economic policy in
the *Atlantic*, Casey was livid. He told me, "I called Reagan
and I said, 'It's got nothing to do with me, it's got nothing to
do with the CIA; but this guy, Ronnie, is a son of a bitch. He's
a prick. Bury him.' You know what he did? Reagan called
Stockman into the office, and as soon as he walked in Reagan
said to him, 'They took you out of context, right, David? They
didn't print the whole thing. What you gave them was good
and bad in balance and all they printed was the bad, right? I
know the way they work.'" Casey was furious. Reagan immediately took Stockman off the hook, the whole meeting was
relaxed, and Stockman never got yelled at.

Other than that, Casey was a great admirer of Reagan; they
were both hawks. "But Jesus," he said, "you gotta lop guys
off. Stockman stabbed us in the fuckin' back. 'Ey. *'Ey.*" That's
the way Casey talked: 'Ey, Jesus Christ. He lets them off the
hook."

Lyndon Johnson was just the opposite of Reagan. Jack
Valenti told me about getting a call from Johnson at three

in the morning when he was a special assistant in LBJ's White House. Valenti picked up the phone and said a groggy hello.

Johnson said, "What time is it?"

"Two minutes after three," Valenti said after checking his alarm clock.

"Three minutes after three," Johnson said, *"here."*

Johnson was embarrassing; he could dress you down unmercifully. Reagan has none of that ability, which is what made it so difficult for him to get rid of Don Regan. I think North and Poindexter were the first two people he actually fired, and he did that by saying that Poindexter served his country well and that North was a great American patriot. Casey said to me, "It's not easy to be an ass-reamer. I'm an ass-reamer. Nobody likes to bust someone down. But Stockman? On your ass, you're gone." That's New York talking.

This was all said in friendly circumstances, of course. Then Sporkin said, "Bill, why don't you do Larry's show?" Casey had a history of never appearing on TV talk shows, *Meet the Press,* anything.

"I can't," he said. "I'm too truthful, Stan. Whenever I go before a committee I ask for a private session on national security grounds. Part of it's bullshit. But they're gonna hear the truth. If I went on Larry's show, I might be nice for a while, but if he said to me, 'What's a Reagan weakness?' I'm gonna say, 'The guy can't fire anybody.' I don't know how to deal with the flowery shit. I don't know how to do that."

Casey didn't consider himself a public servant. He felt that he worked for the president. I don't know whether he would have done something he disagreed with, but I believe he would have voiced his disagreement. There was no yes-man in Casey. He was capable of saying, "Mr. President, I'll do this, but I think you're dead wrong."

*   *   *

I don't know what sort of president Eugene McCarthy would
have made, because he's sort of lazy, but he has a wonderful
sense of humor and poetry, and he's also a great baseball fan.
In fact, he played semipro ball and hit .342 in the Iowa
League one year.

I had a lot of fun discussing the 1968 campaign with him. I
don't think anyone changed America more than he did at the
time, when he challenged President Johnson in New Hamp-
shire and almost won. Johnson got forty-one percent and Mc-
Carthy got thirty-eight percent, but that was enough to
convince Johnson he shouldn't run, and he quit. Humphrey
entered the race, but he wasn't going to enter primaries—he
had a solid delegate base and the support of the president.
McCarthy won a few more primaries, and then in came
Bobby Kennedy. McCarthy was bitter that Bobby waited until
he had done the hard work of eliminating Johnson from the
contest before he jumped in.

The night Robert Kennedy was killed, McCarthy was staying at the same hotel. Through some weird quirk in schedul-
ing and lack of thought on the part of their assistants, they
both had victory parties scheduled at the Ambassador Hotel.
"I lost California by less than a hundred thousand votes," Mc-
Carthy told me, "but I gave a sort of semiconcession speech. I
was very hurt by Bobby and didn't really want to concede.
Then I went up to my hotel room and watched *his* speech. I
heard him say, 'On to Chicago,' and I shut off my light and
said to myself, I'm on to Chicago, too, you little pip-squeak.
And five minutes later the phone rang."

McCarthy knew it was over for him then, too. He knew he
wouldn't get the nomination because the cleavage between
him and Bobby Kennedy had been so great that the Kennedy
people were not going to come to him. "He beat me in life,"
McCarthy said, "and he beat me in death. Although I came

out of it with one accomplishment I will live with forever: I was the first man who ever beat a Kennedy. I beat Bobby in Oregon."

To be fair to McCarthy, the bitterness never lasted long with him. I think he had a moral issue over the war, but I don't know how much he yearned for the presidency, how much he wanted to greet visiting heads of state or sit in long cabinet meetings on agricultural bills. He may have been too much of a poet for all that.

But I love his wit. I flew down to Miami with him and Al Haig in 1987. There were just the three of us in first class, and a man walked on the plane after we were already seated, just an ordinary guy walking back to the coach section. He obviously recognized us, and as he was passing by, he said, "Shit. If this plane crashes, my name ain't gonna make *any* part of the story."

On that plane trip, McCarthy wrote out for Haig a list of ten things that he thought should bar anyone from running for president. You should be barred if you're a sitting governor, if you've ever held a municipal post, if you've traveled to more than six foreign countries. Haig said he was going to treasure that list. The three of us talked the whole way down—which is kind of odd when you think about it. After all, Haig had been fighting in Vietnam on his way to becoming a two-star general while McCarthy was fighting against the war at home. I asked Haig how he felt about McCarthy, and he said he understood that as long as it was just a political debate, it was all right. "We never felt," he said, "that McCarthy was pro–Ho Chi Minh. We thought he just felt the war was a mistake."

To which McCarthy said, "Would it have hurt you to learn that I was?" They were laughing because they both have a great sense of humor. Anyone who can say upon entering a presidential race, as Haig did, "I'm throwing my helmet into the ring," has to have a sense of humor, even if Mort Sahl gave him the line. They also have a religious background in common—they're both Catholic. Haig's brother is a Jesuit priest, in fact, and both Haig and McCarthy considered the priesthood when they were younger.

McCarthy also gave Haig advice on running. On one primary day, he said, he was convinced that he inadvertently voted for the other guy. The levers were close together, and when you pulled a lever down to vote, it covered the name you were voting for. He didn't want to cover his own name and he's sure he made a mistake. "So watch that," he told Haig.

Haig said that the contra situation was insane. "We're not going to go down there and fight. We're not going to overthrow those guys. But you gotta support it."

McCarthy said, "What do you mean, you gotta support it?"

"Because I believe that once a foreign policy is set by a president, you have to support it," Haig said.

"But what if you disagree? You can't say, 'My country right or wrong.'"

Haig said, "You can disagree all you want in private—you debate the issue, you pound your fist—but you don't undercut a president." Haig is a Kissinger type. He doesn't really want war, despite his military past. Like Eisenhower, the people who have actually fought in a war want to avoid the next one. Reagan never fought in World War II and he's been trigger-happy ever since he got into office. Haig said, "You send guys Ortega likes down to see Ortega, and you call in whoever is leading the fight in the Senate against you, and you tell them what you're doing. You tell them you want a peaceful solution, but you support the president while you're maneuvering behind the scenes." McCarthy disagreed.

I met Nelson Rockefeller only once, but I knew his top aide, Joseph Cannizeri. Joe is a public relations man in Washington now, a good friend of Frank Sinatra, and he worked for the Reagan White House for a while. He's a liberal Republican and he was an adviser to Rockefeller when Nelson was governor of New York. Rockefeller was going over the state budget one day with Cannizeri, and someone at the meeting said to him, "Mr. Governor, you've got to understand the workingman in all this and what he has to deal with."

And Rockefeller said, "*I* know what it is to be a workingman. *I* know what it is to make a hundred, a hundred twenty-five thou a year."

"Governor," Cannizeri said to him, "the average workingman in New York right now, I believe, makes about sixteen thousand dollars a year."

"The director of my museum makes a hundred twenty-five," Rockefeller said, "and *he's* a working man."

Elliott Roosevelt, the son of Franklin and Eleanor, ran for mayor of Miami Beach while I was working there. I drove with him to a speech he was giving to a senior citizens' group and along the way I asked him, "Are you running on your name?"

"No, sir. I'm running as Elliott Roosevelt."

He gave a decent speech, but he didn't quite achieve the full attention of his audience. He ended it by saying, "Ladies and gentlemen, citizens of Miami Beach, I leave you with one thought to remember: The only thing we have to fear is fear itself."

The crowd went crazy. We got back in the car and I said, "Where did you come up with that?"

The ultimate Washington story has to do with the Alfalfa Club. When it comes to being invited to parties and functions in Washington, I probably get more than my share of perks. I

don't have time for most of them, since I work at night, but
there's one annual dinner that I always attend when asked.
It's the epitome of everything that's grandiose, excessive, and
utterly bizarre about life in Washington among the pillars of
society, and I wouldn't miss it for the world.

The Alfalfa Club is based in Washington, although its members come from all over America, and it is not well known
because it is so exclusive. The club meets once a year on the
last Saturday in January, at which time they have dinner, they
nominate a president—alternately a Republican or a Democrat—and they go home. They don't do anything else the rest
of the year. It has about two hundred and thirty members, a
fixed number. New members can be elected only when an old
member dies. Each year they elect at most half a dozen new
members, and they've been doing it since 1913—Herbert
Hoover was a member.

The Alfalfa Club is for men only and so is its annual black-
tie dinner at the Capitol Hilton. Each member can invite
three guests. I have no idea how much the members pay for
this privilege, but it's a sumptuous meal in the company of
about six hundred of the most powerful men in America. The
only reason I know what goes on there is that Harold Stassen
brings me as a guest each year.

At the last Alfalfa Club meeting, you would have found
most of the members of the cabinet, the chief justice of
the Supreme Court, the Joint Chiefs of Staff, Congressional
leaders, about a hundred and fifty presidents, CEOs, and
chairmen of the boards of the cream of the Fortune 500,
David and John D. Rockefeller, Ronald Reagan, George
Bush, Gerald Ford, Richard Nixon, Henry Kissinger, Barry
Goldwater, and George Shultz. As one wag put it, "If a
bomb hit this building, Bella Abzug would be president."
People like I. M. Pei, Armand Hammer, H. Ross Perot, Laurence Tisch, and Jack Valenti are merely invited guests. I
have to admit I feel a little out place. The only other guests

at last year's meeting who were not major political figures or business and industrial leaders were Hal David and Bob Hope—and Hope is practically part of the military anyway.

On the dais at the dinner are the outgoing and incoming presidents of the club, the president and the vice-president of the United States, the cabinet and the Joint Chiefs, a few invited ambassadors and state governors, and several Senate committee heads. Every year it's the same routine: 6:15, drinks; 7:15, enter the room; 7:30, the Marine Band and the Armed Forces Color Guard march through. I'm no gung-ho nationalist, but when everyone stands and the band comes through playing "The Battle Hymn of the Republic," "Semper Fidelis," "Stars and Stripes Forever," and a medley of armed forces marches, and then a black baritone sings the national anthem and "America the Beautiful," I'm ready to say, "Gimme a gun, I'm goin' over the hill, and I'll fight anything that moves."

Newspaper people wait outside for any information they can glean, but all they usually get are terse quotes from exiting members and guests. The only other press person I've ever seen at an Alfalfa dinner was George Will. Lobster is the hors d'oeuvre, and filet mignon is the main course, with baked Alaska for dessert. As befits an event of such propriety, vulgar language is not allowed.

Walter Mondale is a member of Alfalfa, but Jimmy Carter has never attended because no women are allowed and he refuses to go to an all-men's function. Stuart Symington's son James, who is a very witty guy, introduces the new members each year. Last year the outgoing president was Sam Nunn and the incoming president was Howard Baker.

Walter Wriston, then chairman of the board of Citicorp, was seated next to me once, and I remember his saying, "This is my favorite club. You have no decisions to make." At each dinner, the members salute the alfalfa weed, a weed that grows and does nothing. The theme song, which appears on the front of the menu, goes like this:

> Come to the land of Alfalfa
> Come where the clocks never chime,
> Come where ill will is only a rumor
> And sadness is labeled a crime.
> Come where the nights are all gladness
> And sorrows and care are taboo.
> Come to the land of Alfalfa;
> Good fellows are waiting for you.

Can you just picture Ronald Reagan sitting next to Teddy Kennedy and Warren Burger, hands over their hearts, singing along to this little ditty? And they all thought Carter was a schmuck for not coming.

So I was seated between Walter Wriston and Harold Stassen, nine times candidate for president of the United States, the youngest governor in the history of America, and the man who got Eisenhower to run. Stassen now heads one of the largest law firms in the country. One of Stassen's clients, the chairman of the board of Johnson's Wax, was seated next to him. Down the table were David Rockefeller, Edward Bennett Williams, and Howard Baker.

The accent is on wit at these events. I saw Henry Kissinger sworn in as president. Kissinger said, "How lucky you are to have me as your president because if I die, I'll be back in three days." He said, "I've just written my autobiography—the manuscript was twenty-one hundred pages. Then I sat down with my editor, and we decided to take out all the *I*'s. So now it's two hundred and eleven pages. Now that I am no longer secretary of state, I'm my own man. I can travel where I want. I can even travel incognito so I can have a good time. Last week I went to Israel—as Henry W. Kissinger."

Then Reagan got up. "Shucks," he said, "it's so nice to be here. I come from a little town called Beverly Hills. It's just an ordinary town like the ones most of you folks come from. We've got a little white line going down the center of the streets too—of course, it's ermine. . . . You know what still annoys me after all these years? When I ran against Jimmy Carter, there was a night that Carter spent in a Hispanic home in New York. You remember the pictures in the papers the next day—wonderful publicity. When *I* spent the night in a Hispanic home, nobody covered it. I had the same feelings, the same compassion and understanding—and Ricardo Montalban thanked me very much for coming."

The mingling over cocktails is ridiculous. At one point I was standing between Wriston and J. W. Mellon. I like to initiate the conversation in these situations because what are they going to ask *me?* So I asked Wriston, "What's the biggest advance in banking since you've been a banker?"

I thought he was going to say something like debentures. He said, "The twenty-four-hour cash machine. We could've had that sucker twenty-five years ago. It's so simple. The earliest computer could've handled those operations, but we were so dumb. Hey, I came down here, a Saturday night, I didn't have a dime. I put in my little card—I got three hundred bucks. We discovered a whole new concept at Citicorp: Saturday is a day. People walk around on Saturdays. Some of our branches are open on Saturdays now. Banks used to open for your inconvenience: 'For your inconvenience, we're open from nine to three today, but don't come near us at night.'"

Marvin Davis, chairman of the board of United Artists, the company that produced the monumental movie disaster *Heaven's Gate,* was there three years ago. What a conversation that was. He said, "We had a field where the grass wasn't growing too well, and Cimino wanted to spruce it up. We had a very good artist in our studio who could paint grass. It was a twenty-second shot. We ended up flying in grass from Malaysia that cost us a hundred and seventy-two thousand dollars. The paint would have cost eleven fifty a gallon."

One year they nominated Jay Rockefeller for president because Senator Charles Percy is his father-in-law. Percy got up and said, "When my daughter came to me and informed me that she was intending to get married, I said, 'Now, wait a minute. I want to know this boy. I want to know his family and his credentials. I'm a United States senator. I'm a former chairman of the board of one of the major companies in this country. You bring this boy to me. What is his name?' She said, 'Dad, his name is Jay Rockefeller.' And I wept. I flew to New York. I kissed the family ring. They threatened to buy my company with petty cash."

Then Jay Rockefeller got up. He said, "What a night this is, to be nominated for president of the Alfalfa Club. I've had so many dreams come true in my life. When I was a little boy, my number one dream was to be governor of West Virginia. I'd be sitting there playing with my blocks: Forty-ninth Street, Fiftieth Street. . . . And I was spoiled, like so many other kids. I said 'Granddad, I want Venezuela. Why does my brother have to get everything?'"

They all stay to the end, including Reagan, because they want to hear the acceptance speeches. Edward Bennett Williams was hilarious; he said he was going to govern in the great tradition of Maryland politics—from prison. Sam Nunn said he was going to carry on the tradition of great Georgians who have been sent to the presidency, a tradition of remaining just slightly below incompetence. Bush got up two years ago and started off, "It's a great pleasure to be here . . ." Then he leaned over to Reagan and said in a stage whisper, "Okay so far?"

Even the big-name people are excited to be there and leave clutching their programs, which list the names of all the members and guests attending that year. Reagan and Kissinger and Mellon and me, we all left holding on to our programs. I don't know about them, but it can be a rude shock for someone like me to leave that dinner and go back into the real world. The first time I went to an Alfalfa Club dinner, I was still married to Sharon and she had stayed home with the kids. I pulled into the driveway on a real high after having mingled with the people who run America, having eaten a sensational meal and listened to all that sparkling wit. Then I came home to a typical Saturday night domestic scene: one of the kids had fallen and bruised her knee, the older daughter was out late, Sharon had burned the meal and was in tears. I wanted to tell her what a wonderful night I'd had and what a weird and wild scene it had been, and the first thing she said was "Hey, get out of that tux and gimme a hand here."

The drain was clogged and the pipe was leaking under the sink. "I don't give a damn *who* was there," she said, "I've got water everywhere."

CHAPTER 8

THE LARRY KING SHOW

"I can evoke Larry with two words: 'Why comedy?'

"That's the kind of question he likes to ask. Or 'Why Los Angeles, Brooks?' But the thing I love most about Larry is that he never runs out of questions. I just don't understand how a person can ask that many questions of everybody.

"'Tonight we're gonna do six hours with a traffic cop,' he'll say. And then he'll start with 'Why blue?' and 'Are those sticks composite wood or what? How long does it take to make a nightstick?'

"What's most amazing is that he doesn't have prepared questions. Out of all the people doing interviews, I don't know anyone else who works that way. It's kind of the way it should be. It's the way it is in life, and he just does it."

—Albert Brooks

I've talked a lot about the people who come on my show. Let me take just a short time-out here to talk about the show it-self.

I've been interviewing people for almost thirty years, and I still have trouble explaining how I do it. Maybe part of the reason is that the essential talent required is inborn. You're either curious or you're not. Either you can listen well or you can't. You have a sincere interest in what people have to say or you don't. I don't believe those qualities can be taught, and you sure can't fake them.

Without question, the single most potent influence on my style of broadcasting was Arthur Godfrey. Godfrey, above and beyond everything else, was a high risk-taker. He knew how to be himself and he stuck to it, no matter where it led him. The difference between talent and mediocrity is the willingness to be yourself, to show emotion, to react—in short, the willingness to go to your gut.

I first met Arthur Godfrey when he came down to Miami in the sixties. He had heard me broadcast a few times and he put me on his radio show. Then I cohosted with him for a week, which meant that he let me interview people. Godfrey was never afraid to let me do anything; he let me emcee his birthday party. He was forever boosting me to the public and to people in the industry, and for that I have always been grateful to him. He was a very generous man, in part, I think, because he was always in control and had the confidence that came of knowing he was in control.

The producer of his radio show would hand Godfrey a commercial to read on the air every six minutes or so. One time when I was cohosting with him and the producer handed him the commercial, Godfrey took it and said, "Ohhhh, it's time for a product message." Then he tore up the paper on the air and threw it away. "Larry, my boy," he said to me over the microphone, "I hope that my next sponsor goes out of business. In fact, I hope that from this minute on they never sell another product, have to eat every product they've got, and file chapter eleven. And I hope that people go into stores and say, 'Remember them?' as they clear the products off the shelves and burn them, because that, Larry my friend, will mean that they've cured the common cold. Till then, all we have is Contac."

That was twenty years ago and I still remember it. He mentioned the product only once, and it was the last word in the commercial. I don't think Godfrey was a great interviewer, but he was a great personality, maybe the greatest ever on radio. One day when we were on the air, I said to him, "What does it say on your driver's license under occupation? Broadcaster? Television host?"

He said, "Salesman. And that's all we are, Larry. I'm just honest enough to put it down."

"I want to tell you something," I said. "One day when I was twelve years old and stayed home from school with a cold, I was listening to you. I listened to Godfrey every morning. Peter Pan peanut butter was the sponsor. I was lying in bed, sick as a dog, and you said, 'I've been talking about Peter Pan peanut butter for five years. How do you know I really like it?' Then you asked your guest in the studio to confirm that you were holding a jar of Peter Pan peanut butter, and he did. Then you said, 'Okay. I'm going to eat it for the next minute, without any bread. You may not be able to hear me talk, but I'm going to do my best.'

"All I could hear was the sound of peanut butter in your mouth, and the sounds of a man enjoying himself immensely. I got up, I got dressed, I went downstairs, walked four blocks to the corner store, and got some Peter Pan peanut butter and brought it back. And I couldn't wait to taste that peanut butter because you had put that peanut butter in my mouth."

And Godfrey said to me, "I don't remember doing that." I said to myself, Holy Christ, will I ever get to that stage, where I can do something that will stay with someone his whole life—and not remember it myself? Could you ever picture Dick Clark doing that, saying, "I'm going to eat some peanut butter on the air now, and you're not going to hear anything for a few minutes"? Talent does that, and Godfrey was an extraordinary broadcast talent. And the best thing he did was that he did *himself*.

It's hard to convey how outrageous he was twenty-five years ago just by being honest. For example, one day he played the Pepsi-Cola jingle:

> Pepsi-Cola hits the spot,
> Twelve-ounce bottle, that's a lot.
> Twice as much for a nickel, too.
> Pepsi-Cola is the drink for you.
> Nickel, nickel, nickel, nickel, nickel.

"Ladies and gentlemen," he said, "that was played for you on an electric transcription disc. Hear this?" And then he broke the disc on the air. "I've been drinking Pepsi downstairs for the past week, and it costs seven cents. The bottles are seven cents. It's seven cents in the grocery store. It ain't a nickel. It's a great drink, it's worth more than seven cents, but it ain't a nickel."

Why would that stay with me? Because it pounded in that same principle: be yourself. Once you learn it you'll never be nervous again. It sounds simple, but the minute you start to think of being someone else, you're in trouble. If you're trying to make your voice sound deeper than it is, you're not being yourself. If a listener calls in and says to me, "Larry, did you hear about what happened today?" what's wrong with saying, "No, I didn't"? The people who feel they have to pretend to know what they don't or put on a face that isn't their real face because they think that's what the public wants are the people who are nervous all the time. They could be on the air for thirty years and they'll still feel panicked tonight because they are not sure of themselves. Whatever else may be off-balance or lacking in my life, I know that tonight I'm going to be me—whether people like it or not—so I'm not nervous. If you go on the air thinking, Will I be liked? you will be ordinary.

Johnny Carson once told me, "If the show doesn't please you, it'll never please them." Godfrey's show always pleased him. He communicated with his audience. He was Arthur Godfrey. The best I could say about my career is that I hope I'm Larry King.

I try to follow a few other rules for interviewing. For openers, I ask short questions. The longer you take, the less the audience is learning. Good questions start with the words *Why* or *How*. Bad questions start with the words *Did* or *When*. With *Why* or *How* questions, I can get some elaboration from the guest. With the others, I'm inviting one-word answers, which everyone hates.

This may sound corny, but you have to make good eye contact because it draws the guest to you. I interrupt whenever I feel the interview is dragging. I have to think of myself as the audience and rely on my own gut feelings. If I'm getting bored, probably my audience is, too. Finally, I never attack. Attacking is a gimmick that wears thin. If you probe guests without offending them, you're more likely to get truthful answers to your questions. When you attack, you create hostility and a return thrust, but you don't get much information.

I've never been a producer and I've never involved myself in the process of getting guests for the show, for a number of reasons. If I got involved in booking guests, the temptation would be to book friends or only people I like. I would want to book baseball managers a lot. On the other hand, I have never canceled a guest, which is unusual in this business. Sometimes I'm warned that a guest is dull, but I love hearing that. Then it's up to me to make him or her lively, and usually I can. I think the only thing that would bore me would be if my producers booked a week of people who were third or fourth stars in soap operas—twenty-seven-year-old actors and actresses who think they're going to make it. That might really put me to sleep.

I don't prepare any questions. CNN gives me some preparation for certain guests. They're a news network and are oriented that way, so they may give me background, which I'll glance at. Generally, however, the less I know about someone, the more comfortable I am. That makes me more curious, and I have to rely on that curiosity. I hate to know the answer to a question before I ask it. That's why I don't like to read the book before the author comes on. If I've read the book, I'll have no curiosity about it. Hosts who read the book may say something like "In chapter four, you said . . ." If I'm the audience and I haven't read chapters one, two, and three, then I feel lost. Of course, if you're doing a four-minute interview on the *Today* show, you don't have a choice—you have to be able to zero in on one area of the book. But I have the luxury of time.

Sometimes I'll have the same guest on radio and TV on the same night, and I find that difficult. The radio audience may be totally different, but *I* don't like asking someone twice in the same night: "Why did you write this book?"

I never want to know the questions in advance when I'm being interviewed, and I can't imagine why anyone would. Every time I've been on *Good Morning America* or *Today*, I've been pre-interviewed. Then the interviewer hands the notes to the host: "Ask him about this." I can't work that way. Occasionally an author will ask, annoyed, "How can you interview me if you haven't read the book?" And I try something like "Gee, I guess you don't want to sell any books. Because the problem is, if I had read the book, I wouldn't ask you about it, since I'd already know. I'd have to ask you about another book of yours I haven't read yet." Sometimes that will do it.

*   *   *

Just as there are certain qualities that make for a good interviewer, there are certain qualities that make for a great guest.
If the guest has them, it doesn't matter if he or she is a ballet
dancer, a plumber, politician, photographer, or songwriter,
the show will be a good one.

The first quality is an ability to explain to the layperson
what they do. The second is a *passion* for what they do. Then
they need a sense of humor, preferably one that's self-de-
precating as well, and a little bit of a chip on their shoulder, a
little anger. If they've got all four of those, you've got a great
guest, regardless of the subject. People like Sinatra and Humphrey had all four. But if I get three out of four I can usually
have a good show.

A fine example of someone else who fits all four categories
is Michael De Bakey, the heart surgeon. If you ask him the
right questions, he can put you right there on the operating
table as he's doing open heart surgery, so that even a layperson can understand what's going on. He's got a passion for
what he does, an ability to laugh, and a chip on his shoulder
based on the long rivalry he's had with Dr. Denton Cooley in
Texas. They used to work for the same hospital and then they
broke up and developed a rivalry. Mention Cooley's name and
it drives De Bakey crazy.

De Bakey told me that he may do as many as seven open
heart surgeries a day. The chief surgeon is there for only
forty-five minutes of the operation—that's the time when the
heart is out of the body. He's the one who holds the heart in
his hands and hooks up the new valve. He's not there for the
rest of the operation, but he is there seven times a day for
forty-five minutes, holding someone's life in his hands.

I asked him, "Do you take your work home with you?"

"Absolutely," he said. "And if you know a doctor who
doesn't, then he shouldn't be in the profession."

"Does that mean that if you and I are having dinner tonight, you know all your surgery tomorrow?"

He said, "Oh, I know every one. And while I can have dinner with you and talk to you, half my mind is thinking, At eight o'clock tomorrow is James Phillips. James is a railroad worker, his wife's name is Audrey, and there's one tough aspect he's going to have with a certain valve procedure. And Bill Brooks, he's second. Bill flew in from Philadelphia. You know? If you *don't* have that feeling for your work, don't be in this business."

I remember asking De Bakey if there is such a thing as a will to live that keeps someone alive.

"Yes indeed," he said. "Patient A can have a better heart, less of a problem than Patient B. But maybe Patient A has had a lot of stress and he's getting tired of it. Patient B wants to live. I could look at the charts and the angiograms and tell you what *should* happen, but it doesn't matter: A dies and B goes home."

He told me a story about a man who had three valves almost totally shut off and one halfway shut. De Bakey said, "They recommended a quadruple bypass to this man. The guy was living on a thread. A *thread*. But he was breathing okay and he must have had something working for him. He was a traveling salesman. I called him in and said to him, 'Listen, the bypass operation is your only hope. Otherwise you've got six months to live.'

"The fellow said, 'Describe the procedure to me.'

"'Well,' I said, 'we saw through your chestbone, we open it up, take out—'

"'You do what? You're gonna saw through my chestbone?'

"'You'll be under anesthesia.'

"'Goodbye.' And he walked out of my office.

"I said to myself, That man's going to die. Six years later, he was part of a foursome ahead of me on a golf course. I asked myself, Why is that guy alive? He absolutely shouldn't be alive. Every time we think we know medicine, there's that guy. He has no reason to be alive."

And I like De Bakey's anger. He's a conservative southerner who was violently opposed to the Vietnam War. He said, "If only we had taken the money from that war and appropriated it to the construction of an artificial heart, and if only we had given it to the same companies that build trajectory bombs. I mean, we're all looking at an apparatus here— an apparatus that pumps. If we took the eighty billion dollars that we give a guy who can trajectorize a tank shot that lands forty miles away and applied it to creating an artificial heart, we'd have an artificial heart that is inexpensive and so available you could take it off the rack at Montgomery Ward. And we'd save hundreds of thousands of lives installing it. With the *same technology*—and we used it for an idiotic thing like bombing people."

I'll never forget that: "an idiotic thing like bombing people."

Having said what makes a good guest, I should add that the most compelling guests are often the ones who are not afraid to admit their own inadequacies, their own vagaries, their own mistakes. The worst are the ones who can't accept blame. Bob Hope had a line about the public that applies to this situation. "They wanna like ya," he said. "Remember that. They paid twelve bucks; they wanna laugh." Nothing draws in the audience and elicits their sympathy more than a guest who is willing to appear human.

Certain guests give me an eerie feeling, however. They never say wrong, they never do wrong. They say the right thing to me in any given situation—in fact, it's often better than the right thing. I get a chilly feeling whenever I talk to any of them. I call them the Stepford Guests, after Ira Levin's novel *The Stepford Wives*.

Werner Erhard, who founded est, is a perfect example. Erhard is the best I've ever seen at saying nothing. When I taped the show with him, sixteen of his followers were there. They all said, "This was the best show he ever did." Erhard told me he had heard I was the best, and he'd watched my show and *knew* I was the best, but then to actually come on my show and be *interviewed* by me—wow! What can I say to someone like that? My producer Randy Douthit came over to me after the show and said, "What did you think?" I said, "I have no idea at all what he was talking about."

Certain athletes are like that: Steve Garvey, Ray Knight, Gary Carter. They know the camera is on them all the time, and they always do the right thing. Steve Garvey is so *nice*, he's like a Ken doll. When Gary Carter gets the single in the ninth inning that wins the big game, he knows the camera is following him down to first base, and so he does the right thing. Can I say publicly that I know he knows that? No. But I know he does.

Joe Theismann of the Redskins is another. As one newspaper columnist put it, Joe Theismann could broadcast a game he plays in. "I'm fading back. Here comes Gastineau, here comes Lyons. I roll to my left, Lyons is tough, *down* I go. Well, we'll get 'em next time."

Or Ray Knight: "Here I am at third. Backing up now, moving over to the left. There's a cute girl sitting by the dugout. Martinez pitches, ball one. Nice pitch, low. I'm standing up now, gliding a little toward third, checking the outfield. There's Fred Lynn, a guy I admire a great deal."

Although I like them personally, maybe what I don't like about these people as guests: none of them needs an interviewer. They could all do the interviews themselves.

"Hi, this is Gary Carter. My guest tonight is Gary Carter."

"Hey, Gary, nice to be here."

"Gary, what happened in the third inning?"

"Let me tell you, Gary . . ."

They don't need the host. In fact, they're so perfect they have the answer for the one question you might think you could nail them with: "How can you be so perfect?"

"I've heard that, Larry," they'd say. "I don't know what that means. I put my pants on one leg at a time. Tell you the truth, Larry, I stubbed my toe the other day. For the life of me, I can't hang a picture straight, Larry, and yet I keep hearing all this talk about being *perfect.*"

They pose the ultimate dilemma for any interviewer. There's nothing you can ask that will shake them. But, as with the Stepfords, something is missing.

Some talk show hosts are like that, too. Dick Cavett, for instance: he interviews himself. When I watch his show, I learn nothing about the guest. He'll have a dancer on, and he'll say, "I saw the ballet last night, and you were terrific. My companion enjoyed it, my children loved it, and I especially liked the part where you . . ." That's called "Who gives a damn?"

Jay Johnstone, a ballplayer I like a lot, is a great one for pranks, and he knows the only way to get to these people is to do something that will throw them, because they're never thrown. Johnstone shares my theory that these guys know the camera is always on them. Once he took a fudge brownie, let it melt in the sun, and concealed it inside Steve Garvey's glove between innings. Garvey went back on the field and put his glove on. By the time Garvey finished infield warmup, he knew something was dreadfully wrong. He didn't know quite what to do, and by then his teammates were all watching from the dugout. He wasn't going to call time-out because that would draw attention to himself in a negative way. He pulled his hand out slowly and he made a mistake—he brushed it against his leg. Now he's got chocolate all over his uniform.

When the inning was over, Garvey went storming into the dugout. He was so furious he couldn't speak. However, what was really bugging him, I think, was that he couldn't understand why anyone would want to embarrass him. He'd never do anything like that himself. They're errorless, these people. But something is still missing.

I've talked about what qualities make a good guest, but I've also noticed that certain *categories* of guests work better than others. You might be surprised to know that, as a rule, military men make terrific guests. Real military leaders tend to be nonpolitical, so they're very open with me, even about their own frailties. They are also very responsive to questions because somewhere in their training they've acquired the discipline to answer precisely what they've been asked. They don't skirt the question and they don't fudge answers. F. Lee Bailey told me once, "If you're innocent, you'll have a better chance of a fair trial in the military." One reason, among others, is that when a judge tells a military jury that the testimony they've just heard is inadmissible, they dismiss it. They're good at following orders. A civilian juror has trouble doing that, which is why lawyers play tricks to get inadmissible evidence mentioned in court, even though the judge will throw it out.

One of the most fascinating military leaders I ever met was General David Schoup, the commandant of the United States Marine Corps. He was a hero in World War II and is since deceased, but he appeared on my show at the height of the antiwar protests in the sixties. The first thing he said was "Thank God for these protests. That's what we died for. That's what every Marine in World War II gave his life for, so that these people can march in the streets. And by God, if we stop that, I don't want to be part of this country." Do you think Oliver North would ever say that?

Schoup pointed out that we bought Chiang Kai-shek in the thirties and forties—a thief, a fascist, a user of his people. He wasn't implying that we had to buy Mao, but he felt that we

shouldn't necessarily have put all our eggs in one basket with
a guy like Chiang. We could have created moderates in China
by fostering an air of balance. By supporting Chiang, we en-
gendered hatred against ourselves.

Omar Bradley told me that Dwight Eisenhower was the
most interesting military man he had ever seen. Ike didn't
trust the military very much and he wasn't particularly fond of
military people. He was very security-conscious, and his
number one interests as a general were reduction of injuries
and reduction of military expenditures. According to Bradley,
Eisenhower was always cautious on the subject of casualties—
he hated the word. "How many will we lose at Normandy?"
was his refrain. That's why it never surprised Bradley that
Eisenhower was so careful about using troops during his administration. The Korean War ended soon after he took office, and after that I don't think we lost a single soldier during
his presidency. And Ike was fearful of ever giving the military
any political power. Bradley felt that Ike had been a brilliant
choice to lead the armies in Europe because he was a natural
politician and could handle all the different factions.

Bradley had an interesting comment about Patton, too. He
thought that Patton's finest hour came when he saw the death
camps in Germany. Patton went into the nearest town and got
the mayor and all the citizens and made them parade through
the camps. One German reacted with such horror to the sight
and smell that Patton handed him a gun and suggested he do
it the manly way. The guy committed suicide. Bradley figured
that Patton was probably certifiably insane, but he admired
him greatly.

Bradley also thought the only real genius among the
German generals was Rommel. My cousin was captured
by Rommel during World War II and he used to tell me the
most outlandish stories about the experience. He was a lieutenant, and every day he would be asked his name, rank, and
serial number—and then he would have breakfast with the

field marshal. Rommel had his men salute my cousin because he was an officer and Rommel went by the Geneva conventions.

I got to know Chappy James, the first black four-star general, very well. Chappy made the famous statement "Nobody hates war more than warriors." I didn't believe that then and I don't believe it now, but I think Chappy believed it. His approach to prejudice in the service was unique: he just stormed through until he got promoted. He was one of those guys who would say, "Okay, so life gave you a bad break. Now what are you going to do? You've got a couple of choices. You can blow up buildings, you can stand around on the street, or you can say Screw this. And I said Screw this."

Eddie Rickenbacker, the World War I ace who later bought Eastern Airlines, was a classic lone-wolf flying nut and another "Screw this" type. He didn't like World War II as much as World War I because the fighters flew in formation in World War II. "Aww, everybody's gotta stay in line?" he would ask. "And then peel off? Lemme alone."

He had all the guts you could ask for. He told me that when he first flew airplanes they had no radar, so he used to follow the train tracks. One time he was so intent on watching the railroad tracks that he flew right into the side of Stone Mountain in Georgia. He broke every bone in his body, but he couldn't wait to fly again. Like Chappy James, he just said, "Screw that. No one's gonna bust this body up."

Rickenbacker had a true military mind. He was shot down during World War II and wound up on a life raft with twenty other guys. They were out in the middle of the Pacific, and the odds were that it was going to be quite a while before anybody found them. Rickenbacker decided that the only way to keep them all going was hate. So he ran the life raft like a military operation. The guys had to salute him. He handed out chicken-shit details on the raft. After twenty-three days they were finally rescued, and he said he figured at the time

that he had about three days left before they threw him over-
board.

I came close to going into the service myself, but, like a lot
of things in my early life, I just missed. When I was around
eighteen I was drafted, and my friends gave me a little going-
away party. This was during the Korean War, in 1952. I went
down to take my physical, and guys like me with bad eyesight
had to take the vision test last so that we wouldn't hold up the
line. I went through the whole physical and was drafted into
the navy. We were raising our hands to be sworn in when the
guy yelled, "Zeiger!"

I shivered. "What, sir?"

"Go home!"

"Wha'?"

"Go home. You're over twenty/four hundred in the left
eye—that means you're blind."

"I'm *blind*."

"Yes, Zeiger." He explained, "If you lost your glasses in
battle, you could shoot your own men and never be blamed."

It was ridiculous going home. I had my crewcut. All the
guys were saying, "Larry's doin' a bit. This is shtick. Larry
ran away."

The draft board had actually changed the requirements between the time I had taken the preliminary physical two years
before, when I registered, and when I took the physical on
the day of the induction. It was weird more than embarrassing. My friend Hoo-ha—Bernie Horowitz—had given me a
lighter as a going-away present. I don't want you to think that
my friends were cheap or anything, but the first thing he said
when he found out I flunked the physical was "Hey, gimme
my lighter back!" He meant it.

Of course, when you're discussing life-and-death issues, it's
easy to have a good show. And in thirty years on the air,

needless to say, the range of topics that can be discussed in public has broadened, sometimes outrageously. Mine was one of the first talk shows to discuss abortion, at a time when you weren't supposed to use the word *abortion*, or even *pregnant*, on the air. Now we routinely do shows about incest or homosexual priests, and nobody thinks anything of it. Still, when my producers tell me casually that I'll be interviewing people who have sexual relations with animals, I have to do a double take. As it turned out, I was on vacation the night we did the show on bestiality, but you have to understand one thing about the talk show business today—there is no show they would not do, nor is there any show I'd turn down, because I'm curious about a lot of things.

Some of the most surprising interviews I've done have been with our top contemporary psychiatrists, including Karl Menninger, Rollo May, and Thomas Szasz. Szasz began by saying, "There is no such thing as mental illness." He testifies against psychiatrists in malpractice suits. He says that he'd rather be in jail than in a mental institution any day. "The worst thing a defendant in a murder or assault trial can do is to plead guilty by reason of insanity. They'd be much better off in prison."

I never knew until I talked to Szasz that in many states, if you commit *yourself* to a mental institution, you lose your driver's license. You give up many of your civil rights, even by a voluntary commitment. Szasz holds that the amount of violent mental behavior in America is one-half of one percent. Ninety-nine percent of what we consider aberrant behavior is somebody on the street corner laughing to himself. His theory is "If a bag lady wants to go off with her bags, leave her alone. If a man is standing on a corner looking up at the sky laughing, leave him alone. He hasn't done anything to you. Another man is talking to garbage—you think that's crazy. You're running to work every day, getting a heart attack, he's sixty-seven and he's alive. You're going to have him committed? Let him talk to garbage."

I said, "Okay, what if you go home tonight and for no reason your wife takes a lamp, smashes you in the face with it,
and says, 'I'm going to bed'?"

Szasz said, "Let's take that one step further. That happened
on Monday night. You come home on Tuesday and—*bang!*—
she hits you with the lamp again. You come home on
Wednesday—*bam!* If you come home on Thursday, who's
crazy?" Szasz says you always have an option, and so he
doesn't buy the "other person" theory.

Once when I had a prominent behavioral psychiatrist on my
show I decided to ask him exactly what that term meant. He
said, "It means I deal with the problem as it is. I never go
into childhood like the Freudians do."

I asked for an example. He said, "Just last week, a man
came in and said to me, 'She left me. I love her and I can't
live without her, doctor. I want to die.'

"I said, 'Okay.' I put a gun on the desk and left the room.
'I'll wait outside,' I said. 'That's the decent thing to do while
you kill yourself.' I waited and there was no shot. I came back
in and I said, 'Aha! Something's more important than her:
you. Let's start.'"

"What if he had shot himself?" I asked.

"Then I'd know he really meant it."

Karl Menninger believed that no one should ever be committed, and he would never treat a patient who had been involuntarily committed to an institution. He would fight to get
the patient released instead. If a patient is not bothering anyone else, he considers that person to be sane. If a patient is
damaging to himself or herself, he doesn't consider that a
strong enough reason to commit the person. He also believes
in sin: if you do malicious damage to someone else, you
should pay for it. "Punishment is necessary, and it works," he
said. What doesn't work is punishment for punishment's
sake—punishment without reason and without improvement.

"The greatest failure in the history of mankind is prison,"

he said. "It's an abject flop that society perpetuates." He had the figures to back up his statement—recidivism rates, the cost of prisons, the proof that crime has increased rather than decreased. He showed how our prison system is designed to create better criminals. However, he did say he believed in punishment and reward. He had worked with a model prison in England, where an embezzler, for instance, would be made president of the prison bank.

Now that CNN is carried worldwide by satellite, my television program shows up in some interesting locations. Robert Redford said that he saw my show in a hotel room in Singapore. However, I sometimes wonder how my shows, particularly the call-in segments, would work if I did them in foreign countries. I talked about this with Dave Kendall, the chairman of the board of PepsiCo. Pepsi was exporting its products to the Soviet Union and importing vodka. He said, "I just left Anatoly Dobrinin, the Soviet ambassador, who said he listens to you every night. He's a big fan of yours because he likes to learn about America. But he was very upset the other night because you said they couldn't do this kind of show in the Soviet Union. He said you were absolutely wrong, that they could do it in the Soviet Union—except they'd have to have an 800 number."

"Why is that?" I asked.

"Because the Muscovites would never pay to call in."

Speaking of famous Russians, one of the most eye-opening shows I ever did was with the Soviet apologist Vladimir Posner. When Posner was seventeen, his father, a Marxist, moved his family from New York to the Soviet Union, and there they stayed. Posner now is a Soviet journalist who claims to be unbiased, yet he always seems to take the Soviet side in any discussion. He returned to America some years ago as a commentator on Soviet life and politics and made the talk show circuit. The hosts were asking him about Marxism and Afghanistan and all the usual Russia versus America questions. Since I'm as interested in the person as the subject, however, my first question to Posner was "You left New York City when you were seventeen, and you're fifty now—what do you miss most about America?"

He didn't expect the question, so it made him think.

"You know what I miss?" he said. "Number one: baseball. To tell you the truth, I hate soccer and I don't much care for ice hockey. So you know what I do? Every day I get the box scores from the AP. I'm a Yankee fan, and I know Mattingly and Winfield, and I know what they're doing this year. I know where the Yankees are in the standings."

"What else do you miss?"

"I miss that things get *done* here in America. We're such a young country, the Soviet Union, and I believe in the system. But in America if you want a pastrami sandwich, you've got a pastrami sandwich. Things get done. And I forgot how much I like the people. I was born in France and I came to America when I was three, so my formative years were spent here and there's a lot of America in me."

"What don't you like about where you live?" I asked. "You're a journalist and every journalist complains about something. What do you complain about in the Soviet Union?" That question didn't give him an out. He couldn't tell me, "I love my country, I don't bitch about anything." So he came up with something.

"I hate the red tape," he said. "We must lead the world in red tape. Then I see a man like Gorbachev and I hope that things will go faster. I believe so much in the free medical care, and I don't see people starving. But I see them lined up for two blocks to buy a pair of shoes and I don't like that. We have a big problem with alcoholism—but nobody's sleeping on the streets."

What could have been an ideological debate became a dis-

cussion between two human beings. We never got around to
Afghanistan. I'm a New Yorker much like him, but my father
wasn't a Marxist. If I had a father who was a Marxist, I might
have been taken to the Soviet Union too. A few years after I
interviewed Posner, I had on Anatoly Shevchenko, one of the
most prominent defectors in Soviet history. His situation was
the reverse of Posner's. Here was a Soviet who is now an
American, and I asked him essentially the same question:
"What do you miss most about your country?"

"The bread," he said, almost without thinking. "There isn't
a master baker in the United States who can bake a loaf of
bread to compare with the average peasant's bread in Siberia.
The smell of it, the taste of it with hot butter melting on it,
my God! And I miss the chess. They play chess everywhere in
Moscow, in the square, on the street, all day long. And classical music—not one classical music station on the radio, but
twenty."

Then I told him Posner's comments about missing baseball
and asked him if he missed Russian sports. "Oh, the Soviet
hockey championships!" he said. "You think the Super Bowl is
big here? During the Soviet hockey championships, nobody
goes to work. Stores are closed, and nobody's in the street.
Nobody. You can't buy gas, you can't buy food."

I found out that the premier drops the first puck and then
stays for every game. Can you imagine Reagan sitting through
every game of the World Series? I said, "The worst day in my
life was the day Bobby Thomson hit the home run and the
Giants won the pennant." He said, "The worst day in my life
was the day the Czechs beat the Soviets three to two in over-
time," and he named the Czech who scored the winning goal.

What I find valuable about my style of interviewing is that
before I get to the rest of the material—the sort of thing that
everybody else covers in the first ten minutes—I feel that I

have humanized my subject. I've opened him or her up to the audience, and in so doing I've created a context for whatever else they may say. Peter Ustinov told me, "I love the way you interview because you ask me questions that I don't ask myself. You make me think about things I don't think about."

I've said before that I rely on my curiosity to be successful as an interviewer. But it's the particular nature of that curiosity. *Why* did a doctor choose his specialty? *Why* is one a pediatrician and one a dermatologist? I've gotten really fascinating answers to just that kind of question over the years. Michael De Bakey became a heart surgeon because of the instructor who taught him about the heart in medical school. Dr. Harvey Blank, one of the great dermatological experts in America and the man who did the most to help alleviate acne in this country, became a dermatologist because: "I never want to be awakened in the middle of the night."

I've had plastic surgeons tell me that they dreamed of being sculptors but couldn't make a living at it. I've never interviewed an ophthalmologist who didn't have a history of eye problems in his family. Oncologists, cancer specialists, are usually people who like high-risk challenges—they know they're going to lose nine out of ten patients, but they want to make it eight out of ten.

All these people are driven in different ways for different reasons, but nobody ever asks them about it. Nobody asks them "Why?" I asked Isaac Stern, for instance, "Why the violin? Do you believe you'd be as good a piano player?"

"Yes," he said. "But my mother gave me the violin. I believe music is from the heart; the instrument is just the apparatus. I have nice fingers, I could have been a good pianist. My mother gave me the violin."

CHAPTER 9

CALL ME

At the beginning of my shows, I'm the one who gets to ask all the questions, and as you can probably tell by now, I think I'm pretty good at it. After I'm finished, the audience at home gets their chance to show me up. Considering that they don't get paid for interrogating my guests, I think they do a good job of it, too. I follow the same procedure on radio and on television, except that on radio after the guests leave I open up the phones and hold a dialogue with the rest of the country.

Most radio shows screen calls. I don't. I think the main reason other shows do so is to keep older voices off the air. Producers want to make the shows sound youthful, and they have a definite prejudice against older callers. If you sound old, they'll just leave you hanging on the line. I've never been inundated with older callers, but I've never in my life screened a call on radio, either. I believe that if you get in, you should get on. How long you *stay* on is up to me; I determine whether you are relevant or not.

Since we don't screen calls as they come in, I have to screen the calls on the air. When the caller comes on, I have no idea what he or she is going to say. Sometimes they're not the greatest, but I've also had guests tell me the best calls they ever got were on my show. If the caller is off the mark, it's good night and on to the next call. But I don't want someone else determining who is or is not a good call.

Some screening takes place on my television show because television is a much more frightened medium than radio. Television producers have an absolute fear that one bad call will cause viewers across America to hit their remote control buttons and remove me from the screen. I think that reasoning is absurd, but I can't control that aspect of my show.

One of the most unusual calls I ever got on my radio show was from a thief who was in the middle of a burglary. "I've always been a listener of yours," he said in a quiet, breathless voice. "The radio was on in the bedroom of the house I just broke into, and I couldn't help it, I had to call."

We talked for a while and then he suddenly said, "Well, I've gotta go now," and hung up.

The championship call of all time came from a guy who was so excited he sounded like he was about to burst at the seams. "Larry, Larry, Larry!" he said in a kind of suppressed shout. "I think I'm gonna jump out of my skin. I'm a degenerate gambler. You know the sickness you've done shows on? That's me. This morning I was leaving the house and the wife says to me, 'Gamble once more and the marriage is over.' So I told her I was going on a business trip." He was whispering because his wife was asleep in the bedroom and he was calling from the kitchen.

"Did you happen to notice the triple on the last race at Aqueduct, Larry?"

"I don't have it in front of me," I said.

"Go look it up—I'll wait. Twenty-nine thousand bucks, Larry. One ticket. You're talkin' to him."

CALL ME 157

I started laughing, but not because I didn't believe him. For one thing, the story was too wild to be made up. It was just that as a former "problem gambler," I could identify with his excitement—and his dilemma.

"Wait a minute, Larry," he said. "I went to Atlantic City with the twenty-nine grand." There was a dramatic pause. "Larry?"

"Yeah?"

"I've got ninety-six thousand dollars in hundred-dollar bills. I'm looking at it as we speak. But the wife said if I ever gamble again, she's leavin' me. What do I do?"

I said, "Do you want to break up the marriage or not?"

"I'd like to keep the marriage together."

"I can only tell you what I'd do in the same situation," I said. "I'd be at the breakfast table when she came down in the morning, and I'd have the money under the table. I'd say, 'I broke our vow yesterday, I gotta admit to you, honey. I'm so sorry, I don't know what to say to you.' And then I'd start peeling it off. One bill at a time."

I never found out if he followed my advice or how it all worked out. But God, I loved that call. "One ticket, Larry, and you're talkin' to him."

The callers who phone in to ask questions of my guests are usually pretty serious, but once in a while we'll get a crank caller or somebody really off the wall. One night I had Jerry Stiller on, and a woman called in with a classic Bronx accent and began to talk to Jerry. It soon became clear that she had it in for him in the worst way. Was this going to be the kind of call I had nightmares about—someone out of the guest's past calling to insult him? It was obvious that they had a common past, so I just let them have at each other. I tried to help Jerry out as best I could, but the two of them became so involved that I ended up being little more than a glorified referee until the very end. This is the conversation as it happened that night on the air.

"Hello, Jerry. This is Frieda."

"Who?"

"Frieda Fontana. I went to Seward Park High School with you, Gerald."

"Hello, Frieda."

"He was in a play at Seward Park, Larry. He played Hitler."

"Wait a minute. What?"

"Yes, that's right. It was to raise money for war bonds. And you don't remember me at all, Gerald? I went with Artie, remember?"

"It's been a long—"

"We lent you five dollars, remember?"

"That's a long time ago."

"We lent you five dollars. That's back in the forties, Gerald."

"Frieda, I want to tell you something. First of all thanks for the—"

"You're very high and mighty now. And you have never returned the five dollars. In fact, my husband and I once went to spend a lovely weekend—at Grossinger's?"

"Yeah."

"And you and your wife—"

"Anne. Yes."

"—were playing there. We went backstage to see you?"

"Yes, I remember that."

"You stiffed us. Never remembered—I might add, you *chose* not to remember, as many of your ilk in show business tend to forget their roots."

"Frieda, let me tell you something. As a performer, I can tell you that I meet a lot of people in this business—"

"I don't believe performers. I think they put on an act when they're on talk shows, to show how wonderful they are, *and* they forget their real friends in the old neighborhood."

"Frieda, can you send me a card telling me where I can get in touch with you? I would be very happy to send you the five dollars to show you that I'm not that kind of—"

"How cheap! That's an insult. I don't need your five dollars. I and Artie are very well off, we are dealing in futures and commodities, a very big wheel in Wall Street, and we don't need your help."

"Now wait a minute. Frieda, that's unfair for you to attack me here on radio, on *The Larry King Show*. And the other thing, Frieda, you have to remember: it's not a nice world."

"The wife, the person of Irish parentage you married?"

"Yes. My wife, Anne."

"Who, I understand, tends to go off and do things on her own *and* dyes her hair, I believe, if I'm not wrong, correct me."

"Well, I don't think it's fair for anybody to say. A lot of people dye their hair today. Anne is just like everyone else. She does those things, but I don't take it as an offense."

"I don't feel people want to hear about you and your wife. I called to make a point to Mr. King, who interviews many so-called celebrities. And I think the public—who, don't forget, Gerald, made you and can break you—the public likes to know how these celebrities really are as human beings. And to not pay back a debt of five dollars is *snubbing*. To snub a man and his wife—the wife having gone to Seward Park High School with you—is, I think, unconscionable."

"Have you finished? Are ya really finished? Because I want to tell you something, Frieda. This is one of the most unbelievably disgusting things that could ever happen on radio. I come all the way to Washington, D.C., to be on *The Larry King Show* to talk about a movie that I think is one of the finest movies that has ever been done in the whole world. I say, 'Larry, turn on the phones.' And I have to get this kind of abuse from a caller?"

"Well, I don't think you're getting the essence of my message."

"Listen, there's such a thing as profanity, and it can come from this end of the line, too, Frieda. I'm gonna say something now to Larry, I'll whisper it, and—"

"You ought to use humility, you people, because you can go in the flick of a Nielsen, all of youse."

"Hey listen, I wanna tell ya something, Frieda. Guys like me are just as vulnerable and—"

"Oh sure, sure."

"Get her off. Will you get her off the air, Larry?"

At this point I decided to come to Jerry's rescue. "Wait a minute," I said. "I can't. This is too poignant a moment. Frieda, the man is crying."

"They turn it on, Larry, they turn it off."

"Wait a minute, the man has got tears rolling down his cheeks—"

"Oh, crocodile."

"The man was happy, Frieda. You almost destroyed his life. Do you think you could find it in your heart to apologize to him? He really is a basket case."

"I should apologize to a person who stiffed my husband and me—made us feel like nonentities?"

"Maybe he didn't recognize you," I said.

"Paying back is forgiving, Frieda," Jerry said. "Remember that."

"Who should forgive *you*? Because you had the sin of pride and arrogance."

"You've got the sin of sloth, and misery, and hostility, and hatred, and conniving. You planned this, you waited till I got on. You knew yesterday I was going to be on when he was announcing Sergio Franchi, you waited for years."

"Is that true?" I asked.

"I knew he was going to be on. I know it's a part of my past because I went to school with this boy."

"All right," I said. "Do you go around and tell the neighbors what happened?"

"No. I am not a gossip. This will remain between you and Mr. Stiller and me."

"But you're hurting the man's career here tonight, Frieda."

"In the show business you tend to think you are mightier and holier than thou. *I* have a *pied à terre* in New York. We have a summer home in the Hamptons. I am not a riffraff. I also climbed up the ladder of success in my own way. We may not be household names, my husband and I, but we are human beings. But your wife, who was extremely rude, a loud, vulgar girl—"

"Excuse me, I don't think it's fair for you to say that. Coming from your mouth tonight, that's really low, when she can't defend herself. I'd like to do equal time on you, Frieda. Because you tell me where you are and I'm gonna come by, I'll do it with a bullhorn if I have to."

"Is that a threat? I'm getting a threat over the airwaves?"

"It's not a threat that the FCC can do anything about, I'll tell you that."

And at that point I let the audience in on the joke, in case they hadn't guessed already, which I'm sure they had. At first, Jerry really had assumed it was some sort of crank call, but we soon realized it was Jerry's wife and partner, Anne Meara, on the line. I have a private line in the studio, where people who know me can call in and reach me directly, but Anne had called the regular number, so we had no way of knowing it was her, and neither did our audience. I sometimes wonder how many listeners went along for the ride.

My other favorite call occurred on the night I was interviewing Steve Martin and Lily Tomlin. They were there to promote their movie *All of Me*, and I had never met either of them before. After the interview we started taking calls. A guy called up and asked to talk with Steve.

"Steve," he said, "my son is only ten years old. He likes

you a little, but he doesn't appreciate your great talent yet. I'm going to ask you a great favor. I've got a tape machine here. I want to tape a conversation with you like you know me, like I'm an old friend of yours. And one day my son's gonna come in, and he'll say, 'Dad, this Steve Martin is fantastic.' And I'm going to say, 'Son, he's an old friend of mine,' and I'll play him the tape."

It was an unusual call, but an imaginative one. I said, "Steve, would you do that?"

"Sure," he said. "That's really nice. I never heard a call like that."

"Okay," the caller said. "Let me start the tape recorder. My name is Phil."

This was all on the radio, going out to a live audience.

"Steve, how are ya? It's Phil."

"I'm great, Phil," Steve said. "But I was wondering if you could loan me another thousand."

The guy went mute. "I know I owe you a thousand," Steve said. "But we got this movie and it doesn't look good. I'm tapped a thousand, so what I'll do, I'll meet you at the gas station tomorrow at four, all right? You'll meet me, you'll slip it to me—and then *I* won't tell the kid about the drugs."

By now the caller really didn't know what to say. He was in a catatonic state. Then Lily Tomlin came on. "Is that you, Phil? This is Lily, Phil. I told you never, ever, to call me again."

"You know Phil?" Steve asked her.

"Do I know Phil? I had a really unfortunate experience with Phil, and he's got a lot of nerve thinking he can call here tonight. He thinks he can just humiliate me on the air. Well, he can't."

"Were you lovers?" I asked.

"No, we were not lovers," Lily said with a little catch in her voice. "It was something deep and very dark. He has a very dark side to him, Phil does."

"Did it involve," Steve asked, "a popcorn box?"

"He only broke my heart. A note, Phil? That's all you could leave was a note? And now you call, an old friend of Steve Martin's?"

We were in stitches. Steve said, "He's more than a friend."

The guy never said another word the whole time. For all I knew, he'd already turned off his tape recorder in despair. Then Steve said to the caller, "Same time, same place. Be there tomorrow with the grand."

And I hung up on the guy.

Steve and Lily were playing off each other all night, and I never knew who was going to be the straight man next. Lily explained why she had decided to take on her role in *All of Me:* because the themes of intimacy and unconditional love attracted her to the script and because she liked the idea of two human beings inside one body having to learn to adjust to each other. Then I turned to Steve and asked him the same question. "I basically got involved through market research," he said.

One of the callers wanted to know if Steve and Lily ever thought back to the times when they weren't so successful in their careers. This time Steve gave a serious answer, something to the effect that he never took success for granted.

"The only thing I think is unbearable," Lily said, "is that people won't let you be a has-been in this culture. Let's say I wanted to go back and be a waitress, you know? They'd look up and they'd say, 'Oh isn't that sad? That's Lily Tomlin.' What if I, like, really wanted to be a waitress? I couldn't do it with dignity."

Then Steve told a story about one of his earliest gigs, back when he was about twenty. His agent asked him if he would play a show on the Russian River in California.

"It was outdoors," Steve said, "kind of like a drive-in movie, but with a platform and microphone. The audience would drive in and stay in their cars, and if they thought something was funny they would honk. I swear this is absolutely true. I'd tell a joke and I'd hear 'Honk-honk-honk! Honk-honk-honk!' So there is a kind of change from those honking days to 'Your trailer is ready, Mr. Martin.'

"Then there was a little club in North Beach, in San Francisco, where I performed for a while. The way it worked was that I would go on at eight o'clock—whether there was anyone in the club or not. The club had a window to the street, and the theory was that people walking by would see something going on and would come in. So I'm standing up there every night at eight o'clock doing my act for *nobody* for twenty minutes, until someone would stroll in. I worked the lights myself. Just one person laughing in the audience would keep me going. The waitresses or the bartender laughing night after night could be very uplifting, but some nights were so bad, I'd think, Well, I might as well go for the record and have *no* laughs. Try to get *none*."

Steve said that fame was very gradual for him, like growing in height—he didn't really notice it. I said, "But one day you step on an airplane and everybody knows you. And that's changed your life, hasn't it?"

"Sure," he said. "If someone's standing in the aisle, you just push him out of your way. If you go into a restaurant and people are waiting for a table, you just push them aside. Or if someone's sitting at a table, you're allowed to pick them up physically and eject them. You have to crush all those who oppose you."

Then Lily talked about some of her childhood fantasies that she'd been discussing with Steve before the show, like lying on the sofa in her bathing suit.

"That's part of being raised female in the movie star culture," Lily said. "When I was seven or eight, I learned to pin-curl my own hair because I didn't want to wear pigtails—I wanted to have fluffy hair. And I made myself one of those little dressing tables out of orange crates and I thumbtacked fabric around it in pleats. We didn't have a full-length mirror in the house, only a horizontal mirror over my mother's dresser in her bedroom. I'd put on this two-piece bathing suit and pin-curl my hair, and then I'd lie on my side across the top of my mother's dresser in becoming bathing-suit poses that I'd see in *Photoplay*. So now I have a very large dresser in my bedroom, and the top is padded because my mother's had hard lime oak."

Then we went back to the phones and Lily brought down the house when a caller asked if she planned to do any more work with Dolly Parton following the success of *9 to 5*.

"Dolly's working on a movie for me and Jane to rejoin us," she said, "and it's going to be kind of a James Bond movie. We're all going to be secret agents, and we're real excited about it, because the working title is *Octodicky*."

That sort of live interplay is part of what makes my job fun. Apart from news and sports programming, there isn't much live entertainment left on radio or TV. Even most national talk shows are taped ahead of time, so embarrassing moments can be edited out. On television, we don't work with a six-second delay as we do on radio. When I was interviewing the Iranian designer Bijan on CNN, a caller said something to him in Farsi, the native Iranian tongue. Since I don't speak the language, and Bijan couldn't make out what the caller was saying over the phone connection, I asked the caller if he'd be kind enough to translate for us. Without going into detail, let's just say I was sorry I asked.

One of the most embarrassing moments on radio happened not to me but to one of my guests. Jimmy Breslin has won a Pulitzer Prize for his newspaper column and has written several novels that received critical raves, but he had the misfortune to get caught with his pants down on live national radio one night. I had interviewed him about his latest book *Table*

Money and we had started to take calls, when a young caller got on the line. "Mr. Breslin?" he asked and then gave his name.

I immediately knew something was wrong, because when Jimmy heard the boy's name he gave me a woeful look and muttered, "Oh, Jeez."

The call was from Brooklyn, New York. The kid said, "Mr. Breslin, you didn't come." I asked the kid what the story was.

"I graduated from St. John's Prep, and tonight was our graduation," he said. "I was sorta like the student they chose to find a speaker. So I asked my father, and my father, who was a pressman at the *Daily News* for thirty years before he retired, took me down to the *Daily News* building on Forty-second Street to meet Jimmy Breslin. I asked Jimmy if he would be our graduation speaker and Jimmy said he'd love to. He wrote it down on his calendar, and we had his picture put up everywhere, but we had no speaker tonight."

There are a lot of things you can say in a situation like that, and I think Jimmy picked the worst one. "Kid, I'm sorry," he said. "But this has taught you a good lesson. I'm on a book tour to make money, and that's the way the world is out there. It ain't always the best way, and it ain't the most fortunate way, and if I weren't on this book tour, I'da been there tonight. But my talking about this book sells books, and that's the way the world is, kid. So you tell that to your friends at St. John's Prep."

Jimmy kept digging a deeper hole for himself. The kid said, "Well, I won't see them anymore, because we all graduated. But what I was wondering is, couldn't you have called to say you were on a book tour?"

Jimmy said something about getting really busy and maybe forgetting things sometimes.

The kid was not about to be brushed off. "They planned for this," he said in the most earnest voice. This kid wasn't dumb. He was respectful, never discourteous or abrasive. And he never sounded angry—just so hurt. I couldn't cut him off, even though I could see that Jimmy was suffering. Normally, I'd say, "Okay, thanks for calling," and move on, but there was something about this kid.

"Mr. Breslin," he said in his downcast tone, "everyone was so disappointed. But I think most of all, Mr. Breslin, you hurt my father. I don't know ya, and all the kids are going on to college. But my father was a pressman. Thirty years, y'know? He was really sad."

"You tell your father I'll give him a ring," Breslin said, "and we'll go have drinks and I'll straighten it all out with him, kid."

Then Breslin left and all the calls started coming in on Open Phone. "I'll never buy another book by that bum again!" was a typical response. "That kid is my hero." I don't think there was one call in support of Breslin the whole night.

CHAPTER 10

*D*IAMONDS ARE *F*OREVER

I became a baseball fan in 1944 when I was ten years old. I remember my first game. I walked to Ebbets Field, where the Cincinnati Reds were playing the Dodgers. My only association with baseball before that had been through Red Barber on the radio, and I thought the infield was really a diamond. There was no television then, so in my mind's eye I had envisioned it shaped like a diamond, and I was astonished to find it was rounded. My father was a Yankee fan, but he never took me to a game; he just went with the guys. After he died, my uncle took me. I'd been listening to games on the radio since I was seven, and I didn't know what a called strike was. I remember at age eight trying to figure out what Red Barber meant when he said that: "Called strike three."

It was a beautiful, clear, sunny day when I got to Ebbets Field to watch the Dodgers play the Reds, and when I saw the roundness of the dirt and how *white* the foul lines were and how *white* the bases were, I was astonished. The Dodgers lost, 3–2, and Curt Davis pitched for them. I still feel that chill of memory whenever I walk into a ballpark and see the dirt. I don't get that feeling with any other sport or arena, and that is because baseball is a flawless game. Fans of football, basketball, and hockey may argue with me, and subtle changes wrought by artificial turf and the designated hitter may threaten the divine balance of the sport, but it still seems flawless to me. On the other hand, the men who play it are anything but perfect, as some of the stories I'm about to relate should make abundantly clear.

Tommy Lasorda, who played ball in the majors for a while before he became manager of the Dodgers, once told me a disturbing story. He was seventeen, and his father had taken him to the Polo Grounds in New York to see the Giants play. One of his heroes was a Giants player whose name Tommy wouldn't reveal. Tommy waited outside the park after the game for the ballplayer to come out, and when the guy appeared, Tommy went up and asked him for his autograph. "Get the fuck outta here, kid," the player said.

Tommy got back in the car with his father and started to cry. "I used to stand like him," he told me, "used to pretend I *was* him. And he tells me to get the fuck out of his way."

Four years later, when Lasorda was pitching triple-A ball in the Dodger organization, the player in question had been sent down to the same league on his way out of the majors. "He came up to the plate against me," Lasorda said, "and *bam*! I hit him in the shoulder with my first pitch and down he went. His second time up I hit him in the knee. He cursed me out on the way to first base. 'Hey, you fuckin' kid!'

"I ain't walked a guy all day, but I hit him four times. The fourth time, he comes running out to the mound, we start to grapple, and they separate us. He says to me, 'I'm gonna kill you.'

"'Right after the game,' I tell him, 'I'll meet you outside.'"

So they met in the runway after the game and the guy wanted to know what the hell was going on.

"Four years ago," Lasorda said to him, "you broke my fuckin' heart. I want to tell you something. Everybody goes up, and everybody comes down. And when they catch you going down, they don't forget."

Lasorda said that they became friends after that. But he wouldn't tell me the player's name because it was someone who was known for his nice-guy image, and after they became friends Lasorda didn't want to say anything that would tarnish the guy's reputation.

Nineteen eighty-seven was the fortieth anniversary of Jackie Robinson's integration of the major leagues, and a lot of stories were told about him in the press. It was also the year of Al Campanis's infamous remarks about black athletes on *Nightline,* which may have done nearly as much to advance the cause of blacks *off* the playing field as Jackie did *on* the field.

Everybody talks about how Jackie held in his anger at all the racial slurs and physical abuse he had to take as the first black in the majors. Jackie was a fierce competitor, however, and not too many people talk about what he was like once he had successfully broken the color barrier and his competitive feelings began to come out.

Robinson was probably the number one bench jockey in baseball. Leo Durocher, the Dodger manager who later went on to the Giants, told stories about Jackie off the air that no one would have believed and that we certainly couldn't have talked about on the air anyway.

"When Jackie played against us," Durocher said, "he would yell over things to me like 'I smelled your wife's c--- last night, Leo. Your wife fucks black guys, Leo, the darker the better.'" Durocher told me that he liked Jackie and respected him but that he never knew a more vicious competitor in his life. He would do anything to beat you, and if enraging you worked, he'd try to enrage you.

Enos Slaughter told me a story that illuminates this other side of Jackie as well as anything I can recall—and I give Slaughter credit for telling it like it happened, even though he comes off as the bad guy. "I was raised in the South and I never played against blacks," he told me. "I was a segregationist like everyone else."

When Branch Rickey brought Robinson up to the Dodgers, Slaughter said, "All my friends asked me, 'You're not gonna play against no fuckin' nigger, are ya?'"

The first time Slaughter played against Robinson, Jackie was playing first base. Slaughter told me he hit a ground ball to Robinson and they raced for the bag. Slaughter said, "I deliberately stepped right on his foot. He got there first and I was out. I could have stepped anywhere on the bag, but I aimed for his foot and spiked him. Blood came spurting out. I walked off and said to him, 'Take that, nigger.' All Jackie said was 'I'll remember that.' He was in tremendous pain, but he held it in, and I didn't think anything of it at the time.

"Two years later in Ebbets Field, I hit a single off the right-field wall and tried to stretch it into a double. Robinson was playing second then. I went sliding in, and Robinson took the throw from the right fielder. He made no attempt to tag me on the leg for the putout, which he could have done easily. Instead he whirled around and smacked me in the mouth with the ball in his glove. Six teeth went flying, there was blood all over me, and I later had to have gum surgery. As he walked away, Jackie said, 'I told you I'd remember.'"

I interviewed Jackie six weeks before he died in 1972. He was going blind from diabetes. I had interviewed him many times before, and he would often refer to death, as he did on that day. He said, "The thing I've never learned to accept is promises. I don't even like the word. Don't put me in my grave telling me my kids will have it okay. Give it to me, and then I know they'll have it okay. Don't give me any promises."

As I mentioned before, Jackie didn't trust John Kennedy. He voted for Nixon. Nixon was easier for him to deal with because he was a pragmatist. "Kennedy was a liar," he used to say. "Kennedy didn't understand me. Nixon had some hard times, Nixon was poor. Kennedy didn't understand that. Nixon understood me pragmatically. To him, I was a vote and I had clout. That's fine, deal with me that way.

"I sat down with Kennedy and Kennedy said something about 'I have a vision.' Don't give me that crap. Nixon asked me, 'Do you think you'd be more effective in New York or Connecticut?' We discussed electoral politics. Nixon asked me if I wanted to head Athletes for Nixon, and I said I'd rather get involved with something outside of sports—civil rights. Nixon said, 'Fine. You want to be on the commission?' We never talked about equality. 'What do you want? What's the deal? How can we help each other?' That's how Nixon thought."

Robinson was a handsome man with a great presence, a commanding, soft voice, and beautiful phrasing. But what we forget, until we look up the records, is what a ballplayer he was. In my head for some reason, he was always a .280 hitter; in fact, he was .311 lifetime. That's fourteen points higher than Al Kaline, and Jackie didn't come up until he was twenty-eight years old.

And the things he could do on a ballfield! The Dodger pitcher Rex Barney told me about a trick Jackie had that has never been mastered by anyone else in the majors, with all their speed—Lou Brock couldn't do what Jackie could do. On a single to right field that would cause the right fielder to take two steps to his right, Jackie would round first base thirty feet and *stop*. The fielder had to decide in an instant whether he should throw behind Robinson or throw into second base. Jackie would always challenge that fielder, and anytime the guy threw behind him, Jackie would go to second. But he made the crowd look at the fielder, so the pressure was on him.

Apart from the day my father died when I was ten years old, the saddest, most desperate day in my whole life was October 3, 1951. It was the day Bobby Thomson hit the home run off Ralph Branca and the Giants won the pennant by defeating the Brooklyn Dodgers. Like Phil Foster said, we took numbers to go to the Brooklyn Bridge to jump. The Dodgers were thirteen games ahead in August and still we lost. Branca and the rest of the Dodgers were shattered. Do you know what Jackie Robinson did after the home run? He walked in to make sure Thomson touched home plate.

A lot has been made of Al Campanis's remarks on *Nightline* about whether blacks are qualified for front office and managerial jobs. The incident focused attention on the glaring injustices more than all the flowery tributes to Robinson's memory did, and no one would appreciate that irony more than Jackie himself. The truth is, though, that the discrimination begins on the playing field, on the roster. Earl Weaver made the point to me that the last man on any team in the major leagues is never a black. "The backup second baseman who plays once a week is always white," he said. "If there are two .240 hitters, one black and one white, the white guy makes the team. Blacks are never encouraged to be managers, since they have to be stars or they're sent down."

And he's right. Most of the great managers were .240 hitters. Weaver never made the majors. Could a black minor leaguer who never made the majors start as a manager? Sparky Anderson played one year and was mediocre. Davey Johnson had maybe one or two good years. Ordinary ballplayers make better managers. You can see them sitting at the end of the dugout next to the manager, picking up whatever they can learn. It was strange for Frank Robinson even to *think* about being a manager—he was a great star. Great stars don't want to be managers, white or black. For one thing, the pay is too low. Mickey Mantle is a million-dollar-a-year guy; why would he want to be manager?

There used to be a fellow with the NAACP who swore that he could listen to any sports event on radio or TV—he was blind—and, if the announcer was white, could tell from his descriptions alone whether the athlete he was talking about at any given moment was white or black. If the announcer said of someone, "He comes to play," the athlete was white. If he said, "He's a horse," the guy was white. Whites are hard workers, but blacks have "natural talent." Blacks are rarely described as smart or good-looking, unless an announcer goes out of his way to make the point: "I want to tell you something about Magic Johnson: he's really smart." White sportswriters think the same way. A writer from Atlanta who works in Washington named Mo Siegal said to me one day, "You know what's unusual about this David Robinson from the Navy? The *schwarze* has brains!" I asked Mo how, after everything we'd been through, he could still talk about a black athlete like that, but the sad thing is that I don't think he even realized what he was saying.

Speaking of tribute, in front of Busch Stadium in St. Louis stands a huge statue of Stan Musial that was erected after his playing days were over. I once asked Stan how it felt to walk past a statue of himself. He said, "It's funny, but when I'm going in to watch a game I never think about it. But sometimes I'll be driving home from a restaurant late at night. I'll pull into the parking lot and drive around it and say, 'Holy cow.'" Stan's father worked in the mines in Donora, Pennsylvania, and now here he is probably one of the few people on earth to have a statue built to him while he is still alive.

Meeting Musial was one of the biggest thrills of my broadcasting career because I had seen him play against the
Dodgers so many times when I was a kid. He was the best
hitter I ever saw, maybe because I saw more of him than of
Ted Williams or Joe DiMaggio, who were in the American
League. When Roger Kahn was on my show we tried to explain what Musial meant in Brooklyn as a visiting ballplayer.
We worshiped him; our pitchers never threw at him; and getting him out elicited a collective sigh of relief. It was the first
example I ever saw in practice of the biblical command Love
thine enemy. He got his nickname "The Man" in Brooklyn,
not in St. Louis.

So when I met him, I just couldn't believe that I was sitting
next to Stanley Frank Musial of Donora, Pennsylvania. I knew
the way he held his bat, the way he swung it, the way he
moved on the field, all those things that kids think about
when they idolize baseball players. I had seen Musial and
other baseball legends from way up in the stands, but now I
was talking to them as their peer.

Here's an uncanny thing about players' memories. I had
Warren Spahn on my show just a few years ago with Brooks
Robinson, Hall of Famers both, and I asked Spahn about
Willie Mays's first home run, which he hit off Spahn. Baseball
announcers always say that hitters remember the details surrounding their big hits, but I think pitchers have an even
sharper memory. I asked Spahn if he remembered Willie's
first home run, and he said, "Don't remind me."

It was a chance for me to compare my memory with
Spahn's, since I was there when Willie hit the homer. Mays
had gone 0 for 12 since being brought up to the majors, but
Durocher had said, "I'm staying with him if he never gets a
hit." The Braves were at the Polo Grounds on a Monday
night, and I was in the stands with Sandy Koufax, who I knew
from the old neighborhood in Brooklyn. Spahn told me that
he had gone over the hitters before the game and the scout

had said that Mays couldn't hit the curveball, couldn't even see it. Spahn said, "I threw him one of the best curves of all time. He hit it eighty-three tons. And I said to myself, Damn, they were gettin' him out on curveballs, all right—*right-handed* curveballs. I was the first left-hander he faced. Mays had played three games, all against right-handers, and they threw him nothing but curveballs. No one was throwing the fastball because he'd kill a fastball."

On the same show, I asked Spahn, "Did you ever pitch to Brooks Robinson? Because you were in different leagues all your life."

Brooks said, "I don't remember."

Spahn said, "Twice, both in spring training. Once in Miami Stadium he hit a double off me—I hung a curveball and he knocked it off the Esquire Boot Polish sign. And the other time he popped out to first base."

I remember when the Smithsonian Institution in Washington mounted an exhibition by baseball's first great photographer, the late Charles Martin Conlon, who took some of the best pictures of baseball stars of the early part of the century. For the opening of the exhibition, they flew in Lefty Gomez and Bill Terry. Lefty, the great Hall of Fame pitcher who is also one of the funniest natural wits I've ever met, was in his seventies at the time, Bill was in his eighties. Terry was the last .400 hitter in the National League. He managed the Giants and made that infamous statement in 1934 "Are the Dodgers still in the league?"—and at the end of the season the Dodgers beat him in a two-game series and cost him the pennant.

Gomez and Terry did my show while they were in town, and I chatted with them before we went on the air. "Where'd you have dinner?" I asked Terry. He couldn't remember.

"We ate at the Palm," said Lefty.

"Oh yeah, the Palm," Bill said.

"So where are you staying in town, Bill?" I asked.

"Where are we staying?" Bill said. He was talking like Brando at the end of *The Godfather*.

Lefty came to the rescue again. "The Madison, Bill."

"The Madison, I'm at the Madison," Terry said.

So I started saying to myself, Holy shit, what am I going to do? Lefty will be okay, but Bill Terry has got me scared. We went on the air and I did six minutes with Lefty, during which Terry sat there with his eyes glazed, staring into space. He didn't know my name, he didn't know where the hell he was. I turned to him and said, "And now, we also welcome Bill Terry. I guess my earliest memory, Bill, was when you said in 1934, 'Are the Dodgers still in the league?' and then they beat you two straight and knocked you out of the pennant race. Does that still rankle you?"

"I'm on second with an infield hit, Ott's on first with a walk, bottom of the ninth. We're behind 5–1. Mungo's got great stuff but we've got a chance with no outs. Mungo fans Jackson and Watkins. Lefty O'Doul's batting better than .300, so I put him in for Mancuso. He takes a couple of good cuts but he's down on strikes too." He did eight minutes nonstop, crisp as you please, every detail in place.

Lefty liked pranks and he always had a sense of humor about the game. He was a competitor, but the game wasn't that serious to him. He told a story about Tony Lazzeri, the Yankee second baseman who was the kind of player who could get on his teammates' nerves and really drive them crazy. Whenever Gomez was pitching, Lazzeri would be yelling from the first pitch—"Come on, Lefty, throw the curveball, throw the fastball, stay right on him, Lefty, stay right on him!" If a man got on base, Lazzeri would come to the mound and cover every possible situation: "Okay, Lefty, man on first. If the ball's hit to you, you throw to me; if it goes to the first baseman, you cover first," and so on. Lefty knew what he was supposed to do, but Lazzeri would keep reminding him.

So in one game in Chicago, the Yankees had a 6–1 lead in

the ninth, bases loaded with one out. Lazzeri had come to the mound and had given Lefty the usual rundown of options until Gomez was ready to scream. On the next pitch, the ball was hit back to Gomez. Lefty turned around and promptly threw it to Lazzeri—who was standing halfway between first and second base. Lazzeri, of course, had no play. He had to eat the ball while the runners all advanced and a run scored. Lazzeri ran in to the mound. "What the fuck are you doing?" he said to Lefty.

"You're such a genius," Gomez said, "I wanted to see what you'd do."

One last story about old-timers. Bill Dickey once told me about Ty Cobb playing in an Old-Timers Day game when he was seventy years old. A reporter came over to Cobb and asked, "What do you think you'd hit if you were playing these days?"

Cobb, who was a lifetime .367 hitter, said, "About .290, maybe .300."

The reporter said, "That's because of the travel, the night games, the artificial turf, and all the new pitches like the slider, right?"

"No," said Cobb, "it's because I'm seventy."

I once asked Sandy Koufax, "What's it like to pitch against guys we used to go watch? You were in the stands with me the day Mays hit his first homer, and later you pitched against Mays. And you've pitched against Musial."

Sandy said, "Musial is unbelievable. I'll tell you a story about Musial. He's 38 years old and I'm in my prime. It's Musial's last year and he's hitting .260. He can't pull the ball anymore, so he's stroking singles to left field and the good fastball is getting him out. I strike him out on three pitches his first time up, I strike him out on three pitches his second time up. Third time up, I've got one ball and two strikes on him. He has now swung and missed at eight pitches, all fastballs. We're ahead 1–0 in the bottom of the eighth. I'm rubbing up the ball and I say to myself, All I'm getting him on is sheer force. I'm throwing ninety-two miles per hour and he can't get the bat around. I'm going to throw a change-up. I'm going to use my brains and fool him completely. He's got to be thinking fastball because I've thrown eight by him. So I turn around and shake off Roseboro and take my kick and throw the change-up. He never moved his leg. He just stayed in that crouch."

"What did you do?" I asked.

"I did what everybody else did," Sandy said. "We all turned around and watched right field as the ball sailed onto the pavilion roof. He was rounding second base and I said to him, 'You son of a bitch.' And he said to me, 'Ya gotta throw three.'"

Sandy said to me, "How could a guy 38 years old, against the fastest pitcher in the majors, not lunge?"

If anybody in baseball ever had that kind of confidence in his abilities, it certainly was Stan the Man. Joe Garagiola once told me a story that proved the point.

Wally Westlake was a journeyman ballplayer, a .270 hitter who played ten years in the majors. During his travels around both leagues, he spent a little time with the Cardinals. Garagiola was in the dugout one day when Westlake went over to Musial and said, "Stan, I gotta tell ya. I had a great night's sleep last night—I mean, a perfect night. I woke up this morning and my shower was perfect, the bacon and eggs were perfect. It was a beautiful day and my drive in to the ballpark was just wonderful. I hit four home runs in batting practice. I'm in the lineup and I can't wait to walk up to the plate. I feel it in my bones, I'm gonna get three hits today. D'ya ever feel that way?"

And Musial said, "Every day."

A few years ago they threw a little party for me in Oakland at the time of the All-Star Game, during which they gave me the key to the city of San Francisco and an Oakland A's jacket. That was a great honor, but my biggest thrill of all was that DiMaggio came to the party. Joe D! Joe is a guy who walks in the room and the room changes. DiMaggio has never forgotten his image. He's seventy-four years old, and he's one of the last great living legends.

I had an amazing discussion with Joe D in the dugout at the Cracker Jack Old-Timers Day game in Washington a couple of years ago. Edward Bennett Williams is his lawyer and introduced me to him. The night before, I had had Art Garfunkel on my radio show, and DiMaggio had heard the show. He said, "Nice show last night, Larry."

I thanked him.

"You know," he said. "I like those guys, Diamond and Sarfunkel. But I still don't know what they meant in that song." He was talking about the lines in Simon and Garfunkel's hit song "Mrs. Robinson" that say, "Where have you gone, Joe DiMaggio? A nation turns its lonely eyes to you . . . Joltin' Joe has left and gone away." Joe leaned toward me and said, "I'm still here."

I opened my mouth to say something, but he held up a hand. "I know you're going to tell me it's about how heroes are gone, myths are gone. I know, I ain't dumb." He said, "I was gonna sue. But Ed told me that this was the highest of compliments. I don't understand it, though. If I were dead, that would be one thing. But I'm still around."

I was in the locker room when the old-timers were getting dressed for the game. ESPN was taping the game, and they were moving their cameras around the room. Joe D had his undershirt on, and as the cameras started heading his way, he yelled, "Stop! Shut that off. You never take a picture of me in my undershirt. I put on my uniform—that's when you take a picture." Then he turned to me and said, "Can you believe that? Me in an undershirt?"

Talk about ballplayers' memories. While we were in that

locker room, an old-timer came by and said to DiMaggio, "I remember the day you played first base."

Joe said, "It was right here in Washington. One game Stengel said to me, 'Joe, I think you're slowing down a little.' Boy, I was pissed. I hurt my leg in that game and I never forgave Casey. Sherry Robertson hits a ball to my right. The second baseman can't get it and neither can the pitcher, so I gotta grab it backhanded, turn, and race him to the bag—and I hyperextended my leg. I hit the bag, the ump said, 'Out!' and I knew I was out for a month. I went into the dugout and I looked at that old bastard and said, 'Fuck you, Casey.'"

Jimmy Piersall was a great baseball player, but he is probably going to be remembered more for his bouts with mental illness as memorialized in the movie *Fear Strikes Out*. One of the worst fights Piersall ever had was with Billy Martin. Martin called him nuts and they had a real blowout behind the batting cage. When Jimmy was admitted to the mental ward, though, Martin was the first one there and called him every day. Piersall told me that Martin will give him a job no matter where he is in the world. "I'm never out of work so long as Billy Martin's alive," he said. "When he managed in Texas, I was public relations director; in Oakland, I was the batting instructor." Maybe Billy still feels guilty, but it was probably just an offhand comment—and Billy has never been known to back away from a fight.

Piersall later developed a sense of humor about his past. I was in the booth with Jimmy and Harry Caray, the famous White Sox and Cubs announcer, and the Sox were playing the Orioles. Whenever I visited his booth, Harry would bring me right into the broadcast: "Hey, Larry Kinnnggg! Sit down, Larry! The art of interviewing!" So we were doing the game together for a while, and a player bunted. Piersall said, "I never would have bunted in that situation."

"Jimmy," said Harry, "you're crazy."

"Hold it," Piersall said. "I'm the only man in this ballpark with a certificate of sanity. I was released from an institution and I've got the papers to prove it."

Jimmy later got in trouble for referring to the players' wives on television as "bimbos," but he was always his own man. To this day Duke Snider will never forgive Jimmy Piersall. They were both playing for the 1963 Mets, which Casey Stengel was managing. Jimmy told me he was indebted to Stengel for labeling him the best defensive outfielder in baseball—he is very proud of his .997 lifetime fielding average. But he also said that "Casey was seventy-five years old and he would be snoring on the bench by the fifth inning."

"And he never knew our names," Jimmy said. "He'd just say, 'You, grab a bat, you're pinch hitting.' Duke Snider had 399 home runs and we needed a pinch hitter one day, and Casey was asleep so we told Duke to grab a bat and pinch hit. He got his 400th homer, but the next day the paper just carried a little item about it at the bottom of the page. I had ninety-nine home runs at the time and I said to Duke, 'Watch me. When I hit my one hundredth, I'm goin' coast to coast.'

"I told the newspaper photographers to keep an eye on me. A few days later we were playing in the Polo Grounds where the left- and right-field fences were not far away at the foul poles, and I kept trying to drop one in. I hit one over the fence but foul to left, then one to right. The next pitch I just hit a high fly ball but the wind got ahold of it and carried it into the stands. I had practiced running the bases backwards, and I hadn't hit a home run all season so I ran them backwards and the photographers all took pictures of me. The next day the New York papers ran a photo sequence of me crossing each base backwards, and then the national papers picked up the story and photos too. I said to Duke, 'See, what'd I tell ya? I went coast to coast.'"

I first met Casey Stengel at the World's Fair in New York in the early sixties. We were getting ready to go on the air, and I asked the engineer how much time we had left. We had finished all our commercials, and the engineer said we had fifty minutes. Stengel heard him and apparently took it to heart. I asked Casey one question and he spoke for fifty minutes. He didn't realize that I was supposed to ask questions; he thought he had to do the whole fifty minutes himself. The thing with Casey is that you could *not* interrupt him. While I was frantically trying to get a question in edgewise, he ran down the history of baseball, and when he ran out of baseball stories, he moved on to dentistry. It turned out he was a left-handed dentist in Kansas City; he felt he always needed something to fall back on in case his managerial career fell through. He was also an enormously wealthy man who owned the Glendale Bank in California, and he talked about that too.

As everyone knows, Casey could be confusing at times. What I found especially maddening about interviewing him was that he would never name a player. He would just say, for example, "My catcher." As in "They say my catcher can't catch. That's a hell of a position to be in because you can't back up a passed ball."

I've had a lot of fun just standing by the batting cage and talking to players when they take batting practice, and I've also learned things I didn't know, just by asking questions. I was standing with Reggie Jackson at the cage one day and I said, "Does it matter to you who's umping today?"

"Oh, you betcha," he said. "Rich Garcia's umping today. I won't get the low pitch. Gotta swing at it today. So I told the guy throwing batting practice to throw 'em all at the knees."

Then he grabbed a black bat he had sealed with wax and took some batting practice. Afterward, he looked at the marks in the wax on the bat and he said, "*This* was the grounder to short, *this* was the fly to left, and *this* was the home run."

Batting practice is a science he has worked on all his life. I asked him, "Do you mind that Garcia calls a low strike?"

"Oh no," he said. "I just want to make sure he does. What we mind is when he decides not to. Then he screws up everybody on both teams. No two umps are the same. Some umps give me a break. They like me. If I take the pitch, I usually get it from them. Ken Kaiser likes me, so I'll give a little more on my swing—because if I have to check a swing and he's at first base, he ain't gonna say I swung. I get the benefit of the doubt."

If you want to get really crazy sometime, go to a Yankees–Red Sox game, stand at the batting cage, as I have done, and talk to Wade Boggs and Don Mattingly. They're both out of their minds. I talked with Boggs in Oakland not long ago and he said to me, "You know, when it's August out here, the prevailing winds change. They increase a little, maybe eight knots, and they start moving north to northwest. Have you noticed that?"

"All the time," I said. He didn't notice I was joking.

"So if that's true," he went on, "logically I've got to use a little lighter bat."

"Why's that?"

"Because I'm going to get around more with a lighter bat, and with the wind blowing that way I'll get some pulled doubles. That can make four or five points' difference in my average." Wade Boggs always knows what he's hitting. As Red Barber used to say, "Baseball is a team sport played by very selfish people. I've never met a ballplayer who didn't know his average or a pitcher who didn't know his record."

Boggs also talked about the change in his stroke over the months of a season. He would rather be playing a team that's in a pennant race because they're thinking more and they're more worried. "They're more concerned about Baylor hitting behind me," he said, "than about me. So I'll be seeing better pitches. But a team like Oakland doesn't care and they'll pitch us the same."

Don Mattingly is a fanatic, too. He looks at everybody for batting tips. He says he can learn from .020 hitters. He'll watch the weaker hitters at the batting cage and see what they're doing wrong. Bobby Meacham was hitting one time and Don and I were watching him. "See that little hitch in his swing?" Mattingly said. "Boy, tell me if I ever do that." Then he went over and told Meacham what he was doing wrong.

The wild thing about Mattingly, which I learned from talking to a number of pro scouts, is that when he was in the minors, they didn't give him a prayer to make the major leagues. Don was a short first baseman with no power and no speed who couldn't play any other position. He went in the twenty-seventh round. He was an excellent fielder, but he was hitting about .240. Likewise, Boggs was considered a bad fielder at one time, but now he's improved considerably.

Some players won't talk to you around the batting cage, but Boggs has always been very friendly to me. He was fascinated by the fact that I wear a chai around my neck, because he wears one. He's not Jewish, but it's always been his lucky symbol—he draws a chai in the batter's box every time he steps up. When he found out my daughter is named Chaia, he really flipped out. He'll talk to me anytime about baseball. On the other hand, I can't imagine talking to Wade Boggs about South Korea.

I've never spoken with him about anything but baseball, so I can't be certain that he wouldn't want to talk about South Korea, but baseball does tend to be an obsessive game for both players and fans. No matter how intelligent someone is, when he's concentrating on baseball, it's hard for him to think of anything else—and Boggs concentrates on baseball almost all the time. I've been to many games with George Will, for instance. We sat through the whole '83 World Series together and never, *never* mentioned politics.

*   *   *

If baseball is my favorite sport and the Brooklyn Dodgers were my favorite team growing up, then my favorite sports announcer of all time has to be the voice of the Brooklyn Dodgers, Red Barber.

Any voice from your childhood is bound to be important, but no voice was like Red's. He was my link to that giant outer world of baseball. I remember listening to him broadcast away games without going on the road. The announcer couldn't do remote broadcasts in the forties because of wartime travel restrictions, so Barber would announce games off the ticker the way Ronald Reagan did. Reagan always tells the same old story of how he would say the batter was fouling off pitch after pitch because the ticker broke down and he had to fake it. We all laugh at that story, but what Reagan is telling us is that he lied. Red wouldn't lie. Red would say, "The machine is jammed." He would talk about something else, tell you they were working on the machine, but that was all. When I finally got to interview him, I asked him, "Why didn't you have the guy foul off a few pitches?"

"Why," he said, "would I report to you something that wasn't happening? I'm a reporter. All I know is that the machine jammed. I don't know what's happening in the game."

Red didn't fake it with crowd noise or the crack of the bat over his machine, either, as Mel Allen did. All the printout would say, Red told me, was "Double, left field." *Where* in left field? And sometimes they'd get complicated plays—a double, two runners score, the third runner is thrown out at the plate. Red said the secret was never to start talking while the machine was typing, because it could hit a glitch. A player could be rounding third and the machine could die, and he didn't want to be caught like that. So we used to sit and try to figure out what the machine was doing. With Barber, we could actually hear the machine clicking in the background.

The Dodgers would be losing 5–3 in the ninth in Cincinnati, say, with the bases loaded and two out. We would hear Red say, "Here's the pitch to Dixie Walker . . ." and then we'd hear the machine making all these clicks and noises, seemingly endlessly. One of my friends would say, "It sounds like a double! I know it."

And sometimes we would hear nothing. Maybe a long fly ball ended the game and the teletypist would immediately start sending the stats of the game, and Red would always wait for the ticker to finish before he would say anything.

But he didn't like to work far behind the machine either. Some announcers would work half an inning behind the ticker, so glitches never caught up with them. When they were announcing the bottom of the eighth, they might know the final score. Red never did that because he wanted to retain some element of drama. He wanted to react off his own excitement. Complicated things could happen that a ticker didn't explain, though. Red told me that a runner missed second base one time and was called out on an appeal play before the next batter came up. The ticker never reported that, so Red was counting a run that hadn't scored. Maybe the guy at the ticker got up for a hot dog or went to the bathroom and never mentioned the appeal play. So Red would have the game as 5–3, and the ticker would say 5–2.

Red did a lot of things other announcers didn't do back then. If a pitcher had a no-hitter going, Red would remind you every inning. He didn't believe the superstition about jinxing it. Only recently are baseball announcers willing to call attention to a no-hitter in progress. Red wanted you to feel the drama. Aside from that, he was just a great announcer. He taught me that on a fly ball an announcer shouldn't watch the ball, he should watch the fielder. When announcers watch the flight of the ball, listeners hear a lot of "Going, going, caught!" I'll never forget Barber's call of the famous catch by Al Gionfriddo off Joe DiMaggio, when

Gionfriddo pulled the ball out of the seats during the 1947
World Series. Red used the word *back* eleven times.
"Gionfriddo goes back, back, back, back, back, . . . back, he
makes a one-handed catch." I still get a thrill thinking of that.

Red was the master; he never overstated. When Red went
to the Yankees from the Dodgers, the Yankee fans didn't like
him. They liked Mel Allen, who screamed and yelled. But
Red did some great announcing for the Yankees. I recall a
game where the Yankees were in Boston, ahead by two runs,
and Ted Williams was batting in the bottom of the ninth with
men on base. The count went to three and two, we could hear
the crack of the bat, and then Red's voice: "It's a long line
drive. The ball is in right center field—and so is Maris. We'll
be back in sixty seconds."

Because of all those memories, when I got involved in
broadcasting it became one of my all-time dreams to go on the
air with Red Barber. In the late sixties in Miami, I did a taped
interview show with WTVJ-TV called *News Weekend*, which
was the program that really made me there. I would tape an
interview with a famous person during the week, and it would
air in four segments over the weekend during the six o'clock
news. When I was taping, I never knew who would be throwing it to me from the news team—it could be the weather-
man, the news anchor, just about anyone, depending on
where they inserted my tape—so I would start my taped interview by saying "Thank you."

I had done an interview with Wernher von Braun the
weekend that Red Barber joined the station. By then, Barber
was semiretired and had come down to Florida, where he was
going to be the weekend sports anchor. That particular weekend, I was at home watching the news and waiting to see Red
do his first sports report for our show and also waiting for my
spot to come up. They finished the news and didn't throw it
to me, then they did the weather and didn't throw it to me, so
I knew Red would. He finished his sports wrap-up, and I

gripped the chair; my nails dug into the wood as he said, "That's the sports. Larry . . ." And then I saw myself saying "Thank you" to Red Barber and going into the interview. That was one of the highlights of my career, and when he came on my radio show the following Monday night, it was as emotional an interview as I've done.

Great as Red was, though, he could be a petty man. He drove whoever hired him crazy—every *t* had to be crossed in his contract, and he'd hold them to it. Mike Burke, who was president of the Yankees when CBS owned the team, was a former OSS agent and parachutist. When I had Burke on, I brought up Red's name and he said, "Don't mention Red Barber to me. He's one of the few men in my life I ever wanted to kill. Red would come into my office with two weeks left to go in the season and say in that quiet drawl of his, 'Mike, it's been wonderful working with you. See ya 'round, and I'll be back next year.'"

"Burke would be really speechless.

"But Red, there's two weeks left."

"Oh." Red was cool. "But I get two weeks off. It's in my contract."

"Yeah, Red, I know, but you never said anything all year. We didn't think—"

"Oh, Mr. Burke. It's right here, clause eleven—two weeks' paid vacation during the season."

"Yeah, but you never said anything in June or July." By now Burke would be fairly apoplectic. "It's too late to make changes now."

"I'll see ya down in St. Pete," Red would drawl, and he'd walk out. Burke would be left muttering "Son of a bitch" to the back of the door.

Red hated jocks, too. He felt he'd paid his dues as an announcer, and unless a jock announcer was first-rate, he'd give him a really hard time. He particularly hated Joe Garagiola. If you mention Barber to Joe now, Joe fumes. What Barber would do was embarrass Joe. Once the Yankees were in Boston playing the Red Sox, and there was a rain delay.

Red, to Joe: "What did you do today, Joe?"

"Well, Red, I hung around the hotel lobby, then I went with a few of the guys and saw a movie."

"Joe, we're in Boston. Do you know what's in Boston, Joe? Some of the great institutions of learning in America. Did you ever visit Tufts? Boston College, Boston University, Harvard? You know what I did today, Joe? I went and watched the Boston Pops. You know what that is?"

Joe hadn't heard of the Boston Pops.

"It's an orchestra, Joe. Fella named Fiedler. Arthur Fiedler. Joe, there are more things in life than baseball. In a city like Boston there are more things than an afternoon movie with the players. The band played Sousa today." Joe would get more and more sheepish, and Red would grind it into him.

Also, Joe didn't do a lot of preparation, whereas Red would work three hours before the game. Joe would say something like, "Gee, this is an embarrassing situation for Mantle now."

Red would say, "Did you happen to talk to Mantle before the game, Joe?"

"No, Red. I got here a little—"

"Well, I did. He said these situations don't embarrass him. Go on ahead with the game now."

He could be vicious, too, in his own sardonic way. Red tells a slightly different version of the events surrounding his firing by the Yankees, but here's the way Mike Burke told it to me when I interviewed him. The Yankees were in last place, playing at home against the White Sox on a Thursday afternoon in September, and there was a light drizzle. It was the sixth inning. Red said, "We do not have the official attendance yet, but I'd like the cameras to pan to the left-field seats."

The camera panned to the bleachers, and when it got there,

Red said, "Now I'd like the camera to commence panning the stadium. Why don't we all count together?"

Mike Burke was watching the game on TV, and when Red said that, he pushed the TV set against the wall and fired him on the spot. He called Red in and said, "You will not be back next year."

"Fine with me," said Red. "I've got one more year on my contract. Send the checks down to Red Barber, Tallahassee, Florida."

I asked Red about that incident and he said, "I couldn't understand that. We didn't have any attendance figures and I thought it was amusing. I was trying to point out how so few people could be in what I liked to call 'the *big* ballpark,' watching the once-great Yankees."

Red is retired in Tallahassee now. He's eighty and he's a lay preacher. He still does reports every Friday for National Public Radio. He invented many phrases and terms, some of which have disappeared, some of which are still in use. He would say "FOB," meaning the bases were "full of Brooklyns," or "sitting in the catbird seat," meaning a batter was up with the bases loaded and had gotten ahead in the count. He was never a "homer" broadcaster, never said "we" when talking about the team he was announcing for. How can I explain what he meant to my friends and me? We grew up in Brooklyn, the land of *dese, dem,* and *dose,* and we worshiped a broadcaster with a southern accent. Red gave Vin Scully advice while Vin was learning at his feet, broadcasting one inning a game for Red. "Don't get too friendly with the ballplayers," Red said. "Don't listen to other announcers, don't listen to ballgames. Go and watch them sometimes, but don't listen. Don't pick up other people's bad habits. Be yourself. You let them know when they turn that little dial that it's you. You don't have to say your name." He said that what he liked about me was that when he heard me on the radio he never had to ask, "Who's that fella?"

He meant what he said, though, about not getting friendly with the players. He was like a political journalist of today in that respect. He didn't think it was good to have dinner with anyone but the manager, and that was for information. And in the off-season, absolutely no contact. Red went out of his way to tell Jackie Robinson that he should not take it personally that Red was not eating with him, because he didn't eat with Reese either.

In Red's eyes, Pee Wee Reese was one of the bravest men he ever met because of how Reese reacted to a situation involving Robinson. Red was in the locker room in Chicago when they were informed of a death threat against number 42, which was Jackie. The FBI took the death threat very seriously. They said they were going to comb the stands and suggested that Robinson not play that day. Robinson said, "How can I not play?"

And Reese said, "I've got an idea. We'll all wear number 42. They won't know who to shoot at."

Reese didn't realize what a great moment that was in race relations, in life, in humor, in temperament among men. He was just a man of average intelligence, but a team leader.

In 1953, Red turned down the World Series because the sponsor, Gillette, set the price the announcer would be paid and expected the announcer to be thrilled. Gillette would say, "Okay, you're the announcer for the Series this year. The pay is one thousand dollars." There were at least thirty-two announcers in baseball and Gillette picked only two; if you were picked they expected you to be happy and take the money. Red did thirteen World Series, nine of them for Gillette, but in 1953, when Gillette told him what the pay would be, he said, "That ain't enough. My regular-season pay for seven games would be about that much."

"What do you mean, Mr. Barber?" the Gillette man said to him. "We're paying you fifteen hundred dollars."

"I think I should get twenty-five hundred."

"Mr. Barber, we're the sponsor and this is what we pay.

We're being very generous. Last year we paid fourteen hundred. We're paying fifteen hundred this year, and Mr. Allen has accepted . . ."

"I decline," Red said.

Red Barber never worked another World Series.

That story shows both tremendous strength of conviction and the price you pay for it. Announcers have a bit more leverage today. When NBC contacted me to do the pregame football show *NFL '85*, they offered me two thousand dollars a pop, each week for sixteen weeks, for two minutes' work a week. That came to $32,000. I said, "Okay, call my agent, Bob Woolf."

Bob called me back later and said, "I think you deserve more than two."

I said, "Bob! It's NBC! Two thousand dollars for two minutes—that's a thousand dollars a minute!"

"I'll get back to you," he said.

I got three. I would have taken one. Yet Red had the ability in 1953 to say, "That ain't enough." What respect for self that showed.

Red's finest moment may have been one that very few people remember. Just about everyone knows announcer Russ Hodges's famous shout when Bobby Thomson hit the home run off Ralph Branca in 1951: "The Giants win the pennant! The Giants win the pennant!" The reason Russ Hodges's voice carried around the world and is so famous is that the Giants were playing at home. It was a three-game playoff, and there had been no provision in the network contracts for a playoff. The commissioner of baseball had made a deal the Sunday before the playoffs to have Mutual network carry the home team's broadcast. The games were played at Ebbets Field on Monday and the Polo Grounds on Tuesday and Wednesday. That meant that Red was carried nationally and around the world on the armed forces radio on Monday, and Russ Hodges on Tuesday and Wednesday.

Red still did his broadcast on Tuesday and Wednesday,

however, over the local station, for the Dodger fans in New York City. I didn't hear Russ Hodges's screaming until later, on the replays, because I was listening to Red Barber at the time. And this is the way he did it.

At the moment of that home run, Red was bringing us information which, outside of the death of a loved one, had to be the saddest news any Dodger fan in the city could have heard. Barber said, "Home run. The Giants have won the pennant."

I could hear the crowd going wild in the background. Red went on: "Last week in South Korea, five hundred and eleven Americans died. Their sisters and wives and parents don't care about this home run today. This is a game, and there's a lot more out there than a game. There's a war, and the economy, and people who don't have what to eat. Put it in perspective."

I asked Red about that later. Naturally, he'd planned. He'd inquired of the defense department how many soldiers had died. He gave other statistics that he'd gotten from the department of health as to how many Americans were starving each night, and so on, because he wanted to be able to put the loss in perspective.

Then he said something remarkable on the spur of the moment: "In my opinion, the lives of Mr. Branca and Mr. Thomson will be forever entwined. Historians will not be able to mention one without the other, and whatever each does the rest of his life, on the field or off, mention of one will prompt this recollection of the other." And it's absolutely true. Thomson and Branca travel together; they've spoken at hundreds of dinners together.

What a moment that was. Even for the cool old Redhead, it had to be sad. The cursed Durocher, who had left the Dodgers and was now the Giants' manager. What intrigue, and what a spirit of hatred surrounded those two teams. We were raised to dislike the Yankees—we thought they were pompous, that you had to wear a suit to Yankee Stadium. But we learned to *hate* the Giants. I knew I'd matured when I went to a Dodger-Giant game in San Francisco in the early sixties and had no interest at all in the outcome.

Come to think of it, the Yankee-Dodger rivalry was pretty fierce, too. The only fistfight I ever had was with my best friend, Herbie Cohen, when we fought about the Dodgers versus the Yankees. They were about to play in the World Series, so we were comparing the two teams, position by position. Okay, we said, Berra versus Campanella. And we had a vicious half-hour argument. They were so close to each other in every stat, and both were future Hall of Famers. Then on to first base: they had Tommy Henrich, we had Gil Hodges. Big argument. We knew every statistic. Second base: Jackie Robinson versus Georgie Stirnweiss. I said, "Okay, second base goes to the Dodgers, now we go on to shortstop: Reese versus Rizzuto."

And Herbie said, "I'd rather have Stirnweiss than Robinson." I leaped on him. I got him by the jaw and down we went. I banged my chin open, he started bleeding, and we rolled through the street. "I'd rather have Stirnweiss!" I can still hear him saying it.

CHAPTER 11

THAT SPORTING LIFE

I've met a lot of smart athletes in my time. The smart ones are those who look beyond the present and think in the abstract, who can get beyond the sport they're in. They've learned to invest their money, to plan ahead, to be ready to go into business by the time they're too old to play anymore. Of all the intelligent sports figures in the world, however, without a doubt the smartest I've ever known is Muhammad Ali.

Muhammad Ali is one of my favorite people on earth. I've been doing interviews with Ali since shortly after his first professional fight, thanks to Angelo Dundee, who brought him to me early on. I used to do a show with Angelo every Friday in Miami called *Pick the Fights*.

Actually, I had known about Cassius Clay before that. Willie Pastrano, who would go on to be light heavyweight champion of the world, met Clay when Clay was fighting in the 1960 Olympic boxing trials. One of the series of trials was in New Orleans, where Willie lived. Pastrano told me a kid had called him up and said, "Mr. Pastrano, my name is Cassius Clay and I'd like to meet you."

Clay explained to Willie that he was trying out for the Olympic team, and Pastrano invited him to come and work out with him the next day. Angelo Dundee, Clay's manager-to-be, was then Pastrano's manager, and when he heard that Willie had invited him to spar, he was livid. "Willie," he said, "you can't spar with an amateur. You could hurt him and then we'd be in trouble. You're a lethal weapon and he's not. Besides, we'd have to pay him for sparring, but we can't because then he'd be disqualified from the Olympics."

They somehow worked it all out and Clay and Pastrano went a couple of rounds. Pastrano said to me, "Write this name down, Larry. Cassius Clay."

"Why?"

Willie was a smart, crafty fighter, one of the best. He said, "Because I ain't gettin' near him. Maybe I landed a glancing blow, but that was it."

Entirely apart from his athletic abilities, Ali may have been the best public relations man who ever lived, bar none. He was certainly the best ticket seller of this century. If he'd been alive in the last century, he would have outsold Barnum. He knew what Americans bought, how to enrage them, how to sell them. He is also a fine man with a kind heart and deep convictions. His comment on the Vietnam War was the best one-line summation of that conflict I've ever heard: "White men sending black men to kill yellow men."

For a while during the late sixties, Ali wasn't fighting because the government pressured the World Boxing Association to take his title away. He had requested conscientious objector status, saying he had nothing against the North Vietnamese, and as a result was denied the right to fight professionally. (George Carlin put it in perspective: "The government said, 'If you won't kill people, we won't let you beat 'em up.'") The Supreme Court eventually returned Ali's title to him in a 9–0 decision, but during the period when he wasn't fighting, he came on my show and talked about his PR skills. He told me how he hit upon the idea of forecasting fight results and being pompous about it, which he said happened quite by accident.

Ali, still known as Cassius Clay then, was about to go into one of his first fights, in Louisville, and that week he appeared on a local sports talk show to promote the fight. Gorgeous George was scheduled to wrestle in the same arena that weekend, and they appeared on the show together. Ali told me, "I went on that show and I said, 'I'm the Olympic champion and I'm sure looking forward to this fight. I know that I have a tough opponent, but I'm going to do my best.'

"And then the announcer said to Gorgeous George, 'And you're wrestling the Samurai Brothers on Saturday.' George said, 'I'm gonna kill 'em! I'm gonna take their heads and pound 'em into the ring!! I'm gonna bring venom and menace and horror to Louisville Saturday night!!!'

"I won my fight on Friday," Ali said. "George wrestled Saturday, and I don't know who won. But I looked at the attendance: I drew four thousand and he drew thirteen. I said to myself, There's something to this."

That's when he started to predict that he was going to win. He never *knew* he was going to win. He said he was always just as scared as the other guy. "Of course I was scared," he said. "Hey. The guy's trying to hit me. Why wouldn't I be scared?"

He found that apart from being a PR tactic, boasting and predicting the round were very powerful psychological weapons to use against opponents. Ali didn't call the right round in every fight, but he hit enough of them so that if an opponent heard that he was predicting a knockout in the fifth round, that fighter had to be a little more nervous than Ali going into the fifth round.

Although some of the other boxers didn't always understand

what he was doing, Ali's tactics helped make money for him *and* his opponents. Ali later told me about when he was getting ready to fight Joe Frazier for the first time. Joe's a nice enough guy, but he's not the world's smartest athlete. Ali said he talked to Frazier backstage before they made their first appearance together to promote the fight, and he told him, "Joe, here's what we're gonna do. We're going on a show on ABC to promote the fight, and we want to sell tickets, right? I'm gonna say that all the white people are rooting for you—you're the White Hope. And I want you to get mad at me. You say, 'I'm blacker than you. More black people like me, and I like all people to like me.' And then say something funny. Say, like, 'The Chinese are for you.' Then I'll start in, and we'll build up a whole racial argument, and you'll be the white guy and I'll be the black guy."

Frazier said, "Why are we doing this?"

"We're gonna sell a lot of tickets," Ali said. "We're two black guys, Joe. White America has got to come see this fight if we want to make a lot of money. They're gonna come all right, but we want them to come in droves. But they've got to root for somebody, and they ain't got a white man. I'm never gonna be their white man. *You* be their white man."

"I get it," Joe said. "I get it."

"Understand? Let me say that. But you say you're fighting for all people, so you don't cop out on the brothers. And everywhere I go, when I speak to white groups, I'm going to tell them you're their man."

Joe said, "I understand, Muhammad."

Then, according to Ali, they went out on the set of the show. "We take our seats on the set," he told me. "I look over at Joe Frazier and I say, 'You're the white man's fighter.' He leaps on me! Down on the floor we go. I'm telling him, '*Joe!* We're selling tickets, Joe.'"

"But I had that way of doing things," Ali said, "because

I was so good on camera that even though I had just told
him the whole plan five minutes ago, I still incensed
him."

"You mean," I said to Muhammad, "you had the ability to
turn it on like that?"

And he said to me, "Don't ask me questions like that!!" And
he scared me half to death.

Believe it or not, Miami was an exciting place to be back in
the sixties. I had some great nights on radio because so much
was going on in the culture, and for various reasons a lot of
people responsible for it were coming to Miami—the cult figures, the antiwar leaders, the generals, the entertainers.
Miami was still the big R&R place in America then—what
Jackie Gleason referred to as "the sun and fun capital of the
world." The city had been integrated fairly quickly in
the early sixties, and the hotels were pretty well unionized, so
the top labor unions came down there. The jet age had
dawned, but Hawaii still seemed a bit far away. Miami was
cooking, and everybody came through.

A particularly memorable night at Joe's Stone Crab in
Miami Beach was the night of the first Liston-Clay fight, in
1964. I will never again see a crowd like that in a restaurant,
from Frank Sinatra to J. Edgar Hoover to Howard Cosell—
political leaders, boxing freaks, celebrities, with hundreds of
people waiting outside. That was the fight in which Liston was
a fifteen to one favorite and after which Clay said he was now
going to be called Muhammad Ali.

People forget the kinds of things Clay did back then and
why he was such a shot in the arm for the boxing business.
Liston arrived at Miami International Airport and was walking
to his limo, and there was Clay on the roof of the airport
building shouting taunts at Liston through a megaphone. Clay
liked to show everyone how good he was at training, so he

would get up at four A.M., go to Liston's house in Surfside to do road work, and wake him up with a bullhorn. "Sonny, it's only three weeks away, and I'm the king bee."

Liston never spoke to him, but he'd say to friends, "I'm gonna kill that man." Meanwhile, Clay would come on my show at Pumpernik's and spout his poetry about the fight. He would also talk about the Black Muslims. That name meant terrorism back then—whites were scared to death of the Muslims—but Clay would point out that the Muslims had the lowest rate of juvenile delinquency of any religious group in the country. Then he would smile out at the all-white audience and say, "We gonna have a Black Muslim champion, folks."

The fight promotor, Bill MacDonald, wasn't happy to be promoting a fight in which one fighter was obviously not too bright and the bright guy was a Black Muslim. He was worried about the gate. The day of the fight, Clay came to the weigh-in looking like a crazed man, his pupils dilating, *screaming* at Liston, "Fight me now! Fight me now! I don't need the money! Muslims don't need money! I'll fight you right here!"

The word had been circulating that Clay would not show up, that he had had a religious conversion and was cracking up. Everything was bedlam. I was there with my doctor, Arthur Cohen, who was a big fight fan, and we were watching the whole scene together. I felt sorry for Clay because I had grown to like him and I assumed he was going to get killed. My doctor said, "Walk over here with me a minute."

He took me over to the doctor from the state boxing commission, who was putting all his forms in his valise and getting ready to leave. Art said to him, "What's Clay's blood pressure?"

"One twenty over eighty," the state guy said.

Art said to me very quietly, "Bet him."

I asked what one twenty over eighty meant.

"It's normal, baby," he said. "That was an act. Nothing inside of him is upset. I'll bet you right now he's out having a hamburger saying, 'Do you think it worked?'"

It worked.

The fight was jammed. People also forget that Clay almost threw in the towel during that fight. Liston didn't land a blow in the first three rounds, but there must have been something on his gloves, because he hit Clay in the eye in the fourth round and Clay went blind for a while. At the end of the round, Clay sat down in his corner and told Dundee he was going to quit. "I can't fight blind," he said, "because I'm gonna get killed. I'll fight when I can see."

But Dundee kept working on him with water until Clay got some of his vision back for the fifth round, and then Liston didn't answer the bell in the seventh. Once Clay had won, he put on the most remarkable display I've ever seen of an athlete working the press corps. He walked around the ring calling every writer by name. "Mr. Breslin! Mr. Breslin, folks, of the *New York Post*. Write it down, baby: 'Muhammad Ali.' Dick Young, the famous Dick Young: 'Liston in one!' Look at Liston now, Dick Young!"

Later, in a long interview, Ali admitted to me that he had been scared of Liston, that he thought if Liston tagged him, it would be goodbye. He said, "The thing to learn is that when you're insecure, you think the other party isn't." His contention was that if he was scared to death, so was Liston. So he tried to get a tactical advantage using his own fear. He claimed, perhaps with an excess of modesty, that it wasn't bravery on his part; he just never wanted to get his face hurt. Ali was positive that he had made Liston concerned. He doesn't know when it happened, but he knew that in the first round when Liston missed the first four or five shots, he became an angry, frustrated fighter.

Ali said he tried never to get angry. The only time he failed was in the Floyd Patterson fight when he beat Patterson unmercifully because Patterson had engaged in an anti-Muslim campaign before the fight. However, Ali was ashamed of himself after the fight, he said. All he ever wanted to do was to make a living for himself and, usually, the other black guy in the ring.

Then Ali graphically showed me how well he could do his routine. I asked him on television, "How do you do your PR act?"

All he did was look at me and raise his fist. "What PR act?!" I nearly fell off the chair. It was just like after the Frazier fight, but it still worked.

"That's how," he said.

I knew Rocky Marciano pretty well, and I liked him a lot. Rocky was a great guest, but he was also the world's cheapest man. He never picked up a check, and there were rumors that they found hundreds of thousands of dollars in his mattress when he died. He didn't trust banks.

Rocky was so gentle and sensitive that I could never figure how he could be such a killer in the ring. Marciano hated training and he didn't much care for boxing. He wanted to be a baseball player more than anything else in the world. I asked him, "Did anybody ever scare you?"

"Oh, yeah, George," he said. "George was the neighborhood bully when we were kids. I used to be afraid to walk home from school because if George got me he'd beat the hell out of me."

"So you were really afraid of this kid, George?" I asked.

"Oh, yeah. George was a tough guy. I'll tell you the truth. Twenty years later I'm the heavyweight champ, and there's a dinner for me in Brockton, my hometown. George is at the cocktail party—he's an automobile dealer now. And he comes up behind me and taps me on the shoulder. I turn around and he says, 'Rock, you know—'

"I ducked so fast I spilled my drink."

*   *   *

It should go without saying, I suppose, that coping with fear is part of every athlete's life—not only fear of failure but fear of physical injury, maiming, and death. Boxing may be the most dangerous of all sports, but men have died on the ice or carrying a football or even swinging a bat. We may take that danger for granted watching a game on TV, or we may be impressed by the courage of certain athletes without even realizing that their most consuming fears are sometimes the same as ours.

In that respect, one of my most surprising interviews was with Wayne Gretzky, the great center iceman with the Edmonton Oilers. That interview convinced me that Gretzky will quit early in his career unless he is traded to an East Coast team: the man is positively paralytic about flying.

I believe that Wayne Gretzky is the greatest offensive player in the history of team sports, including baseball, football, and basketball. That's a bold statement to make, but I make it without reservation. Over the course of his life in the sport of hockey, Gretzky has averaged close to three points a game, counting goals and assists. The average score in a National Hockey League game is 5–3, so throughout his career, Gretzky has been involved in three goals a game—usually a deciding margin. That is the equivalent of a baseball player with 180 RBI and 180 runs scored—every season.

Like success in most sports, it all goes back to hard work. Gretzky's father started him skating early, from the time he was three or four years old. His story is similar to that of Pete Maravich, who went to bed with a basketball when he was five and whose father used to drive along at varying speeds while Pete dribbled a basketball outside the window of the car for ball control. Gretzky practiced on the ice by himself and developed a knack for being ahead of the play by half a second or so. If you know anything about hockey, you know that is such an overwhelming advantage that it's surprising he doesn't score more often than he does.

But Gretzky's mortal fear of flying threatens to undermine all of his greatness on the ice. I tried to take him one step further, past the obvious questions about his fear. I asked him, "When do you start thinking about the airplane flight?"

He said he starts thinking about the next flight during the third period of the game, which tells me two things. One is that he will definitely quit early; the other is that his scoring record seems more phenomenal than it already is. While we're all watching him skate flawlessly—and he may set up or score the winning goal with a minute left—he has long since begun to be consumed with fear about that airplane flight.

Wayne told me he never looks out the window when he's flying. He stares straight ahead the whole time, no matter how comfortable the flight is. And his condition has never improved: each flight is the worst one yet. He's always been that way; he's tried everything and has no hope of a cure.

Gretzky also said that the first thing he does at the beginning of each season is look at the playing schedule and calculate how much time he'll have to spend in the air. Train trips are out because Edmonton is too far away from other hockey cities. He said that if he played for the New York Rangers, say, he could take trains to Philadelphia, Washington, Boston, the Islanders, and Pittsburgh. If he had two days to travel to Chicago, he could go by train—anything to avoid an airplane flight. He had never flown as a kid, so the problem didn't arise until he started playing hockey professionally. He was scared on his first flight and he's been scared ever since. He doesn't like the sound of the engines being turned on, and he's not comfortable until the plane stops—not even after the wheels touch the ground, because, he said, "it could take off again."

I said, "Wayne, *Wayne—*"

He laughed. "It could, though, couldn't it?" he said. "Couldn't it land and take off? So why would you relax?"

I've done a lot of interviews with people who suffer from phobias and people who treat them, and I've learned that most of us suffer from one phobia or another. Gretzky's fear is fairly serious, but the most remarkable case of fear of flying I ever encountered belonged to a man who came on my show after having been successfully treated. Before he was treated, his fear was so intense that he not only would not get on an airplane, he wouldn't even go to meet a friend at the airport, for fear that he would make a wrong turn and end up on a plane by accident.

At the other end of the rainbow from Gretzky and company would be a member of a club called Aces. Aces is an international organization of fighter pilots who have shot down at least ten enemy planes during wartime. Eddie Rickenbacker, for instance, is the best-known American Ace. The club, which started in America and expanded worldwide, is primarily a social group—the fliers get together and tell war stories. Because there are German Aces and Korean and Japanese Aces as well as Americans at these conventions, they sometimes discover that they have fought against each other in specific engagements. In 1969, Aces convened in Miami—fighter pilots from all over the world, from World War I and II, the Korean War, the Vietnam War. The greeter was a local Ace from Miami; we didn't know we had one until the *Miami Herald* found him. He declined to be interviewed by the *Herald*, but he was a listener of mine, so he agreed to come on my show. A World War II Ace, he had shot down fourteen German planes and now worked as a stock analyst.

The man arrived at the studio for the ten to eleven o'clock segment of my show, and when I shook his hand I noticed that it was dripping wet. The control room was filled with reporters and photographers from the *Herald*, visitors, friends, the whole lot. I knew that during World War II the air corps was voluntary—it was part of the army because there was no air force—so my first question was "What made you volunteer?"

"I liked it." That was his whole answer.

"What was it," I asked, "that you liked about flying?"

"I don't know."

"Did you always want to be a fighter pilot and fly alone?"

"Yes."

I looked up at the clock. Four minutes after ten. We had fifty-six more minutes, minus a few commercials, with no phone calls. I tried some hypothetical questions. "If there were enemy planes flying over the city right now and you could get into a fighter plane and go after them, would you go?"

"Yes."

"Would you be afraid?"

"No."

"Then why are you afraid now?" I was desperate so I took a chance—I went right to the moment. And he said, "I don't know who's listening."

"Then obviously it's fear of the unknown," I said.

"When I'm up in the air," he said, "I know what's there. But I don't know who's out there now."

He started to switch the subject, and instead of talking about planes he talked about fear. And then I did something I would never do ordinarily—use the word *I*. The only time I use the word *I* in an interview is when I need help, and I needed help now. I said, "Man, I'd be scared to death if I had to go up in a plane and fight. How do you do it?"

By twenty after ten, I'd created a major monster in this guy. He was gesticulating like mad and carrying on: "We *dove* through the clouds, *banked* to the left, into the sun." He was wild, and the hour flew by.

*   *   *

I may not know much about flying, but after spending many years doing color for the Miami Dolphins, I got to know plenty about football. Among other things, I learned about the differences between coaching in the NFL and coaching college ball—and one of the biggest differences is in the way college players are recruited. Lou Holtz, the Notre Dame football coach, told me, "The one secret of recruiting is that no matter what you say or what you promise, never lie. If the kid wants to be a photographer and your school does not have a good photography program, then your object is to get the kid to a school that you don't play. But don't tell him you have great photography courses, because when he comes there and finds out, you're dead. Never guarantee he's going to start, either."

Lou used to like recruiting; he liked meeting the parents. Most coaches don't. Don Shula told me he would have gone back to Notre Dame, which was his dream, if recruiting were not part of the job. He didn't want to go visit the parents and say, "Hi, I'm Don Shula, and I think your son should play for me." If you're a pro coach, you don't have that—you just draft. Holtz, on the other hand, didn't like the pros because he didn't like cutting guys from the squad; in college, if you suit up, you play.

Shula used to say, though, that he was never sure how much of the pro system of drafting, trying out, and cutting was really a proper gauge of talent. Sometimes it was a matter of luck, and in some cases pressure may have yielded the wrong results. He once talked about 1970, the year the players struck the preseason but went on to play the regular games. No veterans were at the preseason camp that year, only rookies and free agents, so they had to fill it up with bodies. The coach of Amherst College called Shula and said, "Don, I got a kid on my team here named Doug Swift. He's a nice kid, and he's going on to medical school. Could he come down and just work out during the summer with you? He wants to stay in shape, he's a good ballplayer, and you'll like him. He's big, he'll fill in for you."

Shula said, "You know, all we can pay him is the minimum preseason salary."

"He don't even want the money, Don. Just wants to stay in shape."

Swift came down to camp, and the first day at linebacker he played great, knocking guys down, intercepting passes. The coaches said, "Well, it's a freak, they're all rookies. Let's see how he does against the pros."

Doug Swift wound up starting, wound up All-Pro, and then became the Dolphins' player rep and a wheel in the players' union, and now he's a doctor. He played five or six years and made big money. The thing is, he never thought he'd be a pro—if he had, he wouldn't have gone to a school like Amherst. Shula told me that story and then said, "We got to thinking: How much of it is pressure? How many kids fail because they come to make it? Swift came to work out, so when he went out on the field to bat down the pass, he wasn't looking to impress me. He was just staying in shape and having some fun, because he was going on to medical school. But how much do we allow for the pressure, and are we too quick to cut?"

Don Shula is a great man in my estimation. He used to be a great curser too, but he's mellowed. He had to, after some of the things that happened in his first year with the Dolphins. I had been doing the color on Dolphin broadcasts for the previous two years, when George Wilson was the coach. Wilson was a very nice guy and had almost no rules about the press. My job consisted of doing pregame and halftime commentary and locker room interviews. The first game of Shula's first season, Larry Csonka got hurt and was down in the medical room being wrapped. After the game, I went down to the medical room with my microphone to interview him. I didn't know that the medical room was off-limits to the press under Shula's setup because it hadn't been that way under Wilson.

I was interviewing Csonka, on the air live, when Shula came in on the other side of the room and started yelling in my general direction. "Get the *fuck* out of the *fucking* medical room!" And his team had just won. It was a live mike and he was screaming at the top of his lungs, so I knew it went out over the air. Csonka said to me, on the air, "Who do you think he's talking to?"

"Probably me," I said. "We'll be right back, folks."

I went outside the medical room and Csonka, who was a hell of a guy, came outside with me and finished the interview in the hallway. I folded up my gear and as I was leaving, walking back across the field toward the elevator, Shula came up alongside me. He asked me kind of sheepishly, "Was what I said on the air?"

I nodded. He asked, "I said it twice, didn't I? What did you say about it?"

"I didn't say anything, but Csonka said, 'Who do you think he's talking to?'"

He smiled. "Okay, I gotta watch that." Then he suddenly grimaced. "How the *fuck* could you not know the fucking medical room is off fucking limits?!"

I said, "Well, I didn't know, but I know now."

After that we became good friends, and I watched him mellow.

Besides Shula, I also got to know Joe Namath pretty well when he came down to Florida for training camp. If Joe Namath is your friend, he's your friend for life. They don't come any more loyal. I was there when he guaranteed the Super Bowl in 1969 in Miami. It wasn't quite the way they make it seem today—that Namath went out of his way to predict a Jets victory, like Ali would do. The press goaded him into it.

The Jets were seventeen-point underdogs, and Weeb Ewbank very smartly had them live a really nice, relaxed week—they stayed at a resort hotel with their wives. The Colts, on the other hand, were sequestered by Shula, who was their coach then. The press corps was sitting around the Diplomat Hotel a few days before the game. Namath was having lunch at the hotel, and three writers went over and started needling him. "Well, you're seventeen-point underdogs," they said.

"I guess we shouldn't even show up, huh?" Namath said.

"Think you're gonna win?"

"I wouldn't play if I didn't expect to win," Joe said.

"The Colts have lost one game all year. How can you expect to win?"

"We've got a game plan. We know their weaknesses. I know I can throw the ball."

"Are you saying that Morrall and Unitas are no good?"

"No, I'm not saying they're not good," Namath said. "But you have to think you're the best, otherwise why compete?"

So finally one of the writers said, "So, are you saying you're gonna win?"

"Yeah!"

And that became NAMATH GUARANTEES VICTORY!

Namath gave me an interesting definition of leadership once. He knew he had it, but he said it's the one quality that can't be taught. He said that the best quarterback he ever saw was John Hadl. Nobody threw the ball better than Hadl—he was imaginitive, he took risks. But according to Namath, Hadl lacked leadership. I asked him to give me an example of what he meant.

"Let's say the Baltimore Colts are losing by four points," Namath said. "With three seconds left, they have the ball on their opponent's nineteen-yard line. They need a touchdown to win and they have time for just one play. In the huddle, Johnny Unitas calls a quarterback sneak, and the ten other players in the huddle believe they're going to score. That's leadership."

Joe and I had a mutual friend in Jay Gordon. Jay graduated from the University of Pennsylvania with a degree in economics, but back in the sixties he had become a beach bum playing tennis in Miami Beach and occasionally teaching tennis to make a few bucks. Jay was a sweet guy, but he had the worst luck. One day Jay said to me, "I played tennis today, and this girl came over and asked me if I wanted to play a little. She was a fourteen-year-old kid, but I had a half hour between games, so I played her. Six-love, six-love."

"Jay," I said, "you're out of her league, obviously."

"*She* beat *me*. She told me her father's a tennis pro in Fort Lauderdale, but this is ridiculous. I'm twenty-six and she had me running all over the court. Write this name down: Chris Evert. Whipped my ass."

Anyway, Jay knew Joe Namath from Beaver Falls, Pennsylvania, where they went to school together, and his family knew Namath's family. In fact, Namath named his daughter Grace, after Jay's mother. I'll never forget the time the Jets were in Miami playing the Dolphins, and Jay's mother and father went out to watch the practice. Jay was going through his hippie phase; he had a beard down to his knees and was living in rags. Namath saw Jay's mother and went over and hugged her. And Jay's mother said, "Joe, look at Jay. Will you talk to him?"

It may have been the only time anyone ever accused Joe of being a good influence.

I love the racetrack, so it should come as no surprise that some of my best friends are jockeys. In fact, I even own a racehorse now, a filly called Praises On High, that I bought with Earl Weaver. I was sitting in the dugout with Earl one day, when out of the blue he asked me if I'd like to own a horse. I put up some money and Earl made the purchase. When I went down to Florida to see the horse, Earl met me at the track early in the morning and we patted her and took pictures. It took me a while, but I finally realized that I owned a horse. It was just so strange for this kid from Brooklyn to be standing there having his picture taken with a horse he owns—at the same track where, years ago, I had been kiting checks.

I like the horse-racing colony because it's like a traveling circus. It's a village that moves around and that bettors come to visit. Bill Hartack, whom I got to know very well, was a classic inhabitant of that village. He was a colorful character, in part because he came out of the postwar era that produced athletes like Ted Williams—men who didn't talk to the press, the hard-assed guys. Hartack was definitely a hard-assed guy. There are still some of them around now, men who are basically fine people but who won't talk to the press, like Steve Carlton. Steve is a wine connoisseur and a gourmet, but he would as soon give an interview as wolf down a Big Mac with a bottle of Giaccobazzi.

Hartack was the kind of guy who could shut off the press like that. Hanging on my wall is a portrait of Hartack by LeRoy Neiman, and the arrogance comes across in his pose. He rode in anger. Different athletes take different routes to success. Bill was not a picturesque rider. He didn't sit well on a horse; he didn't look good in the saddle. Some jockeys, like Willie Shoemaker, look as if they were born on a horse. The horse flows with them. Hartack is a little taller than the average jockey, and he is left-handed. The way he rode, he was all over a horse, flip-flopping and banging around—he didn't have a comfortable seat. He had to work at it, like Pete Rose has to work at baseball. He had to use his intelligence to make himself a better athlete. He told me he would think, What dumb things might these other jockeys do that I can use to steal the race? Can I psych the other guy?

"I decided somewhere along the line," he added, "that winning was the only thing, and second place was the same as last, and so I would approach it angrily."

I later found that Bob Gibson, the great baseball pitcher, did a similar thing—it was a conscious philosophy. When I asked Gibson what that opposing batter meant to him, he said, "My livelihood. My rent, food on the table for my kids. That's what he's there to deprive me of. It's not just this game." Hartack felt that way.

If you ask a jockey, "When do you know that it's time to think about quitting?" the great ones will tell you that they know it's time when the hole opens up on the rail and they don't instinctively go for it. When they're young, they are not afraid to come through at the rail or afraid that they might be knocked into the infield by another horse. It still takes courage to ride in the race, but when they hesitate, that's when they know they have to get out.

The emotional involvement of the spectator is much greater in horse racing than in any other sport. You may bet the football game, but it would be illegal, and most people just root for the home team. The whole reason for going to the track is to bet money on the results. The jockey knows you bet on him; and whether they ought to be or not, some of those people at the track are betting the rent. John Rotz, the jockey who was known as Gentleman John because he was always very calm and distinguished and dressed very well, told me about a day he rode the favorite in the last race at Aqueduct and didn't win. As the crowds were clearing out and the jockeys had come back and were weighing out—a fairly placid scene—he suddenly heard out of the crowd a voice screaming, "Drop dead, Rotz!" Gentleman John never forgot it.

The British style of riding is very different from the American. The British don't whip their horses coming out of the gate; they let them run. Oddly enough, their times are about the same, although the Americans have more sprint races, seven furlongs or less. In Britain, they tend to run a mile or more. As a result, American jockeys have a more gung-ho attitude than the British. Lester Piggott is an international hall of fame jockey, Jockey to the Queen, and one of the great riders of all time. He is also a friend of Bill Hartack's. When Lester once vacationed in the United States, he stayed at Hartack's house. Piggott had never ridden a race in America, so he asked Bill to get him some mounts.

For his first American race, Piggott ended up riding the third at Hialeah, a six-furlong race. The gate opened, all the horses broke out, the American jockeys went to their whips, and they left Piggott in the dust. He managed to make up some ground by the end of the race and finished third. After the race, he went into the jockeys' room, took Hartack aside, and said, "Bill, could I have a word with the chaps?"

Hartack got their attention. "Fellas, Sir Lester"—Piggott had been knighted—"Sir Lester would like to speak with you a moment."

Piggott stood up on a little box and surveyed his curious audience.

"Gentlemen," he said, "what is the blooming rush?"

I had Bill on the radio once with Stan Musial and Chuck Connors. Before Connors became famous in *The Rifleman* on TV, he was a major league baseball player who came up through the Dodger chain and then played for the Cubs. At one point during the show, I asked Musial, "When a baseball player gets old, what goes first?"

"For me," he said, "it was the legs. My eyes were okay, and I thought my swing was still okay. But by August, it seemed the more I ran, the farther away first base would get."

Then I said to Hartack, "What goes first on a jockey?"

And Chuck Connors cut in on the air and said, "His ass."

My favorite racing story, however, has to do with another jockey: Con Errico. Errico was always looking for angles to help him win a race. He and Hartack were in a mile-and-a-half race once at Belmont—twice around the track. The track was so shrouded in fog that the horses could be seen only during the stretch run to the finish line. Hartack finished second, and after the race he asked Errico, "The first time around, where were you? I thought I was in front."

Errico told him no, that he had the lead all the way.

"But I never heard you in front of me," Hartack said.

Two weeks later, they went drinking together in a local bar and they both got loaded. Hartack confronted him about the race, and Errico confessed that he had stopped a little way after coming out of the gate and sat there in the fog waiting. "When I heard you guys coming, I took off."

Errico ran a half-mile race.

On second thought, forget what I said about Ali at the beginning of the chapter—maybe Con Errico is the smartest athlete I ever met!

CHAPTER 12

INSIDE
AND OUTSIDE
THE LAW

Edward Bennett Williams, the prominent Washington trial lawyer and owner of the Baltimore Orioles, has represented his share of unpopular clients, including members of organized crime. As a friend of his once told him, "Ed, someday they're gonna build a statue to you—in Sicily."

Nonetheless, Williams is one of the most highly respected lawyers in Washington, a town of lawyers, many of whom happen to be serving in Congress. He is a devout Catholic and daily communicant, and he possesses a delightful mind that constantly challenges assumptions.

Williams has one of the essential qualities of great men, the ability to focus his concentration on what comes next—a quality that became very clear to me one day in 1983. Williams's Orioles had just won the World Series. His life dream had come true. After the celebration in the locker room in Philadelphia, I flew back in his private plane with him, his wife, and one of his daughters. He couldn't have been happier.

He'd had cancer four times and licked it, and his team had just become world champions. The aircraft was a former Israeli jet fighter that had been converted into a passenger plane, so it *really* took off. As we accelerated into the sky, we could look down on the city of Philadelphia and watch the lights going out in the stadium.

It's only about a twenty-minute flight from Philly to Dulles Airport in Washington, but midway through the flight, I saw a look of concern come over Williams's face. I leaned over and asked him what was the matter.

"I've got a trial on Monday," he said. He had already started to focus on his next case. Most people would savor that feeling of victory and accomplishment for at least a few days, certainly a few hours; Williams was already moving on to the next challenge, focusing on the next set of problems. His client wasn't going to have to suffer for his attorney's success in another arena. That is the sign not only of a great mind but of a genuinely compassionate one.

On another occasion, I asked Williams to explain his philosophy of work. "Whether I come out of a courtroom," he said, "or out of a ballpark, I never feel that I've lost, because I always give my best. The result may read one way, but if you give your best, you don't lose. The case may be lost, the game may be lost, but *I* don't lose."

Williams works off a principle of pessimism, based on the assumption that anything that can go wrong *will* go wrong. "Expect the worst," he told me. That's atypical of most successful people, and it seems to go against all those clichés about positive thinking and visualizing success, but it works for him. Williams approaches each witness in a trial as though that witness could ruin his entire case. It revs him up for the witness: he is geared for calamity. I asked him what principle led him to favor pessimism over optimism. He said, "It's called intelligence."

A few weeks before the Orioles won the World Series in

1983, when the Orioles and the White Sox were in the American League Championship Series, I went to the first game with Williams. The game was played in Baltimore, so I watched it from Williams's private box. Chicago won, and after the game everyone was rather depressed. We took the press elevator down together. It's a small elevator and it's supposed to hold only six or seven people at a time, but fifteen of us had jammed into it. As we got to the first floor, the elevator cable snapped and the car went below the floor into the elevator bay. We hit bottom, and although no one was hurt, we were trapped there. The light was still on, but the doors wouldn't open and there was very little air. To make matters worse, we were in the press elevator and the phone was disconnected. If you're in a general-access elevator, people notice right away if something is wrong, but with a press elevator, the other press people simply figure the elevator is broken and walk down—it's only three flights anyway. There was no emergency bell in the car, so we started banging on the doors and calling for help.

Williams said, "Listen, we have to speak one person at a time or else we'll use up too much oxygen. So raise your hand if you want to talk." I was scared because I had angina and I was apt to get short of breath at the least exertion. There was a small hole in the roof of the car, but not much air was coming in and we were really overcrowded. We kept banging on the doors, but we couldn't hear any response at all, not a sound. Maybe half an hour went by. It was a warm day and everybody was sweating, but to save oxygen we weren't talking much. People were beginning to feel faint. Finally, Williams turned around to face us and said quietly that he was going to lead us in prayer.

"We have just watched a very insignificant event," he said, "a baseball game. And we realize how insignificant it is when we know how close we are to no longer being alive. So if you can find it in your infinite mercy, dear Lord, to help us in our hour of need, we would indeed be grateful. And we hope, if we do get out of here alive, never again to take our existence lightly and to put an insignificant event like a baseball game in its proper place. Amen."

The moment he finished saying Amen, the door opened.

We were underneath the ground level and we had to climb up. Then we saw people reaching down to help pull us up out of the elevator bay. When we got out, we saw fire and rescue trucks and ambulances and three television camera crews waiting there. Obviously, they knew what had happened—that the owner of the team and a lot of press people were stuck in the elevator. Because we were sealed in the elevator car at the bottom of the shaft, though, we never heard any of the commotion going on above us. We went right to Williams's limo with no comment. We got in the car and drove in absolute silence back to Washington.

Maybe it was coincidence—after all, while we were praying they were already working to get us out—but the moment Williams finished saying Amen, that door opened, and I thought, Either there's a God or Edward Bennett Williams is God and he was talking to himself.

I suppose I can be forgiven for thinking of lawyers as Godlike, since they often seem to hold the power of freedom and redemption in their hands, and sometimes they do work miracles. And they watch over their clients and protect them from harm. Melvin Belli told me that the first thing, the *only* thing, that counts in a courtroom is the client: get him off. He said he made a mistake in the Jack Ruby trial by putting Dallas on trial; he made the city larger than his client. "Don't divert attention from your client," he said, "but if you do, make the diversion have some meaning."

Percy Foreman, the great Houston lawyer, gave me a perfect example of how to divert attention in the right way. I attended the Mossler trial in Miami in 1963, in which Foreman defended Candace Mossler and her boyfriend, who were accused of having murdered Candace's rich socialite husband. It was one of those classic trials in which many people judged the couple guilty before the trial but the jury found them innocent. How? Foreman did a masterful job of defense—by putting the dead man on trial. By the fifth day, anyone sitting in that courtroom hated Jacques Mossler. Foreman revealed that Mossler liked to see his wife having sex with other people while he took notes. In fact, Foreman's opening statement was talked about all over town for the next few weeks.

He told us that what was about to take place in the courtroom would boggle our minds and cause us to think thoughts that we'd never thought. He said we'd be introduced to the most sordid events we could ever imagine. He never referred to the husband as "the victim." He called him by his name and dragged out the *M* so that it sounded sinister. "When you learn about Mr. Mmmmossler," Foreman would say, "you will know that he had every, I repeat *every*, known sexual perversion except the foot fetish."

People were going around town saying, "He didn't have the foot fetish? Holy shit." And we didn't know what the foot fetish was. Diversion was the name of Foreman's game. The key prosecution witness was a black handyman who had worked in the Mossler home and who testified that he had overheard Candace and her boyfriend planning the murder. On cross-examination, Foreman never asked the witness about his testimony. He did bring up the fact that the witness had been flown in first-class for the trial and put up at a luxury hotel. He kept telling the witness he had no reason to be afraid of telling the truth in a white courtroom. The district attorney objected and was sustained, but the idea was planted in the jury's mind that maybe this witness was intimidated because of his race and that maybe they shouldn't take his testimony too seriously.

On another day, Foreman interrupted the trial to ask the judge for permission to ask everyone in the courtroom to stand in a moment of prayer for his home state of Texas, which was about to celebrate the anniversary of its statehood. When the judge refused, Foreman asked for a recess so that he could go out in the hall and have a moment of prayer by himself. The judge finally decided that it would take less time to let him do it in the courtroom. By the end of that trial, Foreman had the jury in the palm of his hand. He created doubt, dislike of the victim, and diversions.

I asked him whether he himself thought Candace Mossler was guilty. He said that he was not the determiner of his client's guilt. He said it was up to the jury system to determine guilt or innocence, and it was up to him to see that his client got every benefit of the law.

Sometimes the key ingredient in winning a case doesn't come out in the courtroom. F. Lee Bailey gave me an insight into how lawyers think and into the intangibles that sometimes go into winning a case. One of the most interesting cases he handled was Sam Sheppard's murder trial, which he finally won on appeal. Sheppard was a physician in Cleveland whose wife was found murdered. At first Sheppard claimed his wife was attacked, but further evidence was discovered that seemed to incriminate him. Because Sheppard was so prominent a figure in Cleveland, it was a while before he was made to stand trial. One day, the *Cleveland Free Press* ran a headline asking when the DA would bring this man to justice. Bailey requested a change of venue because of all the pretrial publicity, but he couldn't get one and Sheppard was found guilty by the Cleveland jury. Bailey appealed on the grounds that the jury had been prejudiced by the newspaper headlines, and he presented precedents. He told me that the secret of winning that appeal was using B law students to dig up those precedents. Lee felt that C students were just not bright enough. On the other hand, A students don't want to be bothered with that kind of grinding research. But B students want to be A students. B students want to work for F. Lee Bailey, no matter what the assignment.

Louis Nizer, the famous trial lawyer and author of *My Life in Court*, has handled some pretty messy cases in his long career. He told me that the messiest case a lawyer can have is a contested divorce. Nizer feels that a divorce suit is tougher than a murder case with the victim's wife on trial, because nothing is worse to him than two people who have lost love and now hate each other. It's a case most lawyers have to handle and most of them hate.

I asked him once how much luck played a part in the courtroom. "Oh, I get lucky a lot," he said. "I get lucky at four A.M. in the law library."

Nizer believes that jury selection is the heart of every case, that the process of selection is a science—noticing how a prospective juror crosses his legs, knowing how to tell when someone is lying, recognizing which nationalities or races are likely to be more or less lenient. Edward Bennett Williams, on the other hand, contends that jury selection makes no difference in the world. He believes that you could walk out on the street and pick the first twelve people who come along and get the same verdict you would get if you spent six months selecting the jury. The one thing they all have in common, though, is that I've never met a lawyer who said he could forecast what a jury will do. And every great lawyer I've known has had a jury surprise him at least once.

Like Nizer, trial lawyer Melvin Belli—who has specialized in accident cases—is a firm believer in the painstaking art of jury selection. Belli talked at length on my show about who on a jury votes for high awards for accident victims. Belli holds that blacks, Jews, and working-class Italians all vote for high awards, whereas Irish and Chinese jurors tend to be conservative and vote lower. Geography also plays a part. "You can get seventy-five thousand dollars for a broken arm in New York," he said, "but in Cedar Rapids, Iowa, you might get only twenty-five thousand."

Belli also pointed out that the biggest cases are sometimes over matters that seem the most trivial, and his famous chocolate bar case is a perfect example. In that case, a woman who had bought a well-known company's chocolate bar came home and, in the presence of the television repairman, began eating the candy. She looked down and saw little insects crawling on the chocolate and fainted. The woman claimed she suffered extreme stomach problems and could never eat chocolate again. It came out in court that a certain bug lives around the cocoa plant—a nonpoisonous, harmless bug. The odds of the bugs ever surviving in a processed chocolate bar were figured at something like eight billion to one. In the history of chocolate bars, it had never happened.

The company admitted all these facts and agreed to pay the woman's medical bills. However, she was also suing for damages—I think it was close to a million dollars, which was a huge amount at the time. The chief chemist at the company presented very compelling testimony about the precautions the company takes, the extremely unlikely nature of what had happened, and so forth. Representing the woman, Belli felt he was losing the case. The judge pointed out to the jury the laws concerning product liability but explained that the jury could consider the mitigating circumstances. Belli knew that the jury was very impressed with the chemist, and he realized that while he would win some money for the woman, he wasn't going to get a lot.

During a recess, Mel went out and bought one of the company's candy bars. When court reconvened, he approached the chemist in the witness stand and said, "I want you to do something for me. I want you to open this chocolate bar, sight unseen, and eat it before the jury. Don't even look at it—just take a bite and eat it."

The chemist opened it, but before he could take a bite, he gagged involuntarily. That was it. One million dollars! What I like about Belli in that situation is his willingness to take a high risk at a moment of crisis. There were no insects on the chocolate bar, of course. It was a perfectly good bar, but all the chemist had to do was to think: maybe.

If I didn't love what I already do, I'd probably rather be a trial lawyer than anything else. I could never be a prosecutor, though. I have friends who are prosecutors and they amaze me. To represent the state seems like such a meaningless abstraction—I mean, who is the state? But I like to take risks in my work, and good trial lawyers do that almost as a matter of course. I also don't think it's an exaggeration to say that we use similar techniques. As an interviewer, my job is to put the audience in my guest's shoes. The key to great trial lawyers is their ability to put the jury in the victim's shoes—as in the candy bar case—or in the defendant's shoes, as in a murder trial.

That's easy enough to do in a crime of passion. Good lawyers can ring any number of changes on the handling of crime-of-passion murder cases, and the details can get pretty bizarre. One such trial occurred in Miami while I was working there and it made front-page headlines for weeks. The defendant had killed a woman by choking her. He then had put her body in a garbage can and put the garbage can in the Miami River, where it was found three months later with the decomposed body inside. When the defendant was arrested, he admitted strangling the woman and said he was glad to have her out of his life. The verdict, after a long trial, was not guilty. In this case, the defendant made a convincing witness on his own behalf. Here is the story as it slowly unfolded in court.

The defendant, a single man, owned a little clothing store. The victim was a married woman who shopped there. They carried on a furtive romance and eventually slept together, but only once. Then the woman began to hound him, offering to leave her husband if only he would marry her. She would come to his house late at night and harass him. One night, she came to his house at two in the morning and started screaming at him. He panicked, grabbed her, throttled her, and she died. He claimed he was just trying to shut her up and didn't actually mean to kill her, but it looked pretty bad for him. At one point during his testimony, the prosecutor asked him why, if it was just an accident, he put the body in a garbage can and dumped it in the river. The defense attorney objected, holding that what the defendant did with the body was immaterial and would prejudice the jury. Destroying a dead body was a civil offense, the lawyer said; the husband could sue his client for that in a separate case if he wanted to. The judge sustained the objection, but other than that, the defendant agreed to everything the prosecutor said. The reason for the not guilty verdict, I believe, was that the members of the jury were able to put themselves in the defendant's shoes.

A Miami attorney named Neal Sonnett once defended a man whose daughter had been accidentally killed by a motorist when she stepped out from between two parked cars. The police didn't charge the driver—he wasn't speeding, and the girl had been jaywalking. Three months later, the girl's father confronted the motorist in front of the man's office and shot him. He was charged with first-degree murder. The father had followed the guy around for days before he shot him, but Sonnett pleaded temporary insanity on the grounds of irresistible impulse. He argued that it was all part of a deep depression that had set in over the loss of the man's daughter and that the father thought the depression might be relieved by killing the motorist. Sonnett won a not guilty verdict for his client.

Both those cases fascinate me for the same reason the Bernhard Goetz trial does. Goetz was found innocent of attempted murder in his subway shootings. His lawyer put the jury into that subway car with Goetz, surrounded by four youths.

I hold no brief for Goetz, but I've been on the subway. I was sitting on the subway once when I saw two white guys coming toward me, and I knew they were going to do something. Before they got to me the train stopped, the doors opened, and a cop walked on. All I have to do is remember that scene and think about what I might have done if I'd had a gun and no cop came along. In other words, put the chocolate bar in the jury's hands. That's why I admire great lawyers.

The role of the lawyer is not to determine guilt, Percy Foreman said. He's there to see that the defendant gets a fair trial. Good lawyers will tell you that there is no such thing as a technicality. The law's the law, and each part is as important as every other part. Proving guilt is as important as having a search warrant.

That part about getting a fair trial goes for organized crime figures, too, of course, but, as for me, I've always preferred to keep organized crime as much at arm's length as possible. The two times I made exceptions, however, were particularly remarkable.

One of the reasons I enjoy public speaking is that I get to do what I do best—make it up as I go along—so I very rarely turn down speaking engagements. As long as I can fit it into my schedule, I'll speak to just about any group that makes me the right offer. Once, however, someone made me an offer that, as they say, I couldn't refuse. I picked up the phone one day years ago and found myself talking to a man of few words, all of them heavily accented. He said, "King?"

"Yeah," I said.

"This is Boom Boom Giardella," the voice said. The only reason I'm telling this story is that I'm sure Boom Boom sleeps with the fishes these days.

"November 7, War Memorial Auditorium, Fort Lauderdale," Boom Boom said. "Boys Town of Italy is the charity, Sergio Franchi is the singer, you're the emcee. Eight o'clock, black tie." And he hung up.

I never said a word. I went because something told me to go. When I got there, I saw a sign with my name and Sergio's. Boom Boom met me at the door. "Ay, kid, ay," a familiar voice said. "We're glad you came."

I said, "*You're* glad I came?"

I went backstage and said hello to Sergio, whom I knew. "Sergio," I said, "how'd they get you for this?"

"A guy named Boom Boom called me."

Then Boom Boom came to give me my instructions. "You can kid all you like, kid," he said. "Make all the jokes you want. But don't, *don't*, turn up the house lights."

"Why not?" I said.

"We've got three thousand people here," he said, "and a lot of 'em are competitors. You know, some guys in the olive oil business, some guys in jukeboxes—just don't ask to turn the lights on 'em. We had an entertainer do that once and it didn't go over too good."

I went onstage, and I was really cooking that night. They were a great audience. I tried a couple of jokes about the mob and they got big laughs, so I just relaxed and had a ball. Then I introduced Sergio. Sergio sang, the evening was a success, and Boom Boom walked me to my car.

"Thanks, kid," he said. "We'll never forget this."

"My pleasure, Boom Boom."

"We owe you a favor," he said.

"Hey, thanks, Boom Boom."

"What can we do for you?"

"Nothing, it's okay."

He gave me a nasty look. "We don't like to owe favors," he said ominously.

"It's okay, Boom Boom, I don't need anything. Really."

"No good. We don't like it when people hold markers on us. So, what can we do for you?"

By now I was getting a little edgy. I wasn't going to be paid because it was a charity affair, but they still figured they owed me something, and they were going to pay me in the way that was easiest for them. I asked him, "What do you have in mind?"

And Boom Boom said, "Got anybody you don't like?"

I never thought I'd hear those words. But the truth is, the first thing I thought of was names. I thought of the general manager of the radio station I was working for. What power! The power of violence is scary. Then rationality took over. I listened to Boom Boom run down a list of possible "favors," hoping he would get to some nonviolent ones. He finally said, "We'll call you, give you a horse." Not to own, to bet. I felt relieved.

One morning a few weeks later, I picked up the phone and a voice—not Boom Boom's but with a familiar neighborhood tang to it—said, "Cut The Twig in the third at Hialeah." That was it.

I bet a hundred dollars, which was all I had. The horse paid $8.20. I should've borrowed.

Duke Zeibert tells a story about something that happened to him in the fifties. "I had a party of ten in my restaurant one day," he said, "and they were all due to appear before the Kefauver hearings. They were big racketeers from Chicago and they were all eating like there was no tomorrow, the most expensive things on the menu—lobster, caviar, champagne. All of a sudden one of them leaned back, let out a belch, and roared, 'Who says crime doesn't pay?'"

Cut The Twig in the third at Hialeah.

Then there was the time I met Meyer Lansky. Lansky was the infamous Jewish gangster portrayed by Lee Strasberg in *The Godfather*, the guy who all the Italians trusted. Lansky was the champion money launderer of all time; the Feds never found him with cash, never traced a bank account to him. The only time he was indicted was for income tax evasion, and he eventually beat the rap for that. For a while after his indictment he went to live in Israel and ended up being the only Jew the Israelis ever deported. Lansky offered Brazil two million dollars to take him and Brazil refused. He finally had to come back to America, went to trial, and won the case. But he had very good help. On the date the government claimed he was making an illegal transfer of funds, he happened to be undergoing heart surgery in Boston. The government had the wrong date; they screwed up the whole case. Another time, he was arrested for possession of illegal drugs, and the drugs turned out to be a prescription medication.

Lansky was well known in Miami and, in a way, idolized—because he was Jewish and he was not intimidated by the Mafia gangsters. He used to call them "the dumb vops," but they respected him because he made a lot of money for them. *Once Upon a Time in America,* which is one of the most underrated films of this decade, was really about the young Lansky. He never killed anyone himself, but he had a hatchet man called Jimmy Blue Eyes. Jimmy did have beautiful blue eyes, but he was a killer. Lansky himself looked like he could be a salesman for Arthur Adler clothes. The most income he ever reported in his life was thirty-two thousand dollars. He had a little home in Hollywood, Florida, where he lived with his wife, and an apartment across the street from the Fontainebleau. Occasionally, I would see him in the coffee shop of the hotel.

One night in the late sixties, I was having dinner at the Embers restaurant in Miami Beach. I was a pretty well known celebrity then, with shows on radio and television, and I was out on a date with a blond woman named Sandy Anderson.

We were eating at a booth when Meyer Lansky and Jimmy Blue Eyes came in with their wives. The maitre d' seated the party of four at the table next to ours, in such a way that Lansky was practically rubbing elbows with me. Suddenly everything changed. The maitre d' was shaking a little as he handed them their menus, the busboy was clattering the cups and saucers as he put them down. If you were in that restaurant and you didn't know it was Meyer Lansky, you'd wonder what all the fuss was about; he looked like an ordinary little Jewish guy out with his wife and friends. Lansky seemed totally oblivious to the fact that every time he even cleared his

throat, three waiters jumped and said, "Yes?" But when I had
to go to the men's room, I asked Sandy to let me out her side
of the booth so I wouldn't have to risk bumping Lansky's arm
as I was getting out.

On the way back to my table, Herb Kaplan, co-owner of the
Embers, let me know in a quivering voice—in case I wasn't
already aware of it—who was sitting next to me. I went back
to my table, sliding in on Sandy's side. We were eating our
meat and Lansky's party was about to order, when Lansky
grabbed my sleeve and tugged. I thought, Holy shit. I leaned
over. He leaned over. I was about to be spoken to by one of
the great underworld lords of all time. He said to me in his
classic New York Jewish accent, "Ya makin' a dollar?"

So I said, "I'm doing all right."

"Vell," he said, "ya got the radio, ya got the television, ya
writin' the paper, ya should be doin' all right."

I said, "Well, you know, this ain't a union town."

"Eh, ya don't do all right, go do better somevere else."

Then he introduced me to his wife. "This is Larry King,"
he said. "He's a *yidlach*, he's a Jewish boy. Don't go by the
King." He introduced me to Jimmy Blue Eyes and his wife
and said, "Good luck to ya, I like your work."

I went back to my dinner and I could sense a different respect from the crowd because I'd been introduced. I figured
that now I could listen in on their conversation and I'd at least
get a great column out of it. I mean, the FBI follows Lansky
wherever he goes trying to get something on him—they were
outside the restaurant—and there I was sitting next to him
and Jimmy Blue Eyes. Meyer was asking Jimmy, "What kind
of salad dressing?"

Jimmy said, "I can only have the olive oil. No vinegar. I
can't take that strong stuff." The waiter, who was already
quivering, came over and spent ten minutes on the salad. The
rest of the conversation went something like this:

"Jimmy, why don't you move down here?"

"I don't know, I got all my friends in New York."

"Jimmy, it's twenty-two degrees in New York today."

"I don't know, Meyer, what do you do all day here?"

"What do you think? You go to the beach, the wife goes shopping. What else?"

"You're gettin' old, Meyer."

"Jimmy . . . sunshine. How old are *you*?"

"I'm gettin' old, but I don't like bein' around old people. I like my neighborhood, I like the New York papers."

The whole conversation went like that. I've heard saltier conversations on park benches. They were just two aging Jewish guys with wives who like to go shopping. But when Meyer tugged my jacket, my heart did a flop.

I saw him a couple of months later walking his dog on Collins Avenue. I went up to him and said, "Meyer, how are you?"

We started to chat. I said, "I got a deal for you, Meyer. You like my work, why don't you come on my show?"

"What would we talk about?" he asked in all seriousness.

"What a life you've led," I said, playing along. "We could talk about anything you want. We could talk about your work, for instance."

"I'm a business consultant," he said. "I help out some people. Why would you want to talk about that?"

All of a sudden, I couldn't think of a good answer, and Lansky never did come on my show.

My only other brush with organized crime came when Antoinette Giancana, the daughter of Mafia don Sam Giancana and the author of *Mafia Princess*, was on my show. The whole time she was there, off the air at least, I had the feeling that more was going on than just a radio show. Finally, during one of the breaks, she asked me if I wanted to come back to her hotel room after the show and have a drink with her. Clearly, that's not the same as inviting someone out to lunch at Duke's. A voice in the back of my head said, "Don't do it," and so I just smiled and said, "I'll call you."

Antoinette Giancana was a very attractive woman, but I thought, Christ, if I mess up, am I playing out of my league! Without too much prompting I could imagine what might happen. Somewhere I was listening to a voice on the phone, maybe not unlike Boom Boom's, saying, "Whaddaya mean you ain't gonna marry my daughter?"

I didn't call.

CHAPTER 13

STORYTELLERS

Of all the guests on talk shows, I think the most undervalued, and to me often the most intriguing, are writers. Maybe that's because good writers are good storytellers, and what could be more fun than talking to someone who knows how to tell a great story? Of course, there's a lot more to it than that, just as there's more to selling books than being a good writer. The talk show circuit has recently played a role in helping authors get their work across to wider audiences, although I believe that talk shows serve an even more worthwhile function.

Unlike the movies, music, theater, and just about every other form of the arts, a book allows two minds to communicate directly with no interference—no director, producers, actors, musicians, no elaborate settings, no need to buy tickets, get dressed, or show up on time. By the same token, however, there is no chance for any immediate feedback from the audience to the artist. A reader can't boo, applaud, laugh, sing along, or stomp out of the theater in disgust. So aside from the occasional public reading, talk shows with viewer or listener call-ins provide the only opportunity for direct contact between the public and its authors—and vice versa.

Talk shows can help sell a book, but they can occasionally hurt sales as well. Talk shows hurt *The Target Is Destroyed,* Seymour Hersh's book on the Korean airliner shot down by the Soviets. Hersh told the whole story within the half hour or forty-five minutes of each show, and nothing wildly intriguing was revealed that made listeners want to read the book. It was clearly a story of human error caused by a breakdown in communication—a Russian pilot saw a plane over Soviet territory, reported it to Moscow, and the man in charge was out having dinner. The pilot acted on his own and a tragedy ensued. It was a natural set of circumstances; maybe it could even/have happened in the United States. When the essence of the story could be told within the framework of the show, that killed all interest in it.

Jacqueline Susann was probably the first author to use the talk show as a vehicle to sell books. She was on my show a lot in the early sixties, and I'm convinced that she initiated that trend and opened the door for pop novelists, as well as serious writers, to sell books via talk shows. Before Jackie, a talk show host or the show's producer might say, "This is a hot book, let's call and try to get the author on." But Jackie began to sell publishers on the idea of the multicity tour. As long as she was going to a city to sign books in a local bookstore, she thought, why not go on a television or radio talk show while she was there?

Jackie knew how to sell herself very well; she was a master promoter. She figured that if she could titillate the audience by letting them know there was sex in her book, she would always be able to get on talk shows and sell books. She understood talk and she especially understood local talk. She would find out what talk shows were on the air in Omaha, say, and get herself booked on them. She would do disc jockey shows.

What she was doing was putting herself in touch with the community. All she needed was one dirty book—*Valley of the Dolls*—and she was off and running. After that, the talk shows knew they would get the listeners or the viewers if they had Jackie on, and they were happy to book her.

She made writers like Jackie Collins possible. Collins is a doll—happily married and with a great sexual imagination. She is also very defensive about what she writes. She will fight you tooth and nail if you say you closed the book and couldn't remember a single character. You have to like her, and, for what it's worth, I think she's better-looking than her sister. And unlike Joan, she's been married to the same guy for twenty years.

On the other hand, Judith Krantz is a little mouse, and if you met her, you'd wonder where all her ideas come from. You could never imagine having a sexual conversation with her or with her husband—they look like a haberdashery salesman and his wife from the Bronx who made it big and have just moved to Long Island.

The Judith Krantzes of the world all seem to have the same line when they come on talk shows, mine or anyone else's: "The critics don't like us, but the public loves us. We're good storytellers and we know how to keep up the pace. My husband was a little embarrassed by my sex scenes but he understands." And so forth. Judith also thinks she's a gifted writer, and you can't convince her otherwise. They all think they are. Not one of them will admit they've got a great formula and have the public snowed pretty well. They think the critics don't like them because their books sell. They all think their books will be read years from now. I never met one who didn't think that. I like some of these writers personally—Jackie Collins is enormously bright and she's a lot of kicks, as is Sidney Sheldon—but as interviews they get a little boring. They all have very good discipline and good work habits. I don't believe any of them live the lives they write about. I think mainly they have wild imaginations.

One writer told me a remarkable story about his book tour that illustrates the kind of problem more serious authors encounter on the talk show circuit. He had written a novel about a man who, at the end of his life, dreams of what might have been. The character has never been sailing, although all of his life he has wanted to sail. The author was booked on a show in Baltimore, and when he walked onto the set he saw blown-up photos of seven different sailboats. He asked the host, "What's that for?"

"Well, there's so much sailing here in the Chesapeake," the host told him, "that we're going to show the boats and we'd like you to describe each one for the audience."

"Why?"

"Well, you've written a book about sailing . . ."

"I don't know anything about sailboats."

"You don't know anything about sailboats? Your book is all about sailing."

"It's a novel."

"A novel?! We never have novelists on." The host was screaming. "I don't know how to interview novelists! Novelists write fiction. How do I interview a novelist?"

Then, almost *sotto voce*, the host asked him, "Would you please fake it?"

So they gave him printed information to read and he did ten minutes of voice-overs about the boats. And they let him mention his book in passing.

The irony in all this is that the writers who are undervalued as good interviews are the serious novelists rather than the pop novelists and nonfiction and self-improvement writers who get most of the exposure on talk shows. Our best novelists rarely get on talk shows because the hosts, who are used to interviewing writers about the facts in their books, have an awfully tough time interviewing someone who made up the characters. I happen to believe, though, that you learn at least as much from novelists as from nonfiction writers, and some of

my favorite moments on the air have come in the presence of
serious authors.

Of course, even the most serious authors have a few clichés
of their own. They will tell you, for instance, that they write
for themselves and maybe a few close friends and don't much
care about money. Jimmy Breslin told me that he thinks that
kind of talk is baloney. "I'm writing for money first," he said,
"the reader second, and then myself." He also said that all
writers except him claim that their characters surprise them
and change on them as they're writing fiction. He's the only
novelist I've ever interviewed who said, "You control the
characters, they don't control you. That's intellectual bullcrap.
Characters don't take over. It's my hands, my typewriter, and
I determine what they'll do."

I've talked to a lot of writers about their different experiences with famous first books. It can break them, as it did
Thomas Heggen, the author of *Mr. Roberts*. Henry Fonda
told me that Heggen said to him, "Hank, I can't top this." He
wrote a novella and two plays—and then he killed himself.
Like most first works, *Mr. Roberts* was autobiographical—
Heggen had come out of the navy. Norman Mailer had come
out of the army when he wrote *The Naked and the Dead*, an
enormous best-seller whose specter loomed over the rest of
his career. Mailer told Joseph Heller that what made him love
John Kennedy was that Kennedy, at a time when Mailer was
known primarily for that first novel, told him, "I loved your
book *The Deer Park*"—a work that was much closer to
Mailer's heart.

To take the pressure off after his big first success, Mailer
told me, he diversified. He wrote some nonfiction, covered
fights for *Esquire*, wrote think pieces, reported on a political
campaign. The public accepted him in a variety of roles and
he began to hear less about his first book. Consequently, even
though he never wrote a novel to equal the first, he was able
to push the first book out of the way by doing other things.

He developed a style of putting himself into the narrative of nonfiction works such as *Armies of the Night*. He always thought he was a reporter; he felt that *The Naked and the Dead* was simply a pretty good war story based on true experiences and that was why people liked it so much.

Jim Bishop's most successful book, *The Day Lincoln Was Shot*, has sold fifteen million copies worldwide. It was originally rejected by twenty-seven publishers, including Random House. Bishop had a framed letter from Bennett Cerf on his wall, and all it said was "Dear Jim: The Day Lincoln Was Shot? Every schoolboy knows the story. Pass. Best, Bennett." The book won the Edgar award from the Mystery Writers of America, who said, in presenting the award to Bishop, "When we got to the last chapter, we didn't know what was going to happen."

I got to know Jim pretty well in Miami, and he came on my show several times to discuss the way he went about writing his books. When Bishop wrote *The Day Kennedy Was Shot*, for instance, he went to Fort Worth on November 21 of the year after the assassination and stayed in the same hotel room that John Kennedy had stayed in the night before he died. That's what I call research. Jim was awakened by a loud freight train at three-twenty A.M. The next morning, he asked the hotel manager about the freight train. The manager said, "I'm sorry, but we can't do anything about it, we've had it for ten years. That freight train goes by loaded with heavy goods every night. We sometimes tell our patrons they're going to awakened for a few minutes at three-twenty A.M." And that's how Jim came to write that Kennedy was awakened the night before he died at three-twenty.

Then Jim flew to Dallas and got in a car and slowly drove the route that the parade followed, so that when he looked around, he was seeing the things that Kennedy looked at on that day. How far advanced were the trees in losing their color by that time of year? He looked at the Zapruder film over and over to see which direction Kennedy was facing and then went back along that route to see what Kennedy could have seen. I really admire that kind of doggedness—and to be able to write about it in simple declarative sentences takes a special kind of talent and discipline. Jimmy Breslin is a big fan of simple declarative sentences. He told me that most writers find it hardest to write, "He opened the door and came in the room." They have to describe the door, the hand, the room, and everything in it.

Jim Bishop really was a fine reporter, as his many books attest. In fact, he was one of many reporters covering the trial of Adolf Eichmann in Israel in the early sixties. Eichmann was the only person ever executed in Israel, a country that does not have capital punishment; they killed him and then threw his ashes into the sea outside Israel's territorial waters. During the trial, Eichmann agreed to spend a day with one reporter, and only one, so the reporters had a pool and Bishop was picked to speak with Eichmann. He could write his own story about it, but he also had to share the information with the other reporters. Bishop went into Eichmann's cell and listened all morning to Eichmann's rationale for his deeds, trying to get an insight into the Nazi mentality. Lunch came, and Eichmann said to Bishop, "They brought bread again. Three months I've been here, I tell them every day no bread, and still they bring bread."

Then Eichmann banged on the door and asked to see the warden. Bishop went with him to the warden's office. Eichmann saluted the warden and said, "For three weeks, I've done everything in my power to stop having bread sent in with my meals. You know I do not eat bread. Please don't bring me bread."

The warden said, "I'm sorry, but we can't make individual meal requests in this prison. Every meal is made at the same time and delivered the same to each prisoner. Don't eat the bread if you don't want to."

"I'm your prisoner," Eichmann said. "I *have* to eat the bread."

Eichmann ate the bread that day as he did every other day he was there. When Bishop asked him why he ate the bread, he just said, "I'm a prisoner. I must do what I'm told."

I liked Erskine Caldwell a great deal. He was a tough interview, but once I got him going he was very honest with me. He said, "A good novelist is always a good journalist first." Caldwell thought of himself as a reporter who happened to tell a good story, in that regard not much different from a Jim Bishop. He told me that no one worth his salt ever sat down to write a great book. He said, "When I wrote *Tobacco Road*, I never said to myself, This is the great American novel. I never felt it was a novel that was going to change the way we think about the poor South. It was a story about people I knew. I am first and foremost a reporter—the novelist is just the reporter of his age. Sometimes I learn more about history by reading the novels of the period than by reading the history of the period."

Caldwell also said that he never compared a film with a book. When I asked him how he liked the movie *Tobacco Road* compared with his book, he said, "I didn't watch it as my book. I watched it as a movie and it was a pretty good movie. How do you film thoughts, anyway?"

I asked Caldwell how he went about gathering material for a book like *Tobacco Road*. He said, "I go down to the corner and I watch the parade. I listen to what the people say about the parade and I come back, and I give them different names. In *God's Little Acre*, I did the same thing. I understood the poor in the South; I knew that life and I knew those people. And I like making things up along the way."

*   *   *

Elmore Leonard, who writes perhaps the most convincing, realistic American crime novels, told me that he cannot fictionalize being in a city. He must be in a city to write about it. Leonard won't just go to Miami to take notes and then go home and write. He had to write *LaBrava* in Miami. You can't just tell him about some streets in New Orleans; he wants to be there while he's writing about it. Leonard said he could smell New Orleans, and when he wrote *LaBrava* in Miami, he opened his window so he could smell the Spanish flavors coming through. In that respect, he is a little like James Michener, who never writes about a place without being there. Michener sets up shop near a university and invites all the local scholars to come by, answer his questions, and tell him everything they know. When he wrote *Texas*, he found a place to live near Austin. "Always set up near the state school," Michener told me. "The people want to meet you and that's how you get your material."

I should add how much Elmore Leonard is enjoying his success after all those years of being unknown. He is a little like Louis L'Amour, who became a major seller after writing pulp books for years. They both always knew they could write. Mickey Spillane had the most aggressive attitude of all, however. "Writer, shmiter," he would say. "Do you tell a good story? Do people understand it, do they enjoy it?" If so, you're a good writer. By my yardstick, sales are very important. Do more people like to read my books than like to read your books? If so, I'm a better writer."

I said, "Do you mean to say that if a movie sells more tickets than another movie, it's a better movie?"

"Yeah. That's right."

"Okay, then," I said, "by your way of measuring, you're a better writer than Faulkner."

"Yeah, *much* better," he said with sincerity. "I tell a better story. My sentences don't lag and carry on. My characters are as real as his."

"Come on," I said.

"Hey! All of this is a fantasy trip. You ever meet any of Faulkner's people?"

"No. I never met Mike Hammer either."

"Fine!"

He was unflappable. Spillane was enjoying every minute of it, and he was really spirited. "I'm the best writer in the English language," he would say. "I don't have to write anymore, but anytime I want to write, I'll write anyway. I'll write a violent scene better than anybody, I'll write a love scene better than anybody, I'll write a death scene better than anybody."

I may not love his books, but I had to admire his chutzpah.

A mystery writer whose books I do love is John D. MacDonald. MacDonald died at the end of 1986, and he'll be sorely missed. He didn't give many interviews, but he used to come over from Sarasota on his boat, dock in Fort Lauderdale, and come down to do my show. When I first interviewed him, he had never been published in hardcover. He was one of the most famous paperback writers in America with his Travis McGee mysteries. I remember his telling me, "I'm having a hardcover book come out next year."

I congratulated him, but he waved it off. "My fans won't buy it," he said. "They're dollar-ninety-five readers. McGee wouldn't buy it."

If there's one common thought that runs through all the best writers I've met, it's that not one of them has ever said that he wanted to make a statement about race relations or some other issue, so he wrote this novel around it. Travis McGee certainly made a lot of political statements about overbuilding and zoning and things like that, but MacDonald never said, "Tonight, Travis McGee takes on the city council." He didn't begin by saying, "Today I'm going to teach

them about . . ." He felt that readers learned a lot from reading him, but the story came first. Every day of his life, he set
out to learn more, and he said that he had to fight his natural
inclination to be lazy. He loved other mystery writers, like
Ross MacDonald and Dashiell Hammett, and he once told
me, "I have trouble passing libraries without wanting to go
in."

James Dickey is a great poet whose claim to popular fame is a
novel, *Deliverance*, which was made into a hit movie. He also
wrote the screenplay for it, and most people may not know
that he played the menacing sheriff as well. Dickey has always
preferred poetry, though, because he doesn't like the wasted
words in fiction. He said, "When you write poetry, at least
theoretically each word has a meaning. There are no
throwaway words."

When I asked him why he wrote *Deliverance*, he said that
he wanted to try another form of writing just to see if he could
do it. "Most of the other poets of my acquaintance wanted to
write plays, but I've never been attracted to the theater. I
once thought of a bad pun when somebody asked me why I
never had wanted to write drama. I said, 'Because too many
American poets have been damned with faint plays.'"

His description of writing was unique. "So much of what I
do is just day labor," he said. "The way I write is predicated
on simply sitting there with the material and being in prox-
imity to it for a *long* time, trying one thing and then another
thing and then another thing and choosing among them."

John O'Hara was so bitter he surprised me. He thought he'd
never gotten his due, the way O'Neill and Steinbeck had, because he was writing about a particular type of person who
was often wealthy and lived in Pennsylvania, instead of some-

one like the Irish poor, as his contemporaries did. He felt he should have won a Nobel Prize and that he was the best damned writer of dialogue who ever lived. One thing I will say for John O'Hara is that he had a natural ear. I can read any one of his short stories—it could be about two people standing at a bus stop—and by the third page I know both of them. And there may be no descriptive writing at all, just conversation. O'Hara was one of the few great writers who *thought* he was a great writer. Mailer is another.

John Steinbeck did not think he was a great writer. Steinbeck told me, "I am a storyteller." He was the one who said Dostoyevsky was just a good storyteller.

I said, *"The Grapes of Wrath* changed American society. *Of Mice and Men* probably taught us more about interpersonal relationships—"

He cut me off before I could finish. "They were two damned good stories," he said.

CHAPTER 14

THE SOUL OF THE MATTER

Religious leaders have always interested me, though I'm not particularly religious myself. I don't have much respect for certain television evangelists, but some of the people I've encountered, even though I don't believe as they do, have made me question some of my own assumptions.

Archbishop Makarios, of the Greek Orthodox Church, caught me completely off-balance once. His attitude could be summed up in the question "How could you not believe?" He said to me, "Do you attach to anything? Are you plugged in? There's life coming out of you, but you're not attached. You sleep, you wake up, you eat, you function, your heart is beating—that's an accident? You demean yourself, you demean all of us to think it is an accident."

He said this without ever putting me down. That was twenty years ago and I can still remember the look on his face: "That's it? You really think this is all an accident?" And I remember the Greeks who came with him. I like to watch parishioners around someone they exalt, whether it's the people around Makarios or the people around Louis Farrakhan— all followers have the same kind of fervor.

Bishop James Pike scared me because I think that if I had spent a lot of time around him I would have become at least a partial believer. Pike was so honest and he was the only religious guest I've ever had who seemed to get in touch easily with his feelings. I said to him, "You know, you sound Jewish to me. Your thoughts sound Jewish."

"Oh," he said, "I *am* Jewish. All Christians are Jewish. Most of us forget it. If Christ appeared now and I told Him I was an Episcopalian, He would say, 'What is that?' We'd have to go find a rabbi. He wouldn't know what a priest is, what *Catholic* means. The only ceremonies He'd know would be Jewish, the only food He'd know would be kosher—Passover food. How could any Christian be anti-Semitic? We're Jews because our leader is a Jew."

Pike believed in séances, and after his son died he went to see a medium who put him in touch with the boy. I later interviewed the psychic who conducted the séance. In the second session, the psychic went into a trance and said to Pike, "Harvey wants to tell you that Poopsie's okay." Pike nearly fainted.

"When I was in England," he told me, "I bought my son a dog. The dog was given a household name that everyone called him, but we decided that we would have a name for the dog that just he and I would know—my wife wouldn't know this name, his wife wouldn't know. Only when we spoke to each other in private would we call the dog Poopsie. No one else knew that. How did the medium know?"

Pike called Billy Graham after the séance and said, "Billy, I love my faith and I love my Lord and I love my church, but there are two things I've always doubted. I've doubted the virgin birth, and I've doubted the Resurrection—life after death. And today I believe in the Resurrection, because I've communicated with my late son."

Graham said to him, "Aw, Jim, you don't want to believe all these psychics. You don't buy that, do you?"

"But Billy," Pike said, "it does mean that there is life after death—that's what we've been telling them."

"Yeah," Billy said, "but come on."

It struck Pike as humorous. He said to me, "The trouble with us religious leaders is that *we* want to be the ones. If my son had come to Billy Graham in a vision that Billy could bring to me, that would have been different. But Billy couldn't stand the psychic bringing it to me. If we get the message that Christ is returning tomorrow and *someone* is bringing Him here at two o'clock, and we all line up and hear two sets of footsteps on the cobblestones, each of us will be saying, 'I hope it's an Episcopalian' or 'I hope it's a Catholic priest.' By God, what if it's an agnostic black woman? What if it's a rabbi? Who's bringing Christ?"

I think Lenny would have liked Bishop Pike—they would have made a great pair. A lot of Lenny Bruce's biggest fans were young priests. Lenny was a great debunker, an exposer of moral and political phoniness, and maybe the priests responded to that.

Or maybe the young priests just liked the way Lenny thought. Once, for instance, I was having dinner with Lenny when he gave me a whole routine about how arbitrary sexual prohibitions were. I never saw him do this on stage, but he certainly could have. Lenny's theory was that society picked out the vagina as a taboo because it was a convenient thing to single out. But he said, "Suppose they picked out . . . elbows. You can never see your mate's elbow till you're married and never touch it. But they never mention or forbid any other body parts, including the genitals—just elbows. Now here's a typical scene in society: A man comes home a little early from work. His wife's in bed with another guy. That's all right. The husband hides in the closet looking for those elbows, man. Elbows covered! Whew! She's loyal! In the early days, they'd shoot you if your elbows touched at the dining room table by accident. And those goddamn hookers—just give you a quick glimpse of that elbow to get you all horny."

Lenny's point was that society built that fear into you, but it could be anything—elbows, chins, knees. I don't know whether Lenny knew it, but I've heard that for a long time it was the custom in the Vatican that when a woman had an audience with the Pope, her elbows had to be covered.

This was the kind of thing the hip young Catholic priests who came up in the early sixties, during the Vatican Council, responded to. They went to see Lenny perform and I would talk to them outside the clubs. The priests would say to me, "Why would God care about the word *fuck* as opposed to the word *war*?"

Lenny also felt that the Catholic hierarchy was out to get him—the Spellmans and their like. It's hard to prove, but it's not farfetched. Certainly, in his view, the kind of moral corruption he attacked was embodied in such men. They can't have taken it well.

However, I think it wasn't just the Catholic Church, but the religious leaders in general, who had it in for him, and the reason is that, back in 1958, Lenny had discovered the guiding principle behind the television evangelists of the world. He knew what they were all about: money.

Now, I don't think all television evangelists are hypocritical. For instance, Jerry Falwell is very easy to be around; I don't particularly feel any animosity toward him, no matter how much I may disagree with what he's saying. These preachers must have some quality about them to rise up in their field, and I would call their field "sales." Jerry Falwell is a wonderful salesman. If I went into a shoe store and Jimmy Swaggart was over there and Jim Bakker was over here and Jerry Falwell was next to both of them, I'd go up to Falwell. I

would trust that he would get me a good pair of shoes and that
he wouldn't con me all that much. In other words, I don't
believe that Jerry Falwell has a gold lamé rug in his car. I
don't think that's where his interest lies.

What I don't like is that his Sunday morning sermons differ
from his interviews. When he's interviewed on a talk show,
he'll say, for instance, that a homosexual could be president.
He said that to me. He said, of course, that he regarded homosexuality as a sin, but he wouldn't say that it affected a
man's ability to be a good president. Yet when he preaches,
he talks about homosexuality as a disease. I think that's just
his Sunday morning shtick. That's Jerry on stage. Like Herb
Cohen says: "It's all wrestling."

I also think Billy Graham really does believe, and I don't
think Graham ever liked the money aspect of his ministry. In
fact, I never heard Billy make a pitch. He always examined
himself, too. I was with Billy when he was examining his
thoughts about Martin Luther King. In the beginning, he was
a typical southern Baptist: "Who is this guy upsetting the ap-
ple cart?" he would say about King. He was a Nixon Republican. But then he sat next to Martin Luther King on a long
plane trip to South America, and that was when he began to
change, began to understand what King really wanted.

It would be an understatement to say I have mixed feelings
about many of these people, though. For instance, when
Jimmy Swaggart came on my show, he tried to convert me.
"Are you a believer, Larry?" he said.

"I'm Jewish," I said.

"I love the Jews," he said. "All you've got to do is take that
one step. Christ was Jewish—you gave us our leader. Larry,
take that one step."

When I had my heart attack, Oral Roberts said a prayer for
me on the air. But he had a funny way of putting it. "We're
gonna say a prayer today for a Jew person," he said. "He's not
a believer of our faith, but he's been very fair to us."

Recently when Oral came on my TV show, I asked him if a

person had to be Christian to be a healer or if there could be, say, a Jewish healer. He said yes, there could be a Jewish healer.

"Is there anything wrong with you physically?" I asked.

"I've had bursitis for some time," Roberts said, "and it's bothered me quite a bit lately."

I put my hand on his shoulder, on the air, and said, "Lord, take this man's bursitis away!"

And he said, "I feel better already."

"A Jewish healer!" I said. The sad thing about all this is that, while I was just having fun, I think Oral Roberts took it seriously.

After a while most of these religious people begin to seem like an Amway convention, or maybe Herbalife. All the women look the same, all the men look the same. And the product doesn't matter anymore. The purveyors make you feel that your life is going to change because you're going to sell something, which you will then deliver to someone's home. It ain't the Herbalife. It ain't the Amway product. It's them, it's your new friends. In a normal sales organization, the product is usually the thing that is talked about. At a radio convention, for example, the thing most talked about is "What can we do to please the public?" or "What's the hot new format?" At an Amway convention, you will rarely hear the word *soap*. Go to a meeting of television evangelists. How many times will you hear the word *God*? Maybe when they preach, but on the floor? God is just the vehicle. They're in the sales business.

To paraphrase *How to Suceed in Business Without Really Trying*, God is wickets to them. Their product is God, but his name doesn't really matter. They buy time on the satellite just like the Home Shopping Club. You and I might send in money for a cubic zirconia ring; other people send in money for God. I think Lenny knew that a long time ago, but I've only recently come to appreciate how insightful he was.

Tammy Faye Bakker falls into the category of satellite sales people. She called me at home after the evangelist Reverend John Ankerberg had been on my CNN show and had revealed the most damaging information so far in the PTL scandal, all sorts of financial and personal misdoings. "*Larrrrry,* why did you put him *onnn?* You knew he was gonna hurt us."

She'd been on my show before the scandal and she liked me. "Tammy," I said, "the producers booked him. I didn't know what he was going to say." And I didn't. When I arrived at the studio on the night of that show, my producer said to me, "You're in for some night. All the press is tuned in and Reverend Ankerberg is going to make some revelations."

"Who's Reverend Ankerberg?" I said.

She started to fill me in and I said, "Don't tell me anything else. I don't want to know anything; I'll just keep going." Most of my questions were "Anything else?" I wanted to re-act. When he claimed that Bakker was homosexual, that was the first I'd heard it—and I still haven't heard anything to substantiate the claim. I told Tammy Faye all this and asked her if she would like to appear on my show to respond. She and Jim were going to come on and then they backed out.

Yet people buy them. Howard Rosenberg, the Pulitzer Prize–winning journalist for the *Los Angeles Times,* put them in perspective: "I'll tell you what's amazing about these people," he said. "I didn't buy Gary Hart for one minute. When he gave that press conference after the Donna Rice story broke, I said, 'Guilty.' But I watched Jim and Tammy Bakker for ten minutes, and I was already writing out a check."

Jim Bakker told a friend of mine that the Fox network had talked to Bakker about his taking over the *Joan Rivers Show.* Bakker's idea was that if he took the show, his first guest would be Gary Hart. To me, that is the epitome of American chutzpah.

It wouldn't be entirely inappropriate, though. Political corruption and spiritual corruption have something in common, because both occupations require a front of sheer probity in ways that, say, show business doesn't. We really don't care if some Hollywood star is cheating on his wife because he usually isn't preaching anything to the contrary, nor does he have his finger on the button. It's more than that, however. Somewhere inside we still retain the cherished illusion that political and religious leaders *ought* to be free of corruption. We retain it, even though we are disillusioned time and again.

For all that, I wasn't surprised when the Gary Hart scandal broke. I had never heard of Donna Rice, but I happened to know the woman whom the *Washington Post* was going to name in the story it never ran, the story that supposedly convinced Hart to quit the campaign. Hart had originally invited this woman to go to Bimini the weekend he took Donna Rice instead. The woman declined, she told me, because she didn't want to hurt his chances in the coming election.

Hart had no regard for caution. The woman I know worked for a member of Congress, and Hart would call and send her flowers with his name on them, as if the people who worked in the office with her didn't know who he was. She told me she used to say to him, "Gary, you drive a red convertible sports car with Colorado plates and it's parked in front of my house at two in the morning."

Hart was on my radio and TV shows a number of times. He is the only candidate or senator I've ever known who always came to the studio alone. No one came with him—no press representative, no aides, no entourage. I asked the woman why that was, and she said, "Because he was coming to my house afterward. He'd call up and say, 'Watch the show, and I'll be over in an hour.'"

So I wasn't surprised when it finally all caught up to him— just that he handled it so badly. How could he not realize that it's the hypocrisy that gets us, every time? Gary Hart would have come out of the whole mess better if he'd just said after the scandal broke, "You're right, I screwed up, I was wrong." It was the lying and the defensiveness, those righteous deni-

als, that got him in deep trouble. Be the first one to acknowl-
edge that you made a mistake, and there's a chance people
will say, "All right, he screwed up, but at least he was honest." It defuses their anger. And he would have left them with
nothing to say. To paraphrase the song title: What can they
say after you've said you're sorry, before they even asked you?

It reminds me of a story Bing Crosby once told me. Bing
went to the Santa Anita racetrack one day, and out in front of
the track he ran into a fellow named Joe Frisco. Joe Frisco
was an old-time vaudeville comedian who used to stutter as
part of his act. Frisco said, "B-B-B-Bing, c-c-c-could ya loan
me t-t-t-twenty dollars? I left the house with no m-m-m-
money today." Bing lent him the money and went inside.

After the fifth race, Bing went back to the pavilion to use
the men's room. On the way, he passed a table and there was
Joe Frisco surrounded by five women, drinking champagne.
Bing asked a waiter what was going on. The waiter told him
that Frisco had hit the daily double and won about four thousand dollars. Bing decided to try to make him look bad. He
figured he'd go over to the table and say something like "Hey,
Joe, give me the twenty dollars I loaned ya in front of the
track today."

He started heading toward the table, and Frisco saw him
coming. Joe took twenty dollars out of his pocket, waved it at
Bing, and said, "Hey, k-k-k-kid, sing 'M-M-M-Melancholy B-
B-B-Baby'!"

Gary Hart could have learned a few things from Joe Frisco.
And so could Tammy Faye Bakker.

CHAPTER 15

NOBODY ASKED ME, BUT . . .

Jimmy Cannon used to have a column called "Nobody Asked Me, But . . . ," and I could do worse than to emulate it here. Trying to string together stories in a book of this sort is a little like trying to put your car engine back together and coming up each time with a few parts left over. However you try to rearrange them, there is no way to fit these remaining stories into a coherent narrative. So here they are.

A couple of years ago, before I had my heart attack and stopped smoking, Larry Hagman adopted me for the Great American Smokeout. It didn't work, but he called me eleven times that day from the set of *Dallas*. I picked up the phone once and he said, "I know it. You have it in your hand, don't you?" Guys who think like that are really bizarre. I'd had him on my show two days before to discuss the Smokeout, and I guess he decided to try to help me, whether I wanted to be helped or not.

Larry was very congratulatory after I quit. Martin Sheen, who still smokes, told me that the only time he ever met Larry Hagman was at a party at Hagman's house in Malibu. Sheen was on the back porch and he lit up a cigarette. Hagman, who was walking on the beach maybe a hundred yards away, came running, hurdling, jumped onto the porch, grabbed the cigarette out of Sheen's mouth, and crushed it out. That's obsession.

I don't smoke at all now, but I don't mind if my guests smoke, and I tell them so. I realize that everyone isn't so casual about it, though. If Tony Randall comes on a talk show, not only can the host not smoke, but Tony doesn't want to *see* anyone smoking. If there's someone in the control room smoking behind the glass, Randall won't do the show. His reason is that he cannot stand to see self-inflicted death. Hagman said to me, "You let people smoke around you?"

I said, "Sure."

"They're killing you," he said.

Sinatra stopped smoking a couple of years ago on his seventieth birthday. He had been smoking since he was fifteen— it's pretty amazing to me that someone could quit after fifty-five years. However, the champion of all time in that department had to be Hal Roach.

Hal Roach is the great director of comedy films who worked with Laurel and Hardy, Charlie Chaplin, Buster Keaton, Harold Lloyd, Our Gang. He's ninety-six years old. He sold his studios when he was fifty-three and he's done very little since. Recently the Laurel and Hardy films have been colorized, so he gets a piece of that. But he always says he's in the business, he's always looking for properties—he just hasn't found any in the last forty years.

We did a show on the colorizing of Laurel and Hardy, and as a favor to me, Roach came on and talked about his career. He happened to be on my show at a time when I was still smoking, and he said to me, "I'm ninety-three, you know, and I quit last Saturday."

I was mildly surprised. I asked him, "How many years had you been smoking?"

"Let's see," he said. "I started when I was fifteen, fifteen from ninety-three . . . I guess I'd been smoking seventy-eight years."

"Seventy-eight years?" I was really impressed now. "Why did you stop? You had the game beat."

"I coughed," he said. "I was playing cards last Saturday and I smoked a couple of packs, and when I got home I coughed my head off. So I said the hell with it."

He cracked me up. Hal Roach made one serious movie in his whole life and it was nominated for the Academy Award in 1939: *Of Mice and Men*, with Lon Chaney, Jr., and Burgess Meredith. I said, "What an achievement. All the comedies you've done and then to make *Of Mice and Men*. You must be so proud."

And Hal Roach said, "It coulda used a few laughs."

Speaking of laughs, nothing could compare with the Miami Beach politics of the fifties and sixties. They were so eccentric that I don't think anyone who wasn't actually there could imagine what the scene was like. Members of the city council would bring pastrami sandwiches to meetings. Senior citizens exerted enormous control over the city. I remember once trying to bring in the Houston Astros to have their spring training at Flamingo Park in Miami Beach. I was put on the committee and had to give the mayor's report to the council. There must have been six hundred senior citizens at the meeting and they were paying no attention to me. If the senior citizens were uninterested, the city council was uninterested, so I was getting no attention from either group. I was talking baseball and everyone there was seventy-two years old. So in a loud voice, I said, "Ladies and gentlemen, the general manager of the Houston Astros has asked me to tell you that he supports Medicare."

I got a standing ovation, and the council voted 7–0 to en-
courage my further efforts to bring in the Astros.

More than in most places, politics in Miami was power-of-
personality politics. We had a mayor named Chuck Hall who
went on to become mayor of Metropolitan Dade County.
Chuck was very handsome, slim with gray hair, and had been
a travel agent. He had no depth, no knowledge of the issues
at all, but he knew how to shake hands and how to look good.
He's dead now, but while he was alive he had an uncanny
ability to focus attention on himself. Dade County consisted of
twenty-seven municipalities and a central government, so
there were twenty-seven mayors, plus the county mayor. I
used to emcee a lot of dinners, and I witnessed the ways in
which Hall would make an entrance; it drove the other mayors crazy. Sometimes he would arrange to come in while they
were serving the baked Alaska. For baked Alaska they would
turn out all the lights and flame the cake. When the flames
reflected off the ceiling, the floor would appear to ripple, and
at that moment Chuck Hall would stroll in—walking on
water.

Here's a true story about Hall that sounds like something
out of a political satire. Lyndon Johnson was scheduled to
speak in Miami sometime in 1965. He had spoken in Tampa
in the morning and then would fly to Miami for the afternoon
speech. Dade County's twenty-seven mayors were lined up at
the airport as a delegation to greet the president—all except
Chuck Hall. The question of the hour was not whether Chuck
would show up, but how he would do it. It turned out Hall
had gone to Tampa that morning, corralled LBJ's PR man,
and said, "I'm the mayor of Dade County and I missed my
flight out. I'm heading a delegation to greet the president at
the airport. Could I please fly down on Air Force One?"

The fellow said they were pretty crowded already. Chuck
said, "That's okay, I'll sit on the john. No problem."

So he flew down to Miami in the airplane lavatory, which

was located right next to the exit door. They landed at Miami International, with the twenty-seven mayors waiting by the plane for the president. A flower girl ran up to the airplane. The door opened, the stairs were rolled up, the band played "Hail to the Chief," and Chuck Hall walked off the plane. Hall walked directly to the microphone that had been set up for Johnson to deliver his address, and announced, "Ladies and gentlemen, my good friend the president of the United States, Lyndon Johnson."

We could see Johnson leaning over to his aide, probably saying, "Who the hell is this?"

Miami was crazy in other ways, too. Ben Novack and Harry Mufson were two Miami Beach hotel owners who had been partners at one time, but they broke up and grew to hate each other. Ben Novack went on to build the Fontainebleau Hotel on the old Firestone estate. Harry Mufson built the Eden Roc next door. Novack hated Mufson so much that he built an extra building on the side of the Fontainebleau, just to put Mufson's pool in the shade. To have a pool in the sun, Mufson had to restructure his whole setup, run pipes down to the beach and build a new pool next to the water. It then was as long a walk to the pool as it was to the ocean.

I was part of all that nonsense because I was broadcasting a show called *Surfside 6* from a houseboat off the beach. That was an extraordinary time to be in Miami, the late fifties and early sixties. The city was the playpen of America—nothing mattered, nothing was real. We had palm trees and Hialeah, money and women. It will never be like that again. But the memories are just plain silly sometimes. Like George Jessel, who was in his sixties, coming to do my television show accompanied by a twenty-three-year-old woman. He was being made up while she sat there watching. He leaned over and whispered to me, "I know what you're thinking. You look at

her, you look at me, I'd think the same thing. Don't worry—if
she dies, I'll get another girl."

I emceed Jackie Gleason's birthday party every year in
Miami, and at the second one we did there, in 1965, Bishop
Fulton Sheen was one of the entertainers. The theme of
Bishop Sheen's speech was repetition. He said, "Sometimes
we're all accused, even the Church, of doing the same thing
over and over again. I've known Jackie a long time. My
brother had a baby, and the baby got to be four or five years
old. And whenever there would be a family gathering, Jackie
would come and he would do something funny to amuse us,
and the baby would say, 'Do it again!' Jackie would do it again
and the baby would say, 'Do it again!' Why do you think the
baby wanted Jackie to keep doing it again? Because it was
funny and he was comfortable with it, the way we are comfortable with our church, comfortable with those we love, and
we're comfortable with people like Jackie Gleason. So, when
he comes on this stage, whether he comes as the Poor Soul,
or Reggie, or Ralph Kramden, or just Jackie, why don't we all
say, 'Do it again.'" He had me crying.

I once emceed a dinner honoring Gleason on the roof of the
Doral Hotel, one of the most spectacular settings in all of
Miami Beach. The owners didn't trust that there would be
stars out every night, so on the ceiling of the rooftop dining
room—called the Starlight Room—they installed seven thousand little lightbulbs to imitate the stars. At this dinner, the
owner of the Doral, Alfred Kaskel, came around to meet
Gleason. Jackie and I were sitting together with Hank Meyer
when he came over and said, "Mr. Gleason, it's an honor to
meet you."

And Jackie said, "Mr. Kaskel, one of your lightbulbs is
out."

Kaskel went crazy. He looked up at the ceiling with all its
little lights. "Which one?!"

"Hey," Jackie said, "it's your hotel, I don't want to tell you."

Duke Zeibert has a story about Jackie, too. "You know, Toots Shor's restaurant was very famous," Duke said, "but it had a reputation for bad food. I'm not going to comment on that one way or the other, but it's a fact that everybody used to kid Toots about the food. So one afternoon Jackie Gleason was holding court at the big banquette that separated the bar from the dining room, and there were about six or seven of us with him. A loud electrical storm was raging outside during lunch, and suddenly there was a tremendous clap of thunder and the lights went out in the restaurant. Gleason jumped up and went into one of his theatrical poses, his arms spread wide and a look of mock terror on his face. 'My God!' he shouted. 'They electrocuted the chef!'"

In his time, Jackie was one of the most powerful people in television. Everybody—sponsors, networks, stars—had to bow to him. I once asked Gleason, "When do you have clout?"

"When you have it," he said. "If you ask the question, you don't have it. If you have it and you know you have it, you have it. If you don't have it and think you have it, you have it. But if you have it and don't know you have it, you don't have it." Think about that.

Speaking of clout, the first time I went to San Francisco, I was working in Miami and not making a lot of money, just enough to take my first wife, Alene, for a trip. Jesse Weiss, of Joe's Stone Crab, said to me, "Hey, we'll do it up right. When you land, there'll be a nice surprise for you."

We flew coach to San Francisco, and as we were getting off the plane, a man in a tan overcoat and hat came up to me. I don't know how he knew who I was, but he said, "Mr. King, Mrs. King? Come right with me."

He took us to a limo and once we were inside he introduced himself. "I'm agent Sanders with the Federal Bureau of Investigation, and I'll be happy to take you anywhere you'd like to go while you're in San Francisco."

Hoover was a great public relations man, it was later explained to me. "You're hosting a talk show in Miami," Jesse said. "You're writing a column. How do you think the FBI builds friends around the country?"

Their thinking was fairly sound. After all, how could I hate the FBI after that? A PR expert I later interviewed explained that what the FBI gets out of its courtesies is attachment and loyalty. As a result, if, as someone in the media, you hear something bad about the FBI, you're apt to go to the FBI before you run with it.

The one time Hoover's PR gesture could have helped him, though, it all happened so fast I didn't have time to think about it. Back in the fifties and early sixties, it was part of the public mind-set to believe that J. Edgar Hoover could do no wrong. I suppose the stories about how strange he could be had already begun to circulate, but I had never heard anybody knock him publicly. He was the classic American hero. As the sixties wore on, that mind-set was severely shaken, to say the least. People began to realize that the government could make mistakes, that we could lose a war. And I could have a guy like Los Angeles Chief of Police Parker on the radio.

In 1965, Miami hosted a national convention of police chiefs. It was right after the Watts riots in L.A., and I thought it would be interesting to have the Los Angeles police chief on to discuss them. He was one of those typical tough old cops who seemed to proliferate then, as patriotic as they come. The show went pretty much as expected, until I asked what I thought was a harmless question. "You must work with the FBI a lot in a city the size of Los Angeles," I said. "Tell me, what is it like dealing with them?"

"Phoniest organization I ever met in my life," Parker said,

without missing a beat. "They're all PR. Dubuque, Iowa, probably has a better police force than those guys. I'll take any cop walking a beat in Los Angeles and stack him up against any agent of the FBI in a criminal investigation. All they know how to do is ask for funds. They investigate only the cases they think they can crack—they never take the really tough cases. J. Edgar Hoover is a phony and a fraud."

Even if I had wanted to return a favor to the FBI, Parker gave me no chance—he just went on nonstop. I had never heard anything like it, especially from a police official. The next day, two FBI agents came to the studio and asked for a copy of the tape.

I don't know what became of Parker, but I never heard from him again.

Once I interviewed three men who had been stationed at Pearl Harbor on the day the Japanese attacked and who were now tour guides there. One of them had a particularly hairy story.

On December 6, 1941, he had gotten leave until seven A.M. the next day. He went into Honolulu, about twelve miles away, met a girl there, and spent the night with her. The next morning, he didn't get up until six-thirty. It was a lovely Sunday morning, but he didn't have time to enjoy it because if he didn't make it back to base by seven o'clock sharp he'd be doing time in the brig. He got dressed in a hurry, said good-bye, and began driving his car down the highway to Pearl Harbor. His reveries were interrupted by the sight of a lone airplane flying above the highway toward him.

While he was trying to figure out why one of our fighters would be out drilling so early on a Sunday, the plane started shooting at him. The bullets went through his windshield, just missing him. He rolled out of the car and down an embankment, from which he watched his car go up in flames fifty yards down the highway. He didn't see the zero on the plane until it was past him. And from that embankment, he watched the Japanese bomb Pearl Harbor. He couldn't go anywhere because the planes were all over the place, strafing and bombing. He got back to the base three hours later, to find that his barracks had taken a direct hit and that most of his buddies there were dead, along with several friends who had been aboard the USS *Arizona*.

The man served in the Pacific through the war, came back to Honolulu, and never left again. He's now a retired automobile salesman and he works part time as a guide on the *Arizona*. He told me that about seventy percent of the visitors are Japanese. Although he sometimes breaks down and starts crying while conducting tours, few people ask him what he was doing that morning—yet, he said, the experience of having his entire life change in a matter of minutes was something he never got over. The worst of it, he said, was the great guilt he suffered from having slept late and not being in the barracks when his friends died.

Mike Burke, who was president of the Yankees, gave me one of the best images of fear I've ever heard. During World War II, he was in the OSS, working with the French Resistance. One time, he parachuted into France behind enemy lines and was supposed to be picked up by the French underground. He bailed out of his plane alone in the middle of the night— he was the only one going in. As he got near the ground, he saw seven guys standing there with guns on their shoulders. There was no point in trying to yell to them. He just had to wait till he hit the ground—or until they opened fire. He told me it was the most helpless feeling he had ever experienced.

Feelings of another sort were the subject with Rollo May. May, the psychologist and author of *Love and Will*, told me that sex is in the brain—not only that, but the number one element of sex appeal is a sense of humor. He felt that someone who can make you laugh has as much chance of attracting you as someone with the best body in the world. It wasn't surprising for him to see Ava Gardner marry Mickey Rooney. May said it was completely logical. In fact, he felt that a Mickey Rooney might grow tired of an Ava Gardner faster than the other way around.

Sophia Loren had much the same idea. It's a myth, she said, that pretty women are always attracted to handsome men. She gave the lie to that myth herself by marrying Carlo Ponti. Sophia said to me, "Do you know what a magnificent man Carlo Ponti is? If I could only tell you how little looks mean to a woman beyond the first meeting. The first time I met Carlo Ponti, I said, 'Who is this little guy?' After talking to him for five minutes, he wasn't little and he wasn't funny-looking anymore. His voice, his charm, and his sense of humor were so appealing that I started falling in love almost from the beginning."

Sophia's best line, however, was when she quoted a friend of hers who really understood this principle. Her friend once said, "What the hell does Arthur Miller see in Marilyn Monroe?"

Speaking of sex, when David Ogilvy of Ogilvy and Mather, the advertising agency, was on my show, he told me about what turned out to be one of his most successful advertising campaigns. Back in the sixties, Comet was the number one cleanser by far in the country. I don't remember exactly, but I think he said Comet had something like eighty percent of the market. Needless to say, this had the people at Ajax rather uncomfortable, so they hired Ogilvy and Mather to do something about it.

When David got the Ajax account, he began doing a lot of research, and one of the areas his people studied was the sexual fantasies of American women. They found that women in this country fantasized most when they were washing dishes. From that bit of information, they came up with their ad campaign—the White Knight riding into town brandishing his lance. The lance, as Ogilvy explained it, was the penis. The White Knight stuck his penis through the kitchen window, and suddenly the dishes got sparkling white. He was all in white on a white horse—the knight on a white charger, he said, was the ultimate female fantasy at that time.

When he gave the concept to the company that made Ajax, they went nuts. "Are you crazy?" they said. "We're gonna put a penis in our TV ad?"

Ogilvy said, "Look, if it's easier for you to see it as a magical way for these housewives to clean dishes by touching them with his gleaming lance, fine. But what it is basically is that they're getting laid."

Within six months of launching the campaign, Ajax had turned things completely around and had eighty percent of cleanser sales.

I've had some amusing revelations on my show. Rosemary Clooney and I were talking about one of her biggest hits, "Come on-a My House," which came out in 1951. She completely surprised me when she told me who had written the lyrics to that song. She said that she went into the studio and Mitch Miller showed her the song and said, "This is going to be a hit."

She took one look at the silly lyrics and said, "You gotta be kidding."

"My friend wrote the music," said Mitch, "and William Saroyan wrote the lyrics."

"Saroyan? But he's won a Pulitzer Prize."

She recorded the song, but as she was leaving the studio she said, "This is the dumbest song I ever heard." Two months later she was walking down Broadway and every record store had it coming out of their speakers.

That story reminds me of Erroll Garner. Garner may have been the greatest technical piano player who ever lived, but he couldn't read or write a note of music. He told me he was driving in his car one day when he started humming a tune. His friend said, "Man, that's pretty."

Garner said "Yeah, I heard it somewhere."

A week later they were in the car again, and Garner was still humming the same tune. He said, "I've got to find out where I heard this song. I can't get it out of my head."

His friend said, "Are you sure you heard it?"

"I'm positive," Erroll said.

His friend said, "Let's write it down, just to be sure."

Erroll didn't know how to write music, so the friend wrote it down for him. It turned out to be "Misty," which would become Garner's most famous tune.

Ella Fitzgerald isn't a great interview, but she has a kind of simplicity that, in comparison to the extraordinary complexity of her talents as a singer, makes her all the more captivating. Barbra Streisand once said to me, "Ella Fitzgerald is not only the best singer in the world, but there's no one in second place."

Streisand could sit and analyze music for hours, as she did the first time I met her: interpretation of music, what people like, hitting high notes, keys, all of that. But like a lot of great musicians, Ella doesn't know from music theory. She just sings a song and blows everyone away. I asked her what she focused on when she was singing "How High the Moon," when she went into her scat singing. She said, "Mostly, Larry, I'm just really having a good time."

"But are you aware," I asked, "that Count Basie said you are a genuine musical instrument and that your voice is doing things voices aren't supposed to do?"

"I've heard that, but I can't see it. I get up and I just love to sing."

Ella has absolutely nothing of the egotistical performer or the show business celebrity about her. She is more like an aunt that you grew up with who'd come to your house and crochet and bake muffins. But then Aunt Ella picks up a mike and sings better than anybody ever sang. I treasure her for that.

From what I've been told, being born blind is less of a handicap than going blind at some time in your life. If you have never seen anything, it's still an *enormous* inconvenience, to say the least, but it's not as bad as going blind. Jazz pianist George Shearing explained to me the difference between the way objects are perceived by you and me and by a person blind from birth. He said, "A table is a form or structure to you, but to me it's a passage outlet." What he meant is that a table is not a three-dimensional object, but something he moves around or sits next to. He doesn't have the same frame of reference. "A table is just a point of spatial reference to me. I can't dream in color because I don't know what color is. But I dream in images."

I once asked Ray Charles how far back in his life he experienced racial prejudice. When he was a kid, he said, he was sent to a segregated school for the blind in Florida. At that time, there would have been separate schools for the two races, but for financial reasons—because there weren't enough blind kids—there was only one school, but it was segregated inside. The black kids sat on one side of the classroom, the white kids sat on the other, even though they couldn't see one another. If a kid sat on the wrong side by accident, he would have to be told by the teacher to go to the proper side. The teachers had to explain race to the kids, who couldn't understand it because they had no concept of color or what the difference between black and white could be. I told the story to Shearing and he almost died laughing.

Another funny story came from Danny Kaye. It was about his heart surgery and began this way:

"I'm sitting home watching Johnny Carson one night around eleven thirty, and I start to get tingles in all my fingers. My wife isn't home, the butler has the night off, and so does the driver. I call my doctor. I say, 'Doc, I got these tingles in my fingers.' He says, 'Danny, I don't like that. You're seventy years old . . . meet me in Cedars of Lebanon emergency room. Better safe than sorry.'"

"Okay," Danny said, "I don't have my driver, so I drive over myself, park in the lot across the street, and go inside the hospital. My doctor meets me there, gives me an examination, can't figure it out, and they check me into the hospital to run some more tests. Five days later, they determine it's a blockage and do open-heart surgery."

Somewhere along the line, however, Danny contracted hepatitis, so instead of staying in the hospital for two weeks, he ended up staying there from February till August, until he got rid of it. It turned into a long, drawn-out siege.

Sometime in July, a friend came to visit, and the friend said, "Danny, you been here so long—what the hell happened?" Danny told him.

"Well, I'm sitting home, I'm watching Johnny Carson, and my fingers start to tingle. I call my doctor, he says, 'I don't like that, Danny. Meet me at the hospital.' I drive over to— My *car*! My *car* is in a pay lot!" He hadn't thought of it since February. The slip was still in his jacket pocket, so he told his friend to go over to the lot and get the manager. The manager came back.

"Is the car still there?" Danny said. "Is it okay?"

The manager said, yeah, fine, and he handed him the bill. He owed them nineteen hundred dollars for the parking! He asked the manager, "Didn't you think there was something funny about this car? Didn't you inquire? Wasn't it a little unusual?" The guy said, "Yeah, Mr. Kaye, we thought it was a little unusual. But it was a new car, we figured someone's bound to come for it someday. So we just sort of, uh, took care of it. We washed it once a week." Nineteen hundred dollars.

I went to the racetrack with Bing Crosby the day after I interviewed him, and he told me how a racetrack can reduce your ego if you're a celebrity. He said he once walked into the grandstand on a bet that he wouldn't be recognized. A friend of his had bet him that nobody would come up to him at the track because when people are betting the horses they don't care about anything else. As Earl Weaver once put it, when the horses go into the home stretch, six naked women could walk across the grandstand and not one head would turn. Sure enough, no one came over to Bing, asked for an autograph, or even stared. Finally Bing got on line to place a bet, and because he hadn't been concentrating on betting—he was looking around in astonishment that he wasn't being recognized— he took a little time at the window getting his bet down. When he finished, he turned around to the guy behind him on line to apologize. He said to me, "I took my face—Bing Crosby's face—put it right in this guy's face, and said, 'I'm sorry.' And the guy said, 'Move, creep.'"

Crosby was fascinated with practical jokes. He knew some classic practical jokers, and he loved to tell stories about their exploits. One of his favorites was about the days when Victor Mature had just come to Hollywood and was hot to trot, making it with every woman in sight. A fellow Bing knew wanted to teach Mature a lesson, so he invited him to a classy dinner party and told him, "We're having an orgy at such and such a house, and here's how we do it." He then told him to come in an overcoat with nothing underneath, because they liked to eat dinner in the nude and then screw all night, and to arrive at nine o'clock sharp.

The dinner actually started at eight, and the guy playing the joke didn't bother to let anyone else in on it, aside from the butler. He told the butler that Victor Mature was coming at nine and that he was a little eccentric, so the butler should answer the door nude for him and then go get dressed. According to Bing, Mature arrived at nine, saw that the butler was nude, took off his overcoat, and handed it to the butler, who pointed out the door to the dining room. Mature strolled in to face eighteen studio heads and stars having a sit-down dinner in full formal attire.

Crosby also told me about an accountant who worked at Paramount and who was the world's most meticulous man. Everything about his work had to be just so. His clothes had to be perfectly fit as well, and his hat was custom-made with his initials monogrammed on the inside band. Crosby, Hope, and a couple of other guys who knew the accountant pretty well went out and got a hat two sizes bigger—the same make and style, with the same initials monogrammed inside—and switched hats. The accountant came out of his office, put on the hat, and it slid down to his ears. He was chagrined beyond belief, but when he looked inside the hat he saw his own initials. He started feeling his head as if maybe it had shrunk. He put paper inside the brim for the time being, so it would fit all right until he could get it sized. The next day he came in and hung up his hat with the paper in it, and while he was working in his office, they took his old hat, put paper in it, and hung it up. He came out, got his hat, and now it's a beanie. The guy went berserk.

Remember Howard Morris, the second banana on *Your Show of Shows*? Carl Reiner told me that when he hired Howard

he welcomed him to the show but warned him about Mel
Brooks, who was a writer for the show. "Mel is a little crazy,"
he said. "If he does something crazy, never mention it either
to him or to us because it will pass. Don't even tell me because you'll lose your job."

Reiner then went to Mel and told him what he'd told Morris.
Mel said, "Wonderful." Three days later, Mel took Howard to
lunch, and as they were walking back, Mel grabbed Howard,
pushed him into an alley, and said, "Gimme your wallet!"

Howard gave him the wallet and nobody said anything
about it for five years. Mel kept the wallet, Howard quietly
got new ID cards, driver's license, and whatever else was in
it. He never mentioned the incident to anyone, and Mel
never did another crazy thing, but Howard would never go
out alone with him again. When the show went off the air,
they gave the wallet back to him with the money and everything else intact.

Harry Morton, who is in his eighties now and lives in Florida,
used to operate nightclubs and manage performers such as Jan
Murray. He was a funny man himself, although he never did a
stage act, and he pulled off one of the most elaborate practical
jokes of all time. Because of the nature of his work, Harry
kept late hours and liked to sleep till noon. There was a guy
on his block who made a lot of noise in the morning, and no
matter how nicely Harry asked him, he would never let Harry
get any sleep. The guy drove him crazy and Harry vowed that
he'd get even someday. The guy came over to him one day
and said, "Look in my driveway, Harry, and tell me what you
see."

"I see a Volkswagen," said Harry.

"I got a Volkswagen, Harry. *You* should get a Volkswagen.
This car gets good mileage." He went back in his house and
Harry got an idea.

"I get home late at night," he told me. "So every night I stop at a gas station and buy gallons of gas. I get to this guy's house and I pour the gas into his tank. Two weeks later, the guy comes up to me and says, 'Har-*ry*, this car! I'm getting three hundred miles to the gallon, Harry, this car don't lose gas! I've got the magic car of all time.'"

Then, for the next two weeks, Harry siphoned gas *out* of the guy's car. "Harry," the guy now said, "I was getting two, three hundred miles a gallon, now I'm getting six, seven. I'm running out of gas on street corners. You gotta help me."

Harry suggested they go to the Volkswagen dealer he bought the car from. "I walk a little behind the guy," Harry said, "and signal to the head of the service department that this guy is a little crazy. The guy says to the head of the service department, 'Listen, I'm having a little problem. The first two weeks I was getting three hundred miles per gallon, now I'm getting six.'"

A year later the guy was quietly getting thirty-eight miles to the gallon and was very happy about it.

My sports guests have done some pretty surprising things over the years, but none so impulsive as Joey Giardello. He had been middleweight champion and had served a year in prison for malicious assault. Before we went on, I said, "Joey, I'm going to have to ask you about the prison term."

"Go ahead," he said, "I've got a standard answer."

I got to the point in the interview when I wanted to ask about prison, and I said, "Well, Joey, there came a time in your life when you went to prison."

He grabbed his microphone *and* my microphone and shouted into them, "I was framed! It was a no-good, dirty, lousy frame. The Mafia was involved—it was a setup!" He raved on while I nearly fell off my chair.

*   *   *

Then there was Earl Weaver, who was just talking sports
when he suddenly told me about the time he said to Hank
Peters, "Get me Garry Templeton from the St. Louis Cardinals and I'll win three pennants in a row."

"Earl, it's not generally known," Hank said, "but Garry
Templeton is a cocaine user."

"Yeah?" said Weaver. "A hundred hits left-handed and a
hundred hits right-handed? Get me him *and* his dealer."

Jon Miller, the sportscaster for the Baltimore Orioles, was
once asked by a writer for *Sports Illustrated* if he ever pictured the audience to whom he was broadcasting. Miller said
he always pictured one person. The writer asked if he visualized the person—was it a man or a woman or what? Miller
said, "It's Larry King."

The writer said, "What?"

"I broadcast the game to Larry King. Larry King is my favorite radio personality, he's a great fan of baseball, and he's
an objective but involved listener. Many times I look up at
the outfield and visualize Larry driving in his car or Larry
sitting home with his legs crossed. One time I even visualized
Larry sitting with his arm around Angie Dickinson and they
were listening to me broadcast the game."

Life magazine wrote an article about me once and hired a
photographer named Michael O'Brien to take my picture for
it. He told me he had to come and study me first, so one
night, while I was having dinner at the Palm, O'Brien was
sitting at another table not far away. No camera, just looking
at me. I understood what he was doing; he just wanted to get
a "concept" of me. So he sat at another table and told me,

"You don't even know I'm here." He just ate dinner and observed me.

When we finally did the photo session, which was before my heart attack, he made me blow smoke from a cigarette for hours, which nearly drove me crazy. He had decided from watching me at dinner that since I make my living through my mouth, he wanted to emphasize that part of me. Because I was a heavy smoker, he wanted to capture me with a gust of smoke billowing out from between my lips.

Ironically, after all the agony he put me through, he told me that he didn't shoot people anymore and had taken the assignment only because he liked my show. Normally he preferred shooting objects, like Dole pineapple juice. I've got to admit, though, that he did get his subject. It was a great photograph, after all, and I think it won some kind of award for him. You could hardly see my face in it, just lips and smoke. And he got the tiredness in my eyes. But how would you like to know a guy is in a restaurant staring at you while you're eating dinner?

I had a whole bunch of guys staring at me at dinner not long ago. It was at a roast of me in San Francisco at the Other Café emceed by a comic named Bob Sarlatte. They did the roast like *Meet the Press*, with me up on the throne and four "reporters" questioning me. The part I remember most was the beginning. The lights went dark and all we could hear was a voice, sounding exactly like mine, saying, "Ladies and gentlemen, welcome to the Larry King Roast."

Then a spotlight flashed on the speaker sitting in a chair with a microphone, and all he said was "Wichita, Kansas. Fuck you."

Tom Selleck told me that he contributes one hundred thousand dollars a year to the University of Southern California just to keep one subject in the curriculum: the study of ethics in the press. Where does the private life of a public figure begin and end? That's what he wants to know.

That question applies to a prominent former cabinet member who talked to me off the air about feeling trapped in a Catholic marriage. He is not happy with his wife, but because of his religious beliefs he doesn't fool around and he won't get a divorce. He said to me, "I see the dynamic between you and your ex-wife—there's a lot of tension, but there's also a lot of attraction. I don't have either. We've been married a long time, I like my wife a lot, we struggled together to get where we are, but . . ."

This was not told to me in confidence, so theoretically I could reveal the person's name here. I'd be lying, though, if I said I didn't realize that such a revelation might cause him and his wife some pain. The only question is whether I feel that the public deserves to know something of this sort. Since he is not an elected official and since he has done nothing morally or ethically wrong in his private life anyway, what business is it of the public's to know about his troubles? What if he were in a sensitive position, however, dealing with national security or the armed forces? What if he were Cap Weinberger or Henry Kissinger? Would that make a difference?

Ted Koppel told me about a time Henry Kissinger was flying to a major conference in Europe. During the last hour of the flight, one of his aides was feverishly trying to get his attention. Kissinger kept shooing him away, telling him to be quiet and leave him alone. The aide looked more and more perplexed and finally wrote out a note, which he handed to Kissinger as he was about to walk down the stairs off the plane. Henry took the note and Ted watched him stop at the top of the stairs, look down and see that his fly was open. He zipped it up quickly, and when they arrived at the conference, Kissinger said to Koppel, "That boy is going far, that aide. Those are the things you look for, Ted. The rest is bull-shit."

Ted told me that one of the strangest things that ever happened to him occurred one morning about three or four years ago. Richard Nixon called him up and talked to him for twenty minutes about politics, then said goodbye and hung up. Nothing else—no requests, no mention of doing his show. It was a quarter to eight in the morning. Koppel had never spoken to Nixon outside the context of his news program; his guess was that maybe Nixon's aides had dialed the wrong Ted and Nixon didn't even know who he was talking to.

Ted Koppel is an exception—a very tough, brainy news-caster—but so many of his colleagues are airheads. They make happy talk and joke with each other and do shtick, and they have no notion of what is going on.

A lot of those airhead newspeople do shows like *Good Morning Des Moines*. Now if I tell you it's called *Good Morning Des Moines*, that it's on from nine to ten, and there's a male host and a female host, you already know what they look like. And, dear reader, you're right.

So picture this. The cohost, who of course is a blonde with lots of hair, is interviewing me. The blonde is an airhead. She anchors the four o'clock news and she occasionally does fea-ture interviews on that show, too. I see she's got five ques-tions written out, and I can tell that somebody else wrote them for her. She introduces me and asks me the first written question. While I'm answering, she looks not at me but at the monitor, and as soon as she sees that I'm on the monitor and she isn't, she starts fixing her lipstick. Then she goes to ques-tion number two. The crew know me from my show and they can see that I'm aware of what's going on. I've been on the road a lot lately and I'm really tired. She is everything that I think should not be in broadcasting. Her third question is "What in your opinion makes a good talk show host?"

She is holding a pencil against her chin, trying to look very bright. The camera goes back to me and this time she starts fiddling with her hair. I say, "Well, I don't know about the other talk show hosts, but in my case it's helped a lot to be an agent of the CIA at the same time."

I know she's not listening. The crew starts to crack up.

"What the CIA does for me," I explain without being asked, "is that they get me guests. And what I do for them is that, once or twice a night, I say certain words that are clues to operatives that we have in and around the Western Hemisphere."

Now the camera is bouncing because the cameraman is laughing so hard, and I can hear the director laughing too. The interviewer, oblivious to anything resembling an ad-lib, smiles and says, "That was interesting, Larry. So tell me, how do you like the single life?"

It could have been a sketch out of Bob and Ray.

I think you stop being a newsperson when you become an anchor, with a few exceptions—such as Walter Cronkite, who continued to write his own material. Mike Wallace anchored for a while in Los Angeles for much better pay, but he felt he was just a reader when he did that. He told me that all he wanted was to get back to the pavement. Probably the most famous moment in Walter Cronkite's career, the one most people remember him for, was when he tore the story of John F. Kennedy's assassination off the wire and went on the air and told America that Kennedy was dead. I asked him, "Would you rather have been in Dallas?"

"Absolutely," he said.

"You would rather have been running down the street to the hospital with forty other newsmen?"

"Absolutely. What did I do? 'Ladies and gentlemen, the president is dead.' But was I able to describe the scene in the hospital? Did I corner a doctor and ask him what happened medically?"

I once interviewed Merriman Smith, the UPI reporter and longtime friend of John Kennedy who called in the shooting from Dallas. He was the first one on the phone, and as a result UPI beat AP by two minutes with the wire story. I asked him, "At that moment, running to the phone, were you sad or were you on a story?"

"A story," he said. "I cried later."

I freely admit that I couldn't be a newsman. Hanging out waiting for a story to break, following a politician around, cornering a woman whose husband has just died in a plane crash, those aren't things I'm good at.

People often ask me what my fantasy job would be on TV if I weren't an interviewer, and I think I'd like to do weather for a week. I would be a riot. I'd look out the window; I would have the clouds falling behind me; I would explain the "cumulus push." And then I would give the world's only guaranteed perfect weather forecast. I would never be wrong: "Partly cloudy, chance of showers." There's always a cloud somewhere; there's always a chance. And I'd do a lot of that silly banter with the anchors. The local anchor usually segues to weather by saying something brilliant like "Well, Larry, you didn't give us a very good day, did you?" Here's a grown man saying that Larry didn't give us a very nice day. "Hey Frank, I'll try to do better tomorrow!" Do they really think the audience likes that?

If I ever do go into television news and have to ad-lib, however, I'll have had a lot of practice through my public speaking engagements. I do a lot of them, and I rarely speak on specific topics; most of what I say is humorous and often improvised. I may slant the jokes to the group I'm addressing, but none of it is serious and I don't always know where I'm going to go with it. Although that approach occasionally gets me in trouble, there are times when it works better than anything I could have planned. At one dinner, for instance, they gave a plaque to the fellow who spoke before me, so I got up and told the following story, which happened to be true.

"Seeing this gentleman receiving his plaque here today," I began, "reminds me of something similar that happened to me a few years ago. When I was in Miami and I spoke before the city of Miami police department, at the end of the speech they thanked me and gave me a certificate making me an honorary chief of police of Miami. I put it in my glove compartment, and three days later I was pulled over by a cop for making an illegal right turn. They had changed the sign that day so that you could no longer make a right turn on this particular corner, and there must have been a dozen cars lined up with one cop writing out tickets for everybody—it was like you had to take a number. I had plenty of time to think before he got to me, and I remembered my certificate. I figured it was worth a try, but I didn't say anything—I didn't want to be gauche—I just put the certificate down in front of him as he was about to start writing the ticket. He looked at the certificate, looked at me, and then he told me what I could do with the certificate. And I said to myself: Thank God they didn't give me a plaque."

Another time I got a call from a Miami Rotary Club member asking me to speak at the club's annual dinner. "Fine," I said.

"What will your topic be?" he asked.

"I don't have a topic. I speak extemporaneously."

"You have to have a topic," he said.

"Wait a minute," I said. "*You* invited *me*. I don't have a topic."

"You have to have a topic," he repeated. "If we were inviting *Eisenhower,* he'd have to have a topic."

I said, "Call him."

I hung up, but the next night the guy called me at the studio just as I was about to go on the air. I could hear a whirring sound in the background, very loud. "I'm at the printer's," he said, "printing up the fliers for our dinner. What is your topic?"

Out of desperation and sheer hostility, and to get him off the phone, I said, "My topic will be the future of the American merchant marine." That was that. I went on the air and immediately forgot about the whole thing.

Four months and ten speeches later, I drove to the country club where the Rotary was holding their annual dinner. The parking lot was jammed. I parked a block away and walked up and there was a sign: "Tonight—the Future of the American Merchant Marine." I said to myself, Holy Christ, either they got two speakers or else I've got the wrong night. The chairman who had booked me came running out very excited. It should tell you something about the Rotary Club that this topic had broken all their attendance records. The Rotarians could not wait to hear about the future of the American merchant marine. And neither could I.

I sat down on the dais, I was introduced, and as the chairman spoke I started to panic. I usually work unrehearsed when I do my show, but I'm prepared for that; this was real panic. The guy who introduced me told the audience that he had taken the day off from work to research the American merchant marine, and he proceeded to relate its past history. "And so," he concluded, "now to talk about the *future*, here is Larry King."

I decided, If you don't know it, leave it alone. For forty-five minutes, I never mentioned the merchant marine. I tried everything else, but they weren't laughing at my jokes. They were waiting for the merchant marine. I finished to thunderous silence. They were still buzzing among themselves as I exited the building, only to discover that the chairman had followed me to my car. He was so pissed that after I got into

my car he started banging on the window. I hit the push button to lower the power window, and he stuck his head inside.
He now had his head in the window and I had my hand on
the button. That was power—I could have twitched and
guillotined him. He saw my hand on the button and he
backed off, but he started screaming, "You never mentioned
the merchant marine! We drew the largest attendance in our
history, and you never mentioned the future of the American
merchant marine!"

"They have no future," I said and drove away.

Finally, I'd like to tell about my experience with Hadassah.
Hadassah is an organization of twenty-two thousand sixty-six-
year-old Jewish women. They're all widows, they all have
blue hair, and they're relentless. If you're an organization and
you want to increase your membership or you're putting on a
fundraiser, hire Hadassah. Hadassah people have enormous
chutzpah.

In June of 1966 Sadie Shapiro, from the Rebecca chapter of
Hadassah, called me. She said, "Larry, in January we honor
the Hadassah Woman of the Year and I'd like you to be our
speaker."

I asked her what this woman did to become Woman of the
Year. Sadie said, "This Hadassah woman raised $750 from the
Seminole Indians for the state of Israel. *And* she got them to
weave prayer shawls for the Israeli fighting men." This is only
a slight exaggeration, but you get the idea.

They have a lot of chutzpah, as I said. Hadassah has a
fundraising office in Harlem. They get a dollar a month from
welfare recipients. So I said to Sadie, "January is six months
away."

She said, "I'm not talking about next January: I'm talking
about January 1968."

"That's a year and a half," I told her. She said, "At
Hadassah, we plan."

Every Monday I got a letter: "Dear Larry, Seventy-six

weeks from Thursday, you're the speaker." I got telegrams, the works. That's how they succeed, by bombarding you. They had me. I was Hadassahfied. I'd get messages at work: Rebecca Tannenbaum called, urgent! If I called back, she'd say, "Sadie asked me to call. It's forty weeks from today, we just wanted to remind you."

Finally, it's the day of the lunch. I leave a half hour early, because God forbid I should be late. I get to the Fontaine-bleau at eleven-thirty. I'm not due there until twelve, and the lobby is already jammed. There are three different lunches going on, so I look around and I spot a lady in a red dress. I *know* it's Sadie Shapiro. I've never met her, but she has that Hadassah look. I've been stretching things a little, but this next part is absolutely true. I go up to her and I say, "Sadie Shapiro."

And she says to me, "Larry King. I thought you forgot."

AFTERWORD

No, I didn't forget, Sadie, and to tell you the truth, I wouldn't have missed it for the world. I love every minute of it—the radio, the television, the public speaking, even the Hadassah luncheons. How else would I get to meet so many fantastic people, to hear so many wild stories?

Not long ago, Jack Paar was on my show, and he said he hoped I could keep up my enthusiasm, because he didn't have it anymore. "The day you lose that enthusiasm, Larry, you'll quit," he warned. "The day you're sitting here and you're thinking, I've asked all the questions and I've heard all the answers, then it's time to go."

That's what worried me most about my heart attack: Would it depress me? Would it make me too careful? If it did, I was doomed. I couldn't just go through the motions with something I love—and if I lost my curiosity, it would be like falling out of love. If I didn't care what my guest said that night—if I didn't poke and probe and *listen*—then the interview would be terrible. I might as well go join *Good Morning Des Moines*.

As I lay in the emergency room, I had plenty of time to think about whether I wanted to go back to listening every night. It seemed ironic that after coming so far, I had trembled within a heartbeat of throwing it all away. Had I tried to sabotage my own success? Had I loaded my schedule with so many commitments that the only way to get some rest was to have a heart attack? Was my work worth all the energy and emotion I put into it, or would I be happier retiring to a horse farm in Virginia?

Well, you know the answers, of course. You can see and

hear them just about every night of the week on your TV and radio. It didn't take me long to realize that there was nothing else I would rather be doing and nowhere I would rather be. I've been on the air for thirty years; if I get the chance, I'll be on for thirty years more, probing, questioning—and listening.

And if that ever changes, I'll be the first to let you know.

Partly cloudy, chance of showers.

1-4-3, and *Arrivederc'!*